REALISM AND RELIGION

This book draws together a distinguished group of philosophers and theologians to present new thinking on realism and religion. The religious realism/antirealism debate concerns the questions of God's independence from human beings, the nature of religious truth and our access to religious truths. Although both philosophers and theologians have written on these subjects, there has been little sustained investigation into these issues akin to that found in comparable areas of research such as ethics or the philosophy of science. In addition, the absence of any agreed approach to the problem underlines both the need for fresh thought on it and the fruitfulness of this area for further research.

The editors' introduction sets the context of the realism debate, traces connections amongst the essays which follow, and proposes lines for future development and enquiry. The contributors present a variety of contrasting positions on key issues in the religious realism debate and each opens up new and important themes. Gordon Kaufman, Peter Lipton and Simon Blackburn provide the opening chapters and the context for the collection; Alexander Bird, John Hare, Graham Oppy and Nick Trakakis, Merold Westphal, and John Webster explore topics that are central to the debate. This volume of original essays will both introduce newcomers to the field and suggest new lines of research for those already familiar with it.

Realism and Religion
Philosophical and Theological Perspectives

Edited by

ANDREW MOORE
University of Oxford, UK
and
MICHAEL SCOTT
Manchester University, UK

ASHGATE

Published by
Ashgate Publishing Limited
Gower House
Croft Road
Aldershot
Hampshire GU11 3HR
England

Ashgate Publishing Company
Suite 420
101 Cherry Street
Burlington, VT 05401-4405
USA

Ashgate website: http://www.ashgate.com

British Library Cataloguing in Publication Data
 Realism and religion: philosophical and theological perspectives 1. Religion – Philosophy
 2. Realism I. Moore, Andrew II. Scott, Michael
 200.1

Library of Congress Cataloging-in-Publication Data
Realism and religion: philosophical and theological perspectives/[edited by] Andrew Moore and Michael Scott. p. cm.
 ISBN 978-0-7546-5221-2 (hbk: alk. paper) – ISBN 978-0-7546-5232-8 (pbk: alk. paper)
1. Realism. 2. Philosophical theology. 3. Knowledge, Theory of (Religion) 4. Philosophy and religion. I. Moore, Andrew. II. Scott, Michael, 1970–

BT50.R42 2007
210–dc22

2007004390

ISBN 978-0-7546-5221-2 (hbk)
ISBN 978-0-7546-5232-8 (pbk)

Printed and bound in Great Britain by TJ International Ltd, Padstow, Cornwall.

Contents

List of Contributors

Alexander Bird is Professor of Philosophy at Bristol University.

Simon Blackburn is Professor of Philosophy at the University of Cambridge.

John Hare is Noah Porter Professor of Philosophical Theology at Yale University.

Gordon D. Kaufman is Mallinckrodt Professor of Divinity Emeritus at Harvard University.

Peter Lipton is Hans Rausing Professor of the History and Philosophy of Science at Cambridge University and a Fellow of King's College.

Andrew Moore is a member of the Theology Faculty at the University of Oxford.

Graham Oppy is Professor of Philosophy at Monash University.

Michael Scott is Senior Lecturer in Philosophy at the University of Manchester.

Nick Trakakis is a Postdoctoral Research Fellow at Monash University.

John Webster is Professor of Systematic Theology at the University of Aberdeen.

Merold Westphal is Distinguished Professor of Philosophy at Fordham University.

Chapter 1

Introduction

Andrew Moore and Michael Scott

The religious realism/antirealism debate concerns the questions of God's independence from human beings, the nature of religious truth and our access to religious truths. Religious realists typically maintain that religious claims represent a mind-independent religious reality to which we have epistemic access (at least in part), and that religious truth should be robustly construed as a relationship between religious sentences and the reality that they describe. Religious realists also usually maintain that at least some religious claims are actually true. Religious antirealists variously reject different components of the realist's theory: religious claims are primarily expressive rather than genuinely representational; religious truths are inaccessible to us; religious truth is a matter of the satisfaction of internal standards of religious language (or 'language games'); religious claims are systematically false. It is this last issue that has played and continues to play a dominant role in philosophy of religion, usually in the form of arguments about either the existence of God or the coherence of claims made about God.[1] Our concern in this collection is with the other aspects of the debate. That is, we will primarily be interested in the meaning and accessibility of religious claims. Although they are less commonly discussed, it is these other aspects that in an important respect raise more fundamental issues. When one asks whether God exists or whether we have a coherent conception of omnipotence, one already assumes that talk of God is in the business of representing (or aiming to represent) a religious reality; when one asks whether religious beliefs can be reasonable and warranted, one assumes that their truth is accessible to us.

Religious Realism in Context

The debate between realists and antirealists is a focal point of contemporary philosophy that has occupied many major contemporary analytic philosophers. Extensive work has focused on identifying the core points of disagreement between realists and antirealists and providing a framework in which the debate can be helpfully pursued. Moreover, the interpretation and relative importance of the various aspects of the realism problem, as well as the types of antirealist opposition, differ with each philosophical setting. In philosophy of science, for example, the realist's belief in the existence of entities posited by scientific theory is contested by antirealist sceptics; in ethics, the aptitude of ethical claims to express truths is as much at issue as the existence of ethical properties; in the philosophy of mathematics, the status of

---

1   For classic texts, see Richard Swinburne, *The Existence of God* (Oxford: Clarendon Press, 2004, 2nd edition) and J. L. Mackie, *The Miracle of Theism: Arguments for and against the existence of God* Oxford: Clarendon Press, 1982).

mathematical truth is a central issue. An understanding of the realism problem is pivotal to current research in these topics.

Against this background, work on religious realism has lagged behind. Although theologians have written on the problem,[2] there has been no sustained philosophical investigation of religious realism akin to that found in ethics or the philosophy of science. Philosophers of religion have made little use of the considerable technical resources for understanding the problem advanced in recent years.[3] Philosophers working on realism in other fields have shied away from developing detailed arguments on religious realism – even those who have strong (realist) religious convictions or who take a position which in principle commits them to controversial views about the subject. Numerous texts on realism cite religious discourse as an example, but fall short of a satisfactory engagement with the topic. This lack of engagement with the problem is all the more surprising given the resurgence of interest in the cognate areas of religious epistemology and ontology, and the fact that religion, alongside ethical and scientific discourse, presents the most natural context in which to address and evaluate realist and antirealist arguments.[4]

The current lack of an agreed framework for discussion of the religious realism problem coupled with poor communication not only between philosophical fields which should have something to say on the topic but also between philosophy and theology, underlines both the need for new thinking and the potential fruitfulness of this area of investigation. This collection of essays by philosophers of science, philosophers of religion, moral philosophers, and theologians attempts to promote communication between these fields.

There are several critical problems raised in this collection that merit particular attention:

1. The appropriate paradigm(s) for pursuing the realism debate. Should we be primarily concerned with, for instance, the character of religious truth, the reference of discourse about God, the question of God's independence, or the descriptiveness of religious claims? While philosophers and theologians have taken various positions on each of these issues – sometimes arguing at cross-purposes with each other – little has been done towards identifying the focal problems or explaining the relationship between the different approaches.

2. What can be learnt from comparable debates in science and ethics? Can, for example, the (very different) kind of considerations used to defend scientific or ethical antirealism be applied in support of religious antirealism? Can defences of scientific realism be applied to religious realism?

---

2   See D. MacKinnon, *Explorations in Theology 5* (London: SCM, 1979), chs 5, 10, 11; D. Cupitt, *Taking Leave of God* (London: SCM, 1980); J. M. Soskice, *Metaphor and Religious Language* (Oxford: Clarendon Press, 1985); B. Marshall, *Trinity and Truth* (Cambridge: Cambridge University Press, 2000); A. Moore, *Realism and Christian Faith: God, Grammar, and Meaning* (Cambridge: Cambridge University Press, 2003).

3   For example, C. Wright, *Truth and Objectivity* (Cambridge, Mass.: Harvard University Press, 1992).

4   Though see M. Dummett, *The Logical Basis of Metaphysics* (London: Duckworth, 1991).

3. In what ways is religious realism distinct from other kinds of realism, and what are the implications of this for realism/antirealism frameworks?
4. The relationship between philosophy and theology. Because the status of religious discourse is the province of both disciplines, the relationship between them and their respective contributions needs to be brought into focus.

Approaches and Arguments

A useful way into the realism problem is to consider whether religious statements aim primarily to describe the world, or instead express the attitudes of those who assert them. This debate is standardly construed in terms of whether religious statements have cognitive content. The cognitivist argues that religious statements aim to represent facts, and are true or false according to whether their representations are accurate. Religious non-cognitivism involves a positive and a negative thesis. On the negative side, religious statements do not aim to represent religious facts. In this respect, the content of religious sentences cannot be evaluated for truth because they are not *about* any religious subject matter. On the positive side, the non-cognitivist gives an account of how the claims of religious believers should be understood: they are expressive vehicles, and convey the believer's attitudes, emotions, stances, prescriptions, resolutions, commitments, etc. That is, religious statements have a primarily non-descriptive function.[5] The non-cognitivist can allow that a religious statement may have a factual content in addition to expressing an attitude. For example, the statement that an event is a miracle clearly has a descriptive element – an event occurred which is presumably in some way remarkable. But according to the non-cognitivist, what makes this a religious statement about a miracle rather than merely the report of a remarkable event, is that it expresses an attitude.

Non-cognitivism has been defended for various regions of language other than religious discourse. Aesthetic statements might be construed as the expression of certain feelings of pleasure or displeasure, rather than representing aesthetic facts; claims about what is funny might be seen as the expression of one's amusement or lack of it, rather than a judgement with truth-apt content. Non-cognitivist theories have been set out for truth ascriptions,[6] the modal language of possibility and necessity,[7] knowledge,[8] and most notably ethics.[9] Early versions of ethical non-cognitivism proposed that ethical claims served such purposes as venting one's feelings and persuading others to share them,[10] or prescribing rules of conduct for

---

5   This is distinct from the subjectivist position according to which a religious statement *reports* the believer's attitudes. For the non-cognitivist, religious utterances give voice to the believer's attitudes but do not describe or refer to them.

6   P. Strawson, 'Truth', *Proceedings of the Aristotelian Society*, Suppl. Vol. 24: pp.129–57 (1950).

7   S. Blackburn, *Essays in Quasi-Realism* (Oxford: Oxford University Press, 1993), ch. 3.

8   J. L. Austin, *Philosophical Papers*, 2nd ed., eds J. O. Urmson and G. J. Warnock (Oxford: Oxford University Press, 1970), p. 99.

9   S. Blackburn, *Spreading the Word* (Oxford: Oxford University Press, 1984).

10   A. J. Ayer , *Language, Truth and Logic* (London: Victor Gollancz, 1936), ch. 6.

oneself and others.[11] On these accounts, what the claim 'Honesty is good' amounts to is 'Honesty: hooray!' or 'Honesty: hooray! Be honest!' More recent work by Simon Blackburn and Allan Gibbard has developed ethical non-cognitivism,[12] or ethical *expressivism* as the current versions of the theory are called, into a highly sophisticated theory that is one of the leading antirealist options in metaethics.[13]

It is of interest to note the relative unpopularity of the religious analogue of ethical non-cognitivism. This is in part due to the close association between religious non-cognitivism and an early formulation of the theory by R. B. Braithwaite.[14] Braithwaite contends that a religious statement primarily serves to express the believer's intention to pursue a certain behaviour policy. Unfortunately, this is open to obvious counter-examples: religious beliefs that are not associated with any particular policy, or with no behavioural intentions at all. Moreover, Braithwaite partly justified his account on the basis of a now wholly discredited logical positivist theory of meaning according to which a statement is factually significant only if it is empirically verifiable. Contemporary discussions of religious non-cognitivism, taking Braithwaite as their model, are typically brief and dismissive, and the objections against it are widely considered conclusive.[15]

But it may be that a stronger case can be made for non-cognitivism in religion. Certainly, a potentially more promising model can be found in an unexpected source: George Berkeley's later writings. In his *A Treatise Concerning the Principles of Human Knowledge* Berkeley notes that words can be meaningful without standing for ideas: they may, for example, excite some passion, encourage or deter action, or produce a disposition.[16] However, it is over twenty years later in his dialogue *Alciphron* that Berkeley applies this proposal to religious discourse.

Berkeley's account is intriguing in part because he extends the non-cognitivist aspect of his theory to a very restricted range of religious statements, and second, non-cognitivism is used by Berkeley as part of a *defence* of Christian faith against sceptical inquiry. The argument proceeds as follows. Suppose that words are significant only insofar as they stand for or suggest ideas, and that to know that a statement is true requires a distinct idea (or collection of ideas) corresponding to what is known. A sceptical objection emerges to certain basic Christian beliefs, about which it seems we have no distinct ideas. Take, for example, the notion of grace. Christianity,

11   R. M. Hare, *The Language of Morals* (Oxford: Oxford University Press, 1952).

12   S. Blackburn, *Essays in Quasi-Realism* (Oxford: Oxford University Press, 1993), Allan Gibbard, *Wise Choices, Apt Feelings* (Cambridge, Mass.: Harvard University Press, 1990).

13   One reason for changing the name is that expressivism, unlike its non-cognitive ancestors, can show how a discourse that primarily trades in the expression of attitudes can support notions of truth, fact, description, and even knowledge.

14   R. B. Braithwaite 'An Empiricist's View of the Nature of Religious Belief' [1955] in B. Mitchell (ed.), *The Philosophy of Religion* (Oxford: Oxford University Press, 1971).

15   R. Swinburne, *The Coherence of Theism* (Oxford: Oxford University Press, 1993); D. Stiver, *The Philosophy of Religious Language* (Oxford: Blackwell, 1995); W. Alston 'Religious Language', in W. Wainwright (ed.), *The Oxford Handbook of Philosophy of Religion* (Oxford: Oxford University Press, 2005), pp. 220–44.

16   G. Berkeley, *A Treatise Concerning the Principles of Human Knowledge* (J. Dancy (ed.), Oxford: Oxford, University Press, 1998), Introduction, Section 20.

as Berkeley puts it through the mouth of his sceptical interlocutor Alciphron, 'is styled the covenant or dispensation of grace', and the nature, effects, and extent of grace is the subject of much theological dispute. We can, of course, have an idea of grace in its 'vulgar sense' as 'beauty ... or favour'. 'But', Alciphron continues, 'when it denotes an active, vital, ruling principle, influencing and operating on the mind of man, distinct from every natural power or motive, I profess myself altogether unable to understand it, or frame any distinct idea of it.'[17] But if no distinct idea corresponds to the word 'grace', so the sceptical objection goes, then it is an empty term and cannot be an object of faith or knowledge.

Berkeley's response is to introduce his earlier proposal from the *Principles* that terms may serve a function other than conveying ideas. For example, the term 'grace' should be understood as playing a role in religious statements and beliefs that serves to motivate certain actions. So Euphranor (who stands for Berkeley) replies to Alciphron: 'Grace may ... be an object of our faith, and influence our life and actions, as a principle destructive of evil habits and productive of good ones, although we cannot attain a distinct idea of it'.[18] Euphranor goes on to develop a similar account of the Trinity:[19]

[A] man may believe the doctrine of the Trinity, if he finds it revealed in Holy Scripture that the Father, the Son, and the Holy Ghost, are God, and that there is but one God, although he doth not frame in his mind any abstract or distinct ideas of trinity, substance, or personality; provided that this doctrine of a Creator, Redeemer, and Sanctifier makes proper impressions on his mind, producing therein love, hope, gratitude, and obedience, and thereby becomes a lively operative principle, influencing his life and actions, agreeably to that notion of saving faith which is required in a Christian.[20]

Original sin is also given a non-cognitive account:

Original sin, for instance, a man may find it impossible to form an idea of in abstract, or of the manner of its transmission; and yet the belief thereof may produce in his mind a salutary sense of his own unworthiness, and the goodness of his Redeemer: from whence may follow good habits, and from them good actions, the genuine effects of faith.[21]

Berkeley envisages his non-cognitivism to extend only as far as those Christian doctrines of which we can form no distinct idea, and he takes it little further than these examples. Regarding the rest of religious discourse, Berkeley is a cognitivist: religious terms correspond to ideas that refer to really existing features of a religious reality. He takes the various forms of behaviour that the non-cognitive uses of religious language promote to be in accordance with Christian thinking about proper belief and practice, which, Berkeley believes, is both cognitively contentful and

---

17   George Berkeley, *Alciphron or The Minute Philosopher* (T. E. Jessop (ed.)) in *The Works of George Berkeley, Volume Three* (eds A. A. Luce and T. E. Jessop, London: Thomas Nelson, 1950), VII, 4.

18   Ibid. VII, 7.

19   And, in the course of it, of the divine-human nature of Christ: ibid. VII, 8; cf. VII, 9.

20   Ibid. VII, 8.

21   Ibid. VII, 10.

rationally defensible. The non-cognitive use of religious language is therefore very much at the service of what natural reason, scripture, and theology have established as true, and is justified by its producing the requisite range of Christian behaviour and dispositions in believers.

Aside from providing a response to scepticism about those Christian doctrines where distinct ideas cannot be formed, Berkeley uses the non-cognitive component of his theory to account for the motivational character of Christian belief. Berkeley emphasizes that there is a practical side to faith that shows itself in the behaviour and dispositions of believers rather than in their understanding, 'a vital operative principle, productive of charity and obedience'. He remarks: 'Faith, I say, is not an indolent perception, but an operative persuasion of mind, which ever worketh some suitable action, disposition, or emotion in those who have it.'[22] He argues that religious claims which evoke emotion and guide action are more suited to explain this aspect of faith than ideas and intellectual argument, which he believes are unable to dissuade people from acting in their own self-interest. Ethical arguments about the virtues, good character, the inner moral sense, Berkeley suggests, will do nothing to discourage someone from 'secular interests and sensual pleasures', particularly if that person enjoys the immediacy and convenience of such pleasures. Faith, however, can effect a change of heart and motivate a different way of life – not by intellectual persuasion, but by changing the believer's attitudes. Berkeley thus identifies a much more promising line of defence for non-cognitivism than Braithwaite's logical positivist theory of meaning: the attitudes expressed in religious discourse also explain the motivational force of religious faith.

None of the contributors to this collection have taken on a full-blooded religious non-cognitivism, but Kaufman comes close. For Kaufman, God is not an accessible object of our understanding, and so there no question of religious claims successfully referring to or describing God. Rather, religious discourse is construed as a product of the imagination rooted in human responses to the (natural) world and the vicissitudes of life. Moreover, these must presumably be primarily emotional rather than cognitive responses, since a suitable intellectual response to the recognition that religious statements fail to represent the supernatural reality that they appear to describe would be to jettison religious language entirely – an option that Kaufman takes note of.

In a key respect the argument of Lipton's paper resembles Kaufman's: they both aim to give an account of religious claims which does not require an ontological commitment to a religious subject matter. However, whereas Kaufman regards the subject matter as inaccessible to us, Lipton proposes a way of engaging in religious language without any commitment to a religious ontology. Lipton does not doubt that religious statements are genuinely representational: they describe (or aim to describe) a religious reality. But he sets out a way in which engagement in religious discourse does not require one to believe in the described religious reality. Lipton's model for this proposal is Bas van Fraassen's constructive empiricist position in the philosophy of science. In philosophy of science, a central issue is the status of unobservable entities posited by scientific theories. The constructive empiricist maintains that if

---

22   Ibid.

a scientific theory is empirically adequate – if everything it says or implies about the observable world is true – we can *accept* it while remaining agnostic about the existence of the unobservable entities it posits. This approach seems most attractive when there are two incompatible scientific models in play. For example, a fluid can be modelled as a continuous liquid or as a collection of particles. A scientist may make use of either model as an appropriate tool for predicting or explaining phenomena without believing both to be true. Lipton contends that we can in a similar way accept religious claims, where it is morally and socially desirable to do so, while remaining agnostic about their content or even, where science has established it, believing their content to be false. Lipton's theory is a variety of fictionalism, a theory which has also been applied to ethics and other areas of discourse.[23]

Although Lipton and Kaufman are religious believers, to some they might seem to approach religious belief and practice from an external stance. They each apply non-religious grounds – ethical and social judgements, or our experience of the world – to evaluate which religious beliefs to hold and which practices to engage in. This is highly controversial for a religious believer who, for example, takes scripture as fundamental. Lipton's aim is to show how one can engage in religious discourse without compromising scientific beliefs, rather than to give a general account of religious discourse. Even so, if religious discourse is a mere fiction, why should anyone engage with it? Lipton is alive to this problem and emphasizes the importance of immersion in religious practice: 'The religious story has its life in the context of ritual observance and more generally as part of a religious form of life. It is a story in which the reader herself is also a participant, and it may provide extraordinary support for communal identification and moral reflection.'[24]

Simon Blackburn, although an ethical expressivist and a pioneer of contemporary expressivist theory, takes a thoroughly realist account of religious discourse. Contrary to Kaufman and Lipton, religious discourse involves commitment to a religious ontology and – at least for the ordinary believer in the pew – this commitment is ineliminable.[25] He argues that religious believers do not use religious language merely to give voice to their attitudes, but draw on religion to justify and explain their behaviour. The unacceptable upshot of fictionalism is that the religious 'believer' can 'cite the gift of God as an explanation and justification of his desire, in one breath, and in the next breath admit that it is all a fiction'.[26] As Blackburn puts it, the two-faced nature of this approach gives it away.

A number of papers in the collection, notably Lipton's, propose relationships between the realism debate in the philosophy of religion and science. Alexander Bird explains such connections in some detail, and provides a critical survey of the literature. Two other important components of the religious realism debate are considered in this volume: the analysis that we give of religious truth, and the

23 Mark Eli Kalderon, *Moral Fictionalism* (Oxford: Clarendon Press, 2005) and *Fictionalism in Metaphysics* ((ed.), Oxford: Clarendon Press, 2005).

24 p. 46 below.

25 Though given that Lipton is looking to find a place for religious discourse within a scientific world view, he would perhaps not disagree with this point.

26 p. 58 below.

relationship between religion and ethics. The relevance of the latter was indicated in the earlier discussion of non-cognitivism: religious and ethical beliefs seem to share a similar motivational force, and arguments for religious non-cognitivism are modelled on their counterparts in ethics. Moreover, the religious antirealist often takes the merits of religious practice and belief primarily to be ethical. In his paper, Hare takes up a further aspect of this relationship, whether ethical truths may be grounded in religious truths about God. Hare aims to show how such an account – closely related to 'divine command theories' – can also account for the motivational character of ethical belief.[27]

The significance of our conception of religious truth for the realism debate has been emphasized in recent work by Alston,[28] and is reflected in both Blackburn's paper and Oppy and Trakakis's detailed discussion of the work of D. Z. Phillips. For more than forty years, Phillips developed and expanded on Wittgenstein's lectures and writings in the philosophy of religion, and his many books and articles constitute one of the most distinctive and lively contributions to the field. Central to Phillips's account is that we must understand religious concepts within the practices and language games of the religious believers who use them, and this includes the concept of religious truth. Phillips would deny that he was an antirealist, arguing instead that both the realist and antirealist positions are confused. But the upshot of taking religious truth as a language game internal concept, i.e. a concept tied to the standards of investigation and justification within religious discourse, seems clearly to situate him on the antirealist side. For example, an implication of adopting this account is that religious truth is evidentially and epistemically constrained. That is, there cannot be religious truths that in principle outstrip our ability to determine their truth or which we cannot even in principle know to be true. The realist, in contrast, will argue that there can be evidentially unconstrained religious truths or truths which are unknowable.

Writing from similar theological standpoints, our two final contributors explore questions of God's independent existence and how it should be construed. The figure of Kant lurks behind many of the debates touched on in this volume and in his essay Merold Westphal argues for a Kantian theological anti-realism. This comprises two theses. First, God exists independently of human beings and their cognitive powers: God is metaphysically real. Second, there is a sharp and essential distinction between God's knowledge of what is true and real (including himself) and our knowledge of it. For Westphal the crucial issue in the realism debate is epistemic, not metaphysical. Thus, on his view, whereas God's knowledge defines the real as it truly is and corresponds to its object, ours does not, and therefore we cannot know things as they really are. Westphal's anti-realism is in significant measure theologically motivated: he denies that created, finite human beings with their limited noetic capacities can arrive at the truth about their infinite, divine creator. Moreover, owing to the taint of original sin, we need to beware our tendency to idolatry, for as he puts it, 'we edit

---

27   See R. Adams *Finite and Infinite Goods* (New York: Oxford University Press, 2002).

28   W. Alston, 'Realism and the Christian Faith'. *International Journal for the Philosophy of Religion*, 38 (1995), pp. 37–60.

God to our convenience'.[29] God's transcendence is such that he cannot become an object of knowledge for us unless, as Westphal believes he does (and here he differs from Kaufman's Kantianism), God reveals himself.

Westphal's theological anti-realism will make many theologians think again about the kind of realism that is appropriate in theology and will have a chastening effect on those who think that theological realism is easily won. But they might also want to ask whether his position wavers awkwardly and unstably between being theologically and philosophically motivated. For example, how far is his apophaticism driven by a Kantian metaphysic and how might it be modulated by Christian doctrinal affirmations concerning God's actions in space and time? In other words, might not more be said in the cataphatic mode of theological discourse, precisely on the basis of the divine self-revelation Westphal accepts, or does his Kantianism preclude this?

John Webster's essay explicitly raises the question of the relationship between philosophy and theology and suggests that the tensions between the two disciplines that have so dogged the realism debate might be eased by patient and self-critical self-explanation. The topic of divine aseity concerns God's objective identity in himself, independent of creatures. In a move that eschews the kind of restrictions (frequently self-) imposed on theology by Kantian anxieties, Webster affirms that the triune God of Christian faith is a knowable subject of human discourse because of his self-revelation in Jesus Christ. 'God is from himself, and from himself God gives himself'.[30] Our conception of God's self-existence should therefore be derived from this datum rather than from abstract comparisons between necessary and contingent being, as both philosophers of religion and theologians have tended to do.

D. Z. Phillips was fond of asking philosophers to clarify the grammar of religious discourse before judging it and Webster's essay can helpfully be seen as a piece of conceptual clarification. An important and controversial implication of Webster's argument for divine objectivity is that the realism debate in Christian theology needs to be set in the context of Christianity's specific doctrinal commitments and forms of self-assessment. As he puts it, 'concepts used in the course of explicating the Christian confession should be kept in the closest possible proximity to substantive Christian doctrine, and not simply introduced already full of content derived from their deployment elsewhere' – 'a general metaphysics of causality', for example.[31] In which case, the question arises as to whether Webster's argument is subject to the problems associated with religious language games explored by Oppy and Trakakis earlier in this volume.

---

29 p. 152.
30 p. 161.
31 pp. 156, 157.

Chapter 2

Mystery, God and Constructivism

Gordon D. Kaufman

In this essay I shall not present an analysis of the general problem of religion and realism nor will I canvass the many aspects of this issue that arise in connection with various Christian claims and practices. I will confine my remarks largely to the interconnections and interdependence of the three topics mentioned in the title above. As we shall see, this will provide us with a kind of case study of the problem of religion and realism as it appears in connection with some of the central claims of Christian faith (and some other faiths as well) concerning the 'ultimate reality' with which we humans have to do.

At its deepest level human life, in many respects, confronts us as mystery. From the magnificence of a glorious sunset, of a Grand Canyon, of the nightly star-filled heavens above, to the profound enigma of the origin of our universe in an almost unimaginable 'Big Bang'; and then the later emergence of life amongst the ashes of that mighty explosion, and still later the appearance of our own human reality with its remarkable consciousness and thought, purposive action and creativity: the world into which we have been born – and we ourselves – are profound mysteries, evoking spontaneous awe. We have no settled answers to questions about the meaning of life, about what we humans really are, about the ultimate reality with which we humans have to do, about which of the problems of life are the most important, about how we should live out our lives. We seek to orient and order ourselves, of course, in terms of what we (quite properly) think of as knowledge of the environing world within which we live, and of our place within that world. But the wider and deeper context of our lives is inscrutable mystery – indeed, many mysteries – leaving us with the paradox that ultimately it is in terms of that which is beyond our knowing that we must understand ourselves.[1]

Throughout most of our history it has been what we today call 'the religions' that have provided humans with interpretations of the profound mysteries within which their lives transpire – interpretations that were sufficiently meaningful and intelligible to enable men and women to come to some significant understanding of themselves in relation to the enigmatic context within which their lives proceeded, and which were sufficiently appealing to motivate them to attempt to live meaningfully and

---

1   'A mystery is something we find we cannot think clearly about, cannot get our minds around, cannot manage to grasp... We are indicating that what we are dealing with here seems to be beyond what our minds can handle.... . "Mystery" is ... a grammatical or linguistic operator by means of which we remind ourselves of something about ourselves: that at this point we are using our language in an unusual, limited, and potentially misleading way.' G. Kaufman, *In Face of Mystery: A Constructive Theology* (Cambridge: Harvard University Press, 1993), p. 60f.

responsibly within that context. The human imagination has produced many such visions of the world within which we live and of the ultimate reality with which we must come to terms, and many quite diverse understandings of the significance of human life within this context. Some of these became the basis for religious traditions of sufficient meaning and interpretive power to have oriented the lives of women and men for generations – but none have succeeded in overcoming or setting aside the ultimate mystery of things. In recent centuries, with the rise of the sciences, our knowledge of the world and of the life processes that have brought us humans into being has transformed or displaced much traditional religious thinking about these matters. But however convincing these scientific pictures of human-life-in-the-world may today be, they also – like our long-lived religious traditions – have not succeeded in dissolving away the ultimate mysteries of the world and life.[2]

I

In our western religious traditions this pervasive mystery – to which our limitations of understanding and knowledge call attention – has often been given the name *God*; and in affirmations that God is 'absolute' or 'infinite', 'ineffable' or 'transcendent', believers have reminded themselves that this One whom they worship must be understood, ultimately, to be profound mystery.[3] There is a significant tension at the very heart of the symbol 'God'. On the one hand, this symbol has designated that – whatever it might be – which is believed to bring true human salvation or fulfillment; that is, in speaking of and to God, women and men seek to direct themselves to the mystery of reality in its aspect as source and ground of their very being and their well being, as that on which, therefore, they can rely absolutely. On the other hand, however, as genuinely *mystery*, God is taken to be beyond all knowledge and understanding. This notion of God's ultimate mystery demands acknowledgement of a significant human *unknowing* with respect to God – acknowledgement, that is to say, that we really do not know how the images and metaphors in terms of which we conceive God apply, since they are always our own metaphors and images, infected with our limitations, interests, and biases.

This feature of the image/concept of God gives rise to a profound tension (not always recognized) central to its meaning. To the extent that God is regarded as profound mystery, our concept of God can, of course, never be verified. This does not mean that the notion of God is simply a fantasy, or that God is unreal. It does mean, however (as has often been maintained in our traditions), that our belief in God, our commitment to God, is always an act of *faith*; it is not grounded on proofs or knowledge. Thus, paradoxically, we acknowledge God as indeed *God* – ultimate mystery – only to the extent that we recognize that all our human religious ideas, symbols, and methods of knowing, are our own human contrivances: the images or concepts of God that we have in our minds and our books (including the Bible) are

---

2   For discussion of this claim see G. Kaufman, *In the beginning...Creativity* (Minneapolis: Fortress Press, 2004), especially pp. 76–93.

3   For the historical background of this claim see G. Kaufman, *In the beginning*, especially pp. 5–7, 9–10, 22–6.

all humanly constructed. This does not mean that our human beliefs in and about God are necessarily misplaced or false; as we shall see, there is a kind of 'reality testing' appropriate to the concept of God. But it does call our attention to certain features of these beliefs that must be taken into account when we consider – theologically and philosophically – the roles they play in our lives and their importance to us.[4]

The word 'theology' – combining two Greek words, *theos* (God) and *logos* (words or thoughts) – means simply 'thinking about God', 'words about God', 'God-talk'. We think and talk about many different sorts of things, of course, but it is important to note that there is something distinctive, indeed quite peculiar, in our talking to and about God. We speak of tables and chairs; of humans and other living things such as dogs and cats, trees and flowers; of the sky above and the earth underfoot; and so on; and we know whereof we speak because all of these objects are directly available to us in our experience, in our seeing and touching and smelling and hearing. But what about God? That is a different matter, for God is not directly perceivable by us; God cannot be 'pointed to' like the ordinary objects of experience or easily evoked like feelings or other inner states.

In the Bible God is generally presented as a being that humans cannot directly experience. In only a few texts is it suggested that humans have directly encountered God: for example, it is said that Enoch 'walked with God' (Gen. 5:22, 24); God is said to have 'appeared' to Abraham (Gen. 17:1; 18:1) and spoken to him; God 'spoke' to Job 'out of the whirlwind' (Job 38–41); and so on. However, it is a central biblical theme that humans do not have direct or immediate contact with or experience of God. This inaccessibility of God is frequently reported. Job, for example, in the midst of his tribulations, seeks God for an explanation, but God is nowhere to be found:

> Lo, he passes by me, and I see him not; he moves on, but I do not perceive him…. Behold, I go forward, but he is not there; and backward, but I cannot perceive him; on the left hand, I seek him, but I cannot behold him; I turn to the right hand, but I cannot see him (9:11; 23:8–9).

Even Moses, through whom God is said to have made Godself known decisively, was not allowed to see God's 'face', we are told, but only God's 'back' (Ex. 33:23), for (as the text puts it) no one can see '[God's] face…and live' (33:20). And when Moses asked God to reveal his name, God replied darkly, 'I am who I am' (3:14). If we turn to the New Testament we find very sweeping statements about this matter: in the Fourth Gospel (1:18) and again in 1 John (4:12), we are told flatly, 'No one has ever seen God'. For the biblical traditions in the main God is simply not the sort of reality that is available to direct observation or experience.

If we stop to think about this for a moment, it becomes quite understandable. Can we even imagine what it would be like to experience – to *see* – the 'creator of the heavens and the earth'? What kind of experience could present a reality of that sort to us? By what criterion could *God* be distinguished from any number of

---

4   The questions taken up in these paragraphs are argued more fully in my book *In Face of Mystery*.

other marvellous or fantastic realities that one might encounter?[5] How would one recognize that this – whatever it was that one was experiencing – was *God*? On what grounds, thus, would one ever be in a position to say that it was indeed *God* that I experienced? Questions of this sort suggest that the very idea of 'experiencing *God*' is a serious mistake. And this judgement is reinforced when we remember that for the most part throughout Christian history theologians have held that all knowledge of God is through analogies and symbols; that is, it is not based directly on our *experience* of God but rather on a combination of images and concepts drawn from ordinary objects of experience. Thus God is spoken of as a father, a lord, or a king; as a shepherd, a rock, a wind (spirit); as light, truth, and love; as 'one'; as all-powerful and all-knowing; and so on. All of these words gain their primary meanings not through direct experience of God but rather through our ordinary living (and reflection on that living) – our experience of ordinary objects and properties found in the everyday world. At most, therefore (theologians have usually argued), these sorts of words must be regarded as providing *analogies* with the help of which we can put together a meaningful idea or image of that about which we are trying to speak when we say 'God': the notion of God, thus (as I shall argue below), should be understood as a human imaginative construct.

Another central biblical theme sharpens further these peculiarities of the concept of God by pointing out the difficulties they make for would-be believers. The Old Testament, for example, portrays a kind of ongoing struggle between God and the idols – those deceivers that the Israelites (and others) often worshipped in place of the 'true God'. What or who is the *true God* – the one truly worthy of worship and devotion – is really not all that clear to the Israelites, nor is it clear who are the 'true' prophets, the spokespersons and intermediaries of this true God; and in consequence, which candidates for devotion and worship are in fact *idols*, deceivers whose spokespersons and advocates are 'false prophets', also remains uncertain. The very notions of *God* and of *idol* dialectically presuppose each other, neither being comprehensible without consideration of the other. Although the concept of God has ontological weight not true of the notion of idol, these two concepts help to define and refine the meaning of each other: 'God' names the true and proper object of faith and worship, and 'idols' are false gods to which men and women often mistakenly turn in their lives and their worship. In our weakness and frailty we can never really be certain which is the true God and which an idol – and this confusion further deepens God's profound mystery.

Our very worship and ideas of God can easily become corrupted into idolatrous human attempts to control God. To claim we know with certainty who or what is

---

5   Some might wish to claim that the Bible supplies us with criteria for judging who or what is God. But that is really not the case. The many images and concepts of God presented by the Bible are far from consistent with each other, as every Bible reader knows well; and partly because of this variety and inconsistency many quite different kinds of churches and sects have appeared in the course of western religious history, most of them claiming to base their understanding of God directly on the Bible. For interesting studies of the variety of God-images present in the Bible, see J. Miles, *God: A Biography* (New York: Knopf, 1995) and his *Christ: A Crisis in the Life of God* (New York: Knopf, 2001).

God would be to claim that *our* concept of God, *our* understanding of God, *captures* what or who God really is. Such a claim is nothing more than reification of our own ideas, a disguised pretense to some measure of control over God – the sin to which the ancient Jewish prohibition against speaking the divine name is directed. The questions which the long-standing tradition of negative theology has repeatedly raised about even the most carefully refined and nuanced claims respecting God are a continuing reminder of these problems.[6] At least this much is clear, however: as human imaginations have worked and puzzled in many different directions over the image/concept of God, they have succeeded in producing an exceedingly complex and intricate symbol.

Problems with the concept of God – the mystery of God – of the sort I have been indicating here, raise the question whether this notion is not riddled with such contradictory motifs as to be utterly unintelligible, and hence should be discarded. Why not just forget all of this God-talk? Is it really worth putting ourselves through all these word games and mental hoops? Why should we suppose that concern about God is still a worthwhile expenditure of time and energy? Why not regard the concept of nature or of the universe as adequate for dealing with the ultimate context within which human life falls – and live out our lives in those terms? Many in our time have taken such a position: God-talk may well have been important and relevant in earlier periods of history, they say, but we today can do without it; and we ought, therefore, to drop the whole subject. That is certainly a possible tack to take, and it should be respected.

If, however, we are aware of certain important *values* that God-talk can, perhaps, continue to provide, and certain serious *dangers* against which it can help protect us, we may feel led in our concerns and thinking to move beyond the modern sciences and other philosophical and religious options – as well as beyond today's common sense view of things – in order to struggle with the problems and paradoxes of God-talk. Interest in the significance of the word 'God' may arise simply because one has lived and thought for much of one's life in and with a tradition in which God has been cherished as the centre on which life should be oriented: growing up in a home where devotion and service to God are taken seriously, for example; participation in the ritual and life of a church or synagogue or mosque; meditation on scripture – such experiences and activities may open our consciousness to the importance of this profound Mystery beyond all we know and can experience, as well as to the significance of our frequent temptations to make *idols* of the realities and values found within our world. Or, to take a different kind of example: a deepening awareness of the special import of the word 'God' may emerge as one begins to take note of the important place God has had in the great heritage of western literature and art, or as one studies religious and theological texts in a college class in the philosophy of religion. And so on. Without the awakening of a real interest in that 'X' on which the employment of the word 'God' is intended to focus our attention, without some sense (however vague) of what or whom we are trying to speak – in and with these images and concepts of our traditions – there would be no motivation to pursue the

---

6   For a brief sketch of some pertinent high points of the history of the negative theology, see G. Kaufman, *In the beginning*, pp. 22–6.

sorts of concerns and problems into which we have just begun to dip. Some kind of interest in God, faith in God, a sense of God (however inchoate and problematic) would seem to be presupposed in all serious theological reflection.

II

If what we are talking about when we use the word 'God' cannot be directly pointed to and is not directly experienced by human beings, what is it? And how could we come to think we know something about it? Our conception of God is an *imaginative construct*, that is, an idea or image that is put together and held together by our imaginations. As we learn in childhood to speak our native language – English, let us say – our imagining gradually becomes developed and educated in the use and meaning of thousands of complexly interconnected words that make up the vocabularies of the family into which we have been born, the community in which we live, the schools that we attend. Among these words being learned – along with all their complex grammatical, syntactical, and semantic interconnections – is the word 'God', sometimes (but not always) learned quite early in life. This word is taught in a variety of ways: by telling stories of God's care for humans, stories of what God has done in the past and is doing now, stories of God's 'son' Jesus, etc.; by teaching the child to pray to God, to sing songs of praise and thanksgiving, to be mindful of God's presence and care; by connecting the word 'God' in a special way with many other words familiar to the child (such as father, love, hope, light, king, creator, and other characterizations commonly applied to God); and so on. All these connections, characterizations, attitudes, and practices, become linked to the word 'God' and are gradually pulled together by the child's imagination into a unitary image/concept/meaning, as the child learns how to use the word 'God' in discourse with others.[7]

To say that our idea of God is an imaginative construction does not mean that it is 'just imaginary', that it is not about anything real or true.[8] Our minds are loaded with many different sorts of imaginative constructs that we take for granted represent realities of various sorts – perhaps realities we have experienced or can experience to some extent, such as cities like New York City or London (although we readily *imagine* the vast complex cities referred to by these names, none of us ever directly *experiences* all of that); or realities that no human has experienced at all, and in principle cannot directly perceive or experience, such as, for example, the universe. With this concept we call to mind the vast complex structure of all that is, that within which all events occur and all processes proceed. No one has ever directly *perceived* the universe: it is much vaster, more complex, and more mysterious than anything we can experience, and our idea of it is obviously a creation of our human imaginations;

7   Cf. L. Wittgenstein, *Lectures and Conversations on Aesthetics, Psychology and Religious Belief* (Oxford: Blackwell, 1966), p. 59f.

8   For brief explanations of my notion of imaginative construction, see G. Kaufman, *In the beginning*, pp. 119–22; G. Kaufman, *An Essay on Theological Method* (New York: Oxford University Press, 1995), especially ch. 2; and the Subject Index item, 'Imaginative construction', in G. Kaufman, *In Face of Mystery*, p. 504.

yet we have few doubts about its reality. Or consider the Big Bang, which scientists tell us is the origin of the universe. This is also an enormously complex imaginative construct based on a gigantic extrapolation backwards in time through 14 or 15 billion years – an extrapolation worked out by the scientific imagination as it takes up into its theories many kinds of pertinent clues available to us here on planet Earth. The story of cosmic and biological evolution, running forward all those billions of years, is another awe-inspiring imaginative construct that connects up with and holds together in a unitary concept many of the ideas of astrophysics, astronomy, geology, biology, chemistry, ecology, sociology, anthropology, and so on. Other ideas important to us, such as the notions of Truth, of Beauty, of Justice and the like, are all creations of the human imagination: no one has ever directly experienced any of these; they are abstractions from, and imaginative idealizations of, certain cherished features of experience. And so on and on. All of the great and comprehensive thoughts that we humans have are constructions of our imaginations, constructions without which we could not guide or order our lives; for they help orient us with significant facets of the world, of the reality (two more imaginative constructs of importance to us humans!) within which we take ourselves to be living and acting.

And so it also is with our idea of God. This is a symbol created over countless generations by humans seeking to bring before their minds, and hold in their hearts, what they regard as the ultimate reality behind all that is, an 'X' that works itself out in and through all that is; that 'X', therefore, with which we must come to terms in every moment of our lives; that 'ultimate point of reference', as I like to call it,[9] in terms of which we seek to understand and explain to ourselves all that is and all that occurs; the creator of the heavens and the earth, as Genesis 1 puts it. (An attentive re-reading of this last sentence will reveal that in every clause its meaning is conveyed by one or more important 'imaginative constructs'.) Apart from our magnificent imaginative powers, we would have no way of conceiving God at all; this is the only access we have to that reality – that 'X' – to which our prayers are directed, that before which we may bow down in worship, that on which we call in times of need, that to which we may seek to give ourselves in faith and hope and love.

Whatever we know of God, we know through this image/concept created – over countless generations – by human imaginations; and re-created (occasionally in significantly distinctive ways) by each one of us every time we think or utter the word 'God'. The God of the Bible – the God imagined, that is to say, by the biblical writers and their compatriots – remains, of course, an important source (however variegated, inconsistent, and dubious many of its characteristics may be) for thinking about God today, i.e., for the ways in which we imagine God. So also are the imaginings of the many generations of readers and worshippers from the biblical period to the present. Everything that we humans know or think with respect to God – whether we are illiterate peasants, ordinary middle-class churchgoers, or philosophical theologians – is a product of human imagining. Apart from this profound work of our imaginations, no devotion to God – in our worship and prayers, in the activities

---

9   See G. Kaufman, *An Essay on Theological Method*, pp. 14–19 for discussion of this notion.

of our daily lives, in our hopes and fears, in our most basic commitments – would be possible.

It is important that we recognize that the analysis of the image/concept of God that I have presented up to this point tells us nothing about whether God really 'exists'; or whether 'belief' in God is foolish or wise, good or bad. There is no question, however, about whether the *word* 'God' exists in the English language, and no question either whether the symbol 'God' is living and effective in the cultures and religions of native English speakers (as well as elsewhere around the globe). Though I have been making some claims here about the meaning and significance – and about the distinctive character – of this important symbol in our language, our religions, and our cultures, I have not made any claims thus far about the respects in which it calls our attention to some actual *reality* beyond this symbolization (the word 'reality' in this sentence being taken to indicate something more than a mere 'X'). The fact that we have this powerful symbol in our language tells us nothing at all – either pro or con – about whether it is a vehicle through which we come into significant relation with some further 'reality' of significance for us humans (contrary to the interesting claims of the so-called ontological argument).

We have been noting that our day-to-day lives are guided in important respects by imaginative constructs made available to us through our language and traditions, and that our sciences depend heavily on the constructive work of the human imagination in developing their basic concepts and theories. In both these cases imaginative constructions are widely in play and, moreover, are continuously tested pragmatically – that is, by what they enable us to do, how they enable life to go forward. In the sciences *experimental* testing has become highly refined and reliable, and in consequence the sciences and the knowledges they produce have very high standing in our cultures today. There is also, however, a more general and vague kind of pragmatic assessing (in our sociocultural life) of the many symbols and concepts orienting and ordering human everyday living.[10] But since this is not rigorous or systematic (as in the sciences), dangers and false paths sometimes do not become visible until too late, when they lead to catastrophe. Even then faithful *believers* – those who are said to believe something *religiously* even though they may not consider themselves to be particularly 'religious' – often do not see the handwriting on the wall. I am not in a position to say much more than this about the pragmatic 'reality-testing' of many of our major imaginative constructs – something going on in our cultures more or less continuously; but I do suggest that it will be useful to look briefly at certain examples of this testing that involve the image/concept 'God', the central symbol we are exploring in this essay.

---

10   In an article some years ago (G. Kaufman, 'Evidentialism: A Theologian's Response' in *Faith and Philosophy* 6/1 (1989), pp. 35–46) I argued that a kind of 'soft evidentialism' is clearly present in the Bible, and has always been practised in those religious faiths grounded on the Bible. Moreover, this was not a narrow evidentialism dealing largely with specific doctrinal claims (as many recent 'evidentialist' discussions have been); instead it addressed itself to the broader orienting symbols of faith – a sort of pragmatic 'reality testing' of the kind I am pointing to in the present essay.

III

Given this understanding of the symbol 'God', theology – that is, the discipline of theology, theology understood as critical systematic thinking about God – must itself be seen as basically an activity of the human imagination,[11] and should not be treated, for instance, as simply interpretation of biblical and other traditional ideas (as often in the past). The Bible was given a central place in theological work (as were some other traditions in some cases) because it was regarded as 'God's revelation' or the 'word of God' – that is, the revelation to humankind of the omnipotent, all-knowing Creator of the universe. Given that belief, it is hardly surprising that the Bible was often thought of as the most (sometimes the *only*) authoritative source for knowledge of God. Unfortunately, it was not noticed as often as it should have been that this claim itself was based on the assumption that *final authority* for truth belongs to God alone, an assumption that undermines every other supposed authority, including the Bible. The centre of Christian faith (and of the other Abrahamic religions) is not the Bible but is, of course, *God*, and what God has done and is doing; God is the reality to be worshipped and served. The Bible has been of interest and importance only because it tells a story of God and God's acts. If there is any reason to suppose that in some respects God might be other than as portrayed in the Bible and tradition, or if the Bible and tradition turn out to be significantly unclear or ambiguous in their pictures of God, the believability of these pictures will be seriously damaged (at least with respect to the issues in which these problems have come into view) because it is what or who *God* is that really matters. The Bible's authority and the tradition's importance are thus derivative: there is a principle that can undercut both of these, namely *God*. In this respect belief in God works to weaken the authority of the Bible and other Christian traditions rather than support them.

In the Bible itself the picture of God is far from constant: as new insights and understandings appear – often through the mouths of 'prophets' claiming to speak in the name of God – the picture of God takes on different forms (pertinent to new historical situations and contexts, but frequently not consistent with each other). For Christians, the most decisive transformative events occurred in connection with the life, ministry, and death of Jesus of Nazareth,[12] eventually declared to be God's 'son', the very 'word of God', the 'second person' of the divine Trinity. (This last concept became a veritable seedbed for much further imaginative creativity in future centuries.) The Bible itself, thus, supplies important evidence of the ongoing imaginative construction of the understanding of God throughout the history it reports, and the Christian movement has clearly been engaged in this activity as well.[13] Given the strong monotheistic traditions that this movement inherited, the church's creation of the totally new concept of *trinity* during its early period is quite surprising – an outstanding example of imaginative theological reconstruction of the

---

11 My most extended argument on this point is to be found in *An Essay on Theological Method*. My attempt to develop a full theological programme on the basis of this understanding is to be found in *In Face of Mystery*.

12 For a very cogent argument on this point, see J. Miles, *Christ: A Crisis in the Life of God*.

13 For more historical detail on these matters see G. Kaufman, *In the beginning*, pp. 2–9.

main lines of the concept of God in consequence of the necessity to take into account new contextual developments.

There have, of course, also been many subsequent changes in the understanding of God: very few educated people, for example, continue to believe that God created the heavens and the earth just a few thousand years ago, and that God rules the earth from somewhere in the skies above. The universe God created is now thought to be billions of years old, and billions of light-years across; life on earth, and human life in particular, did not appear simply and directly on God's command but instead through a long slow evolutionary process; and so on. Those who continue to believe in God are enabled to do so only by transforming their thinking about God in ways appropriate to the diverse circumstances in which they are living. Since ongoing faith in God is possible only if God is understood to be pertinent to the conditions and problems of life with which believers must come to terms, the way in which God is imagined must change accordingly. Available ideas of God have always been undergoing reality-testing and corresponding reconstruction of this sort. So the questions concerning how God should be understood today – who or what God is or can be for us twenty-first-century people; whether we can still find images and concepts that can make sense of the notion of God at all, etc. – are really not all that new. During most of the history of God-talk sociocultural problems and developments underlay the theological issues being given attention.

And so it is today. As just noted, the traditional biblical picture of God as a kind of person, who created the world and rules it from the nearby heavens above, does not fit well with our modern understandings of the cosmos as a 14 or 15 billion-year creative evolutionary process through which the universe – and all its contents – came into being. Nor does that traditional picture fit well with our understanding of human existence as, on the one hand, emergent from (though still deeply embedded within) the enormously complex web of life on planet Earth; and as having, on the other hand, developed socioculturally in history to a point where we humans now have the power to wipe out human life – and much other life as well.[14] Unlike the traditional picture of life on earth as completely and safely in the hands of God, it is now us humans – with our powerfully creative imaginations – who have taken over substantial (though by no means all) power on planet Earth. If we take seriously today's ecological understanding of ourselves – as inextricably embedded in the intricate web of life on Earth – it becomes difficult (if not impossible) to imagine any sort of action that God could take, which would set these ecological matters right and enable human life to go on: it is we ourselves who must change the way we are living and acting if the ecological crisis we are causing is to be addressed. For those women and men who accept these understandings of the world and of human life in the world, an intolerable tension between faith in (the traditional) God and our modern/postmodern knowledge is created.[15] This should not be regarded as an unhappy circumstance, however, for it sets up conditions that facilitate radically new

---

14 For further discussion of humans as 'biohistorical' beings (as suggested here), see below, pp. 25–28, section V, and G. Kaufman, *In Face of Mystery*, Part 2.

15 For further elaboration of these problems see G. Kaufman, *In Face of Mystery* and G. Kaufman, *In the beginning*.

imagining of what we today might quite properly mean by 'God'. The claim being argued here, that all theology is in fact imaginative construction by us humans gives today's theologians much more freedom on the question of how they will think of God, and of God's relations to and with us humans, than theologians had during much of the past.

Both the Bible (in some places) and past Christian traditions emphasized that our principal human problem is our immersion in sinfulness and guilt before God, while simultaneously encouraging us with hopes that God would forgive us and bring salvation. Given our enormous power today, however, and our full responsibility for controlling the exercise of that power, our situation vis-à-vis God seems now to be of a significantly different order; and it should not surprise us, therefore, that *reality-testing* of the received image/concepts of God is going on widely. We cannot address these problems by simply rehearsing once more the old stories that recount the way in which God and humanity – and their relationship – were imagined in the past, for we are living in a quite different situation, and it is time for us to rethink – re-imagine – how we should conceive God today. Indeed, it may not be appropriate any longer to orient human life in terms of the symbol 'God'. This is a time when we must attempt fresh imaginative approaches to the question of God, seeking a construction that fits in with – and in fact illumines – our present understanding of life here on planet Earth. Some might ask whether it would be possible – or appropriate – to place our 'faith' in any such humanly constructed understanding. But this question, of course, overlooks the fact that all previous understandings of God have also been human imaginative constructions (as we have been noting); so we should not let this consideration get in the way of our moving forward today with such an approach.

IV

How should one begin such fresh imagining? What kind of moves do we need to make? Is there some way to avoid thinking in and with the traditional images and concepts of God that we have inherited, while still be thinking about *God*? We noted earlier that theological work presupposes 'some kind of interest in God, faith in God,...sense of God' however inchoate these may be.[16] Given this deep but inchoate interest in and sense of God, how should we proceed in our theological construction?

Obviously, we cannot address this question satisfactorily by simply attaching the name 'God' arbitrarily to whatever comes to mind as a plausible candidate. We need to ask ourselves, What is it that has given the word 'God' the importance in our religious and cultural traditions that it has? It has not been simply that God was thought of as the answer to speculative questions like, Where did the world come from? or Is there an ultimate power behind everything? That which the word 'God' names has been much more existentially serious than these questions suggest: God was believed to bring salvation from all ills, fulfilment of life. The name 'God', thus, has been of significant weight, a name to be given a central place in consciousness

---

16 See p. 16 above.

and life. God, that is to say, was regarded as that reality – and the word 'God' was taken to express that complex meaning – which brings wholeness, meaningfulness, salvation to human life.

Attempts at fresh imaginative construction of the image/concept of God can be regarded as appropriate and legitimate only if their use of the name 'God' is warranted linguistically; that is, only if the new conception has significant continuity with what this word has meant in the past. (What constitutes 'significant continuity' in this matter is, of course, a judgement call on which there are sharp disagreements.) It is not possible to engage in serious construction of a new understanding of God in this essay, since that would require us (a) to examine much more fully than is possible here the way in which the symbol 'God' has functioned in human discourse and life in the past, and (b) to develop a rather elaborate argument for the new understanding of the symbol being proposed. The most that can be done here is to suggest briefly what such an approach might reveal.[17] There are, in my opinion, two major themes that have given this symbol its extraordinary power and significance in human life. On the one hand (as we have been noting) God has usually been conceived in quasi-human images, and has been regarded as a kind of focus or centre in terms of which human life can come to fulfilment – God has been thought of as a *humanizing centre of orientation* for life. On the other hand, God has been envisioned (as we noted early in this essay) as mysterious and beyond all human knowing, the all-powerful creator of the heavens and the earth and the determiner of destiny, the ultimate judge of the world – that is, God has been thought of as the *relativizer* (as I sometimes put it) of everything human and finite.[18] Hence, God has been taken to be radically independent of all human striving and desiring – certainly no product of our wishes and fantasies – while at the same time it was believed that only in relation to God is genuine human fulfilment to be found. God has been believed to transcend all things human, indeed all of creation, even while being that which creates, sustains, and nourishes all that is. These two dimensions of our inherited idea of God – humanizer and relativizer – belong together: either taken without the other would undermine and ultimately destroy the function and significance of God as the proper object of human devotion and service.

What seems to underlie these themes in the symbol 'God' is an understanding of humans (both individuals and communities) as needing a centre of orientation and devotion outside themselves and their perceived desires and needs, if they are to find genuine fulfilment. As beings seeking security and satisfaction, we all too easily make ourselves the centre of life, rearranging all else so that it conforms better to our wishes. Our narcissism as individuals all too often leads to corruption

---

17   I have given much more elaborate arguments on this matter in a number of places, beginning with G. Kaufman, *God the Problem* (Cambridge: Harvard University Press, 1972), especially chs. 5, 10, 11; and continuing in G. Kaufman, *The Theological Imagination: Constructing the Concept of God* (Philadelphia: Westminster Press, 1981), especially pp. 34ff; and G. Kaufman, *An Essay on Theological Method*. My fullest statement will be found in G. Kaufman, *In Face of Mystery*; and important further developments of my thinking about God are now available in G. Kaufman, *In the beginning*, and G. Kaufman, *Jesus and Creativity* (Minneapolis: Fortress Press, 2006).

18   See G. Kaufman, *In the beginning*, pp. 59–63, 66–8.

of our relations with others, and our similar ethnocentrism as communities and anthropocentrism as a species lead to warfare among peoples and to exploitation of the resources in our environment. A centre and focus of meaning, which can draw us out of our preoccupation with ourselves and our desires and evoke from us devotion and service, can break through this curved-in character of our human existence. The image/concept of God as entirely independent of all our wishes, and not susceptible to any remaking or reshaping in accord with our desires, has traditionally performed this function. The use of anthropomorphic imagery in depicting God – God being seen, for instance, as a humane, just, and loving parent, and we humans being regarded as the children for whom God has unlimited love and care – contributed to the overall impression that God is thoroughly trustworthy; so men and women could give themselves without reservation in service and devotion to God.

There has always been considerable tension between these two central motifs in the idea of God – humaneness, with its tendencies to employ human-like images, and its emphasis on human fulfilment; and transcendence or absoluteness, with their emphasis on God's radical otherness, God's mystery, God's utter inaccessibility. This tension gave the symbol 'God' much of its power and effectiveness as a focus for devotion and orientation in human life (though it has often been a source of instability in human affairs as well). The rules of our language (I am suggesting) require that if we wish to reconstruct this symbol, we must keep in mind that it is properly employed only when it focuses our attention on a reality with these two central motifs in complex interconnection with each other: that 'X' – whatever it may be – that we today can properly regard as both *relativizing* (calling into question) and *humanizing* us humans, as well as relativizing and humanizing the world in which we find ourselves.

What is meant here by the phrase, 'the rules of our language'? I do not have anything technical in mind – only the fact that we would not be able to understand each other (or to understand ourselves, for that matter) in our everyday use of language, if we did not follow certain generally accepted rules governing the way we put together our words and sentences. When children learn to speak English, they learn the rules of English usage along with the many words they are taught; Chinese children learn to follow quite different rules; and so on.[19] Among the rules that we English speakers learn is one requiring that what we call 'proper names' must designate something quite specific and particular – think of such names as George Bush, New York City, Yale University, the Lisbon earthquake, the sun. If we started using language in an arbitrary way, supposing that we could designate anything we please with such names, it would not only be impossible for us to communicate with each other about such things; it would be impossible for us even to *think* them, for we could never be certain of just what it was that we were trying to think. And so it is with the name 'God': the rules of our language require (I am suggesting) that if we wish to reconstruct our symbol 'God', we must keep in mind that this symbol is used

---

19 The most fully developed, and persuasive, argument for this conception of language and its importance is to be found in L. Wittgenstein, *Philosophical Investigations* (Oxford: Blackwell, 1958).

to focus our attention on an 'X' with humanizing and relativizing motifs in complex interconnection with each other.

Earlier in this essay I pointed out that the concept of God undermines the notion of biblical authority in theology. Now we are in a position to see that the symbol 'God' has no *intrinsic* connections with the Bible at all (though it has, of course, important historical connections). To suppose (for instance), that the various forms of the idea of God found in the Bible must be regarded as in some way authoritative or binding on us today (as we engage in theological reconstruction) would imply that God is taken to be a kind of historical (or literary) figure like Socrates and Plato: with such figures we gain nearly all of our basic information from certain ancient texts, in this case the Platonic dialogues. (Many traditional theologians have, of course, understood their task in just such terms). However, although the Bible may well teach us some important things about God, the name 'God' does not refer (even in the Bible) exclusively, or even primarily, to a character in the biblical text. As we have seen in our examination of this symbol, God is supposedly the ultimate reality with which we humans have to do, the source of all that is, the 'Creator of the heavens and the earth' (as the Bible itself puts it), 'the Maker of all things both visible and invisible' (as some of the creeds echo). These characterizations imply that *all realities* of which we are aware (or unaware!) – not simply those mentioned in the Bible – must be taken into account as we seek to understand what is designated by the word 'God'. And for this reason throughout the diverse millennia that this symbol has been effective in orienting human living, acting, and thinking, it has been necessary to engage repeatedly in imaginative constructive attempts to *re*-conceive – to think through afresh – who or what is really *God*.[20] If we today still think it important and desirable to continue living out our lives in significant relation to God – that is, in significant relation to what we are linguistically justified in calling 'God' – we also must undertake our own imagining, and see whether we can, perhaps, find images and concepts that will enable this ancient, mutilated and soiled symbol to take on new life.

The image/concept of God that we have inherited has been effective in shaping the values and meanings of many basic human activities and experiences, in this way orienting and helping to order certain forms of human life. But the symbol 'God' (as we have noted) is not grounded in any specific type of human experience and – though pious believers often supposed they had, for example, 'experienced' God's 'grace' or 'judgement' directly – particular experiences of this or that sort may not be regarded as evidence of the appropriateness or validity of certain particular understandings of God. However, the broad sociocultural 'reality testing' which the symbol 'God' (in face of new historical conditions) has continuously undergone, has provided a basis for significant reconstruction of this symbol many times in the past; and in this way it has been adapted – imaginatively – to the changing circumstances of human existence in different cultural settings. This is obviously a symbol of considerable durability and flexibility, and it continues to show much more vitality today than some observers had supposed (a few decades back) would be possible.

---

20 Detailed evidence for this claim will be found in the Prologue of G. Kaufman, *In the beginning*, pp. 1–31.

The jury is still out, however, on the question whether it will be able to survive the vicissitudes of modernity/postmodernity.

V

To give some sense of the kind of imaginative construction of this image/concept that I think is now appropriate,[21] I will briefly sketch here a world-picture[22] – including God – that is more in keeping (than our inherited pictures of God, the world, and humanity) with the way in which university-educated people today understand the cosmos, and the human place within the cosmos. We humans today – and the further course of our history – are no longer completely at the disposal of the natural powers that brought us into being in the way we were as recently as ten thousand years ago. Through our various symbolisms and knowledges, skills and technologies, we have gained a kind of *transcendence* over the nature of which we are part unequalled (so far as we know) by any other form of life. For good or ill we humans have utterly transformed the face of the earth and are beginning to push on into outer space; and we are becoming capable of altering the genetic make-up of future human generations. Despite the great powers that our knowledges and technologies have given us, however, it is clear that our transcendence of the natural orders within which we emerged is far from adequate to assure our ongoing human existence; indeed, the ecological crisis of our time has brought to our attention the fact that precisely through the exercise of our growing power on planet Earth we are destroying the very conditions that make human life possible.

To understand ourselves and our powers more adequately, we need to see them in the wider context in which they exist. It will be helpful if I introduce here two (perhaps unfamiliar) concepts. First, I want to call attention to what can be designated as the *serendipitous creativity* manifest throughout our evolutionary universe – that is, the coming into being through time of new realities. I use the concept of 'creativity' here – a descendant of the traditional idea of 'God the creator' – because it presents creation of novel realities as ongoing processes or events, and does not call forth an image of a kind of 'cosmic person' standing outside the world, manipulating it from without. Second, since the traditional notion of God's purposive activity in the world – a powerful movement working in and through all cosmic and historical processes – is almost impossible to reconcile with modern/postmodern thinking about evolution and history, I shall replace it with the idea of what I call *trajectories* or *directional movements* that emerge spontaneously in the course of evolutionary and historical developments.[23]

---

21   For a fuller presentation of this conception of God, see G. Kaufman, *In Face of Mystery*, especially Part 4, and chs. 1–3 of G. Kaufman, *In the beginning*.

22   I find Wittgenstein's use of the concept of 'world-picture' – to indicate the wide and deep linguistic/conceptual network underlying all our experiencing, acting, and thinking – both illuminating and persuasive. See L. Wittgenstein, *On Certainty* (New York: Harper Torchbooks, 1972), especially sections 92–179, 208–15, 229–53, 279–82, etc.

23   These two concepts are developed in detail in G. Kaufman, *In Face of Mystery*: see chs. 19–20.

I am suggesting that we should not think of the universe in which we find ourselves as a kind of permanent structure but rather as constituted by (a) ongoing cosmic serendipitous creativity which (b) manifests itself through trajectories of various sorts – both biological-evolutionary and historico-cultural   working themselves out in longer and shorter stretches of time. There are, of course, many cosmic trajectories, moving in diverse directions; and here on planet Earth there have been many quite different evolutionary trajectories on which the billions of species of life have been produced. Our human existence – its purposiveness, its greatly varied complexes of social/moral/cultural/religious values and meanings, its virtually unlimited imaginative powers and glorious creativity, its horrible failures and gross evils, its historicity – all this has come into being on one of these trajectories, and is what we can quite properly call a 'serendipitous' manifestation of the creativity in the cosmos. We do not know in what direction this evolutionary-historical trajectory will move in the future: the creativity manifest in the universe goes its own way, a way not always in accord with our human wishes and desires. We can say, however, that like the God of our ancient traditions, this creativity (as manifest in our biohistorical trajectory)[24] has been both *humanizing* – it has brought our human reality, with all its values, meanings, and modes of life into being – and *relativizing*, calling into question and ultimately limiting us and our projects. It is this cosmic serendipitous creativity, I suggest, that we should today think of as God.[25]

Construing the universe in this way, as constituted by cosmic serendipitous creativity that manifests itself in both biological-evolutionary and historico-cultural trajectories is important for us humans; for it helps us see that our proper place in the world, our home in the universe, is the evolutionary/ecological/historico-cultural trajectory on which we have emerged. I would like to call attention to two points in this connection. First, this approach provides us with a world-picture within which we can characterize quite accurately the major events in the course of cosmic evolution and history that have been crucial to us humans. Moreover, the ancient cosmological dualisms – heaven and earth, God and the world, supernature and nature – that have shaped Christian thinking from early on and have become so problematical in our own time, are completely gone in this picture.

Second, because this approach highlights the linkage of the *creativity* manifest in the universe with our humanness and the humane values important to us, it can support hope (but not certainty) for the future of our human world. It is a hope about the overall direction of future human history – a hope for truly *creative* movement toward an ecologically and morally responsible, pluralistic, human existence. A hope of this sort, grounded on the mystery of creativity in the world – a creativity that on our trajectory shows itself in part through our own creative powers – can motivate

---

24 I use the term 'biohistorical' to express and highlight the fact that we humans today are products of biological-evolutionary developments *in complex interaction with* historico-cultural developments. For a full discussion of this matter, see G. Kaufman, *In Face of Mystery*, chs. 8–14. For my most fully developed reflection on Christological issues, see my recent book, *Jesus and Creativity* (Kaufman, 2006).

25 For a full analysis and exposition of what this means, see G. Kaufman, *In the beginning*, chs. 1–3; see also G. Kaufman, *In Face of Mystery*, Pt. 4.

us men and women to devote our lives to helping bring about this more humane and rightly-ordered world to which we aspire.

If God is understood as the serendipitous creativity manifest throughout the cosmos – instead of as a cosmic person – and we humans are understood as deeply embedded in, and basically sustained by, this creative activity in and through the web of life on planet Earth, we will be strongly encouraged to develop attitudes and to participate in activities that fit properly into this web of living creativity, all members of which are neighbours that we should love and respect. We humans today are being drawn beyond our present condition and order of life by creative impulses in our biohistorical trajectory suggesting decisions and movements now required of us. If we respond in appropriately creative ways, to the historical and ecological forces now impinging upon us on all sides, there is a possibility – though no certainty – that niches for humankind better fitted to the wider ecological and historical orders on Earth than our present niches, may be brought into being. However, if we fail to so respond, it seems likely that we humans may not survive much longer. Are we willing to commit ourselves to live and act in accord with the imperatives laid upon us by the biohistorical situations in which we find ourselves, in the hope that our actions will be supported and enhanced by cosmic serendipitously creative events? In my view, it is this kind of hope, and faith, and commitment to which the trajectory that has brought us into being now calls us.

Thinking of God in the way suggested here will evoke a considerably different faith and hope and piety than that associated with traditional interpretations of the Christian symbol-system. However, certain central Christian emphases are significantly deepened. First and most important: understanding the ultimate mystery of things – God – in terms of the metaphor of serendipitous creativity facilitates (more effectively than the traditional creator/lord/father imagery did) the maintenance of a decisive qualitative distinction between God and us creatures. The creativity manifest in the world now becomes the only appropriate focus for our devotion and worship, that which alone can provide proper overall orientation for our lives. All other realities – being finite, transitory, and corruptible creatures – become dangerous idols which, when worshipped and made central to human orientation, can bring disaster to human affairs. This distinction between God (creativity) and the created order – perhaps the most important contribution of monotheistic religious traditions to human self-understanding – continues to be emphasized in the symbolic picture I am sketching here. Second, in keeping with this first point: conceiving humans as *biohistorical* beings who have emerged on one of the countless creative trajectories moving through the cosmos – instead of as creatures distinguished from all others as the climax of creation (a claim often made in traditional Christianity) – makes it clear that we humans are indissolubly a part of the created order. In this picture the too-easy human-centredness of traditional Christian thinking is thoroughly undercut.[26]

---

26 The understanding of God proposed here can be developed into a full-orbed *Christian* interpretation of human faith and life if the creativity that is God is brought into significant connection with the poignancy and power of the story and character of Jesus, regarded (by Christians) as what Colossians 1:15 calls the 'image of the invisible God', an image of central importance for the *human* sphere of life. The christic New Testament images and meanings

In my opinion this way of thinking of God, the world, and us humans within the world – though barely plausible when outlined this briefly[27] – is a viable option for Christian faith today. Many Christians, formed to deep levels by traditional understandings of the basic Christian symbols, may regard this option as unsatisfactory and pass it by. There are some, however (I have reason to believe), who find this way of thinking about Christian faith and life to be liberative, indeed saving, for us living in today's world.

VI

In this essay I have argued that the *ultimate* context of human life, experience, and reflection is mystery; that is, that we cannot know or say what is ultimately real, or what is truly the case with respect to what we call the 'world' in which we live or our own human being and situations. Life is not simply and only mystery, of course, and from early on humans have developed images and pictures of themselves, of the contexts of their lives, and of the powers with which they had to come to terms – images and pictures and practices and rules about how life was to be lived. In short, the *religions* were gradually created. The religions have always been human constructions intended to enable life to go on safely, fruitfully, and if possible, happily – despite the profound mysteries of existence. They have often changed in decisive ways so as to come to terms with new circumstances more effectively; and there are many different sorts of religions. In recent centuries, especially with the development of the sciences, more reliable methods of testing our images and ideas of the world, and of humans in the world, have been created; and in consequence tensions between traditional religious ideas and scientific understandings of the world and the human have often appeared.

With *mystery* as backdrop in this way, I turned (in the remainder of the essay) to an examination of the symbol 'God' – an imaginative construct of extraordinary complexity that fuses (on the one hand) our notion of ultimate mystery with (on the other hand) the idea of a single 'ultimate point of reference' for orienting and ordering human life. The concept of *serendipitous creativity* (I suggested) provides a reasonable and appropriate way to think of God today. Complex imaginative constructs of this sort are not simply arbitrary inventions: only as they provide significant orientation for men and women do they become objects of devotion

---

reveal something of great significance to our alienated human life. Notions, stories and pictures of reconciliation, love, and peace, of self-giving, voluntary poverty, concern for our enemies, vicarious suffering, point to our deep interconnectedness with each other. Thus, they show the direction in which communities and individuals must move if our human world is ever to become more truly humane. For a 'wider Christology' (than that to which I have been limited in this brief footnote) which includes the early Christian community as among the 'christic' images and which welcomes all who have 'christic'-like concerns and commitments, see G. Kaufman, *In Face of Mystery*, chs. 25–6, and especially G. Kaufman, *Jesus and Creativity*.

27 A much more detailed presentation of this conception of God, the world, and humanity will be found in G. Kaufman, *In Face of Mystery*; for my latest refinements of this view, see G. Kaufman, *In the beginning*, chs. 1–3, and *Jesus and Creativity*.

and service; they are subject, thus, to ongoing reality-testing as new historical circumstances must be addressed. A brief review of some of the significant changes that occurred in the symbol 'God' during historical periods recounted in the Bible (as well as later developments) revealed that imaginative reconstruction has always been going on in response to new circumstances that raised new questions about the way in which God was understood. The fact that the concept of God has always been an imaginative construct (though this was not clearly recognized through much of Christian history) in no way affects the question – important for this book – of whether God has been, or should be, regarded as *real*. It does, of course, bear on the question whether God's reality can be *known*. But (as we noted) central to the concept of God is the idea of mystery, that God is beyond human understanding or knowing; and our ideas of God are all human constructions. This is entirely consistent with the understanding that the relation of humans to God is one of trust and faith, not knowledge. Of course, humans could hardly trust in God, and could not commit themselves to ordering their lives in such faith, if they did not assume that what they take to be God – e.g., the serendipitous creativity manifest throughout the universe – is (in some very significant sense) real. The constructivism that underlies and makes necessary human faith in no way threatens this conviction. Moreover, recognizing that all our ideas about God are our own imaginative constructs helps protect us from reifying these ideas into *idols*, which we then mistakenly worship and serve.

What is required today for faith in God to continue its orienting and ordering function is not simply proposing further new interpretations of the *traditional* configuration of images and concepts of God, but rather (a) careful assessment of the respects in which the (received) symbol 'God' no longer addresses effectively today's problems; and (b) undertaking, in light of that assessment, fresh imaginative construction of an understanding of God – and God's relation to humanity and to the world – that will more effectively orient and order our lives today. This does not imply that we humans are trying to create God – whatever that might mean. On the contrary, it 'lets God be God': the ultimate mystery, the ultimate reality that we humans can never adequately grasp or comprehend. And it frees us to focus on what we humans can be and do: approach life and its problems as imaginatively and creatively as we can.

I have sought to show that every image/concept of God is best understood as a creation of the human imagination in its search for symbols that will adequately orient human life; and that it is appropriate, therefore, to consider ways of assessing the sort of orientation in life that the received symbol 'God' can provide, and to reconstruct – re-imagine – this image/concept in whatever respects will enable it more effectively to perform this orienting function. In this understanding of constructivism religious symbols (of this sort) are not regarded as mere free-floating fantasies; they are, rather, mediating-vehicles of *realities* essential to ongoing human being and well-being. Without some symbolic vehicles of this sort, self-conscious, responsible human life could hardly continue.

Chapter 3

Science and Religion:
The Immersion Solution

Peter Lipton

Introduction: Two Ways to Handle Contradictions

This essay focuses on the cognitive tension between science and religion, in particular on the contradictions between some of the claims of current science and some of the claims in religious texts. My aim is to suggest how some work in the philosophy of science may help to manage this tension. Thus I will attempt to apply some work in the philosophy of science to the philosophy of religion, following the traditional gambit of trying to stretch the little one does understand to cover what one does not understand.

My own views on science and religion are hardly views from nowhere. My scientific perspective is that of a hopeful realist. Scientific realism is the view that science, though fallible through and through, is in the truth business, attempting to find out about a world independent of ourselves, and it is the view that business is, on the whole, going pretty well. My religious perspective is that of a progressive Jew. The problem I am worrying in this essay is my own problem. I take my other philosophical problems seriously too, but for me the question of the relationship between science and religion has a personal edge I do not feel in my other philosophical obsessions with the likes of the problems of induction or the content of *ceteris paribus* laws. My reply to a charge of self-indulgence would be that my cognitive predicament is, I believe, widely shared.

How do we manage contradictions? The White Queen famously gave Alice the excellent advice:

'I can't believe *that*,' said Alice.

'Can't you?' the Queen said in a pitying tone. 'Try again. Draw a long breath and shut your eyes.'

Alice laughed. 'There's no use trying,' she said, 'One can't believe impossible things.'

'I dare say you haven't had much practice,' said the Queen. 'When I was your age I always did it for half an hour a day. Why sometimes I believed as many as six impossible things before breakfast.'[1]

---

1   Lewis Carroll, *Through the Looking Glass* (1896), in *The Annotated Alice* (New York: New American Library, 1960), p. 251.

The White Queen has nothing on me. I believe many more than six impossible things before breakfast and I do it effortlessly, since my beliefs include many contradictions I have not noticed. Some of them are obvious in retrospect. When I lived in rural northwest Massachusetts, I preferred one route walking to my office and another route coming home, believing in each case that I was taking the shortest route. For an unconscionable time, I failed to put these beliefs together and so failed to deploy my sophisticated geometrical knowledge that the length of a path does not depend on the direction travelled. It is, however, more challenging to believe contradictions once you are made aware of them. Few of us aspire to the White Queen's level of cognitive control in such cases, but there are plenty of other options available. Ignoring the contradiction very often works. Another option is to find a way of compartmentalizing beliefs, effectively preventing contradictory beliefs from coming into contact with each other. But suppose that we wish squarely to face up to a contradiction and manage it directly. In many cases we will try to show that the contradiction is only apparent. One of the maxims in the professional philosopher's tool kit is: confronted with a contradiction, make a distinction that will dissolve it. *In extremis*, however, we might just face the music and give up some of our claims or our beliefs to restore consistency.

When claims form contradictions it is impossible for them all to be correct. Consistency is of course no guarantee of truth, but it is a necessary condition. In this essay I am particularly interested in the choice between two strategies for managing contradictions so as to restore consistency, especially as those contradictions arise between science and religion. This choice is between *adjusting content* and *adjusting attitude*. Adjusting content means giving up some claims. Adjusting attitude means keeping the claims but changing one's epistemic attitude toward at least some of them. It is the second strategy that I am going to favour in the particular context of science and religion. The general contrast between these strategies can be brought out in the context of the astronomer Arthur Eddington's memorable discussion of his two tables:

> I…have drawn up my chairs to my two tables. Two tables! Yes; there are duplicates of every object about me – two tables, two chairs, two pens… One of them has been familiar to me from earliest years… It has extension; it is comparatively permanent; it is coloured; above all it is substantial…. Table No. 2 is my scientific table…. It does not belong to the world previously mentioned…. My scientific table is mostly emptiness. Sparsely scattered in that emptiness are numerous electric charges rushing about with great speed; but their combined bulk amounts to less than a billionth of the bulk of the table itself. Notwithstanding its strange construction it turns out to be an entirely efficient table. It supports my writing paper as satisfactorily as table No. 1; for when I lay the paper on it the little electric particles with their headlong speed keep on hitting the underside, so that the paper is maintained in shuttlecock fashion at a nearly steady level.[2]

My subject is the tension between science and religion, not between science and commonsense, but Eddington's tables help to clarify the contrast between the two

---

2   Arthur Eddington, *The Nature of the Physical World* (Cambridge: Cambridge University Press, 1928), pp. xi–xii.

ways of managing contradictions, the contrast between adjusting content, and leaving content alone but adjusting attitude. In the case of my strange beliefs about walking to and from my office, you will be pleased to hear that I reacted to the contradiction by adjusting content: I simply gave up the claim that one route was the shorter in one direction and the other route was shorter in the other direction (though I never did work out which route was the shorter). In the case of the two tables, to adjust content would be to give up on some of the claims of science, of everyday life or both, insofar as there are genuine contradictions between them. But unlike the case of the two routes, in the case of the two tables adjusting content is not the natural option. In particular, we are not going simply to give up our claims about the everyday table. Unlike the White Queen perhaps, we just can't do it. But however deeply we are immersed in our everyday view of the world, we may admit that certain parts of it systematically attribute more than is really there, and these parts are a kind of projection of our own experience that may contradict the scientific story which we take to be closer to the truth about the table. If this is the line we take, then we might nevertheless continue to use our everyday conceptions since, after all, we have no option, but not fully believe them, at least not when we are doing philosophy (or science). Through this adjustment of attitude, although the contradiction between the scientific and the everyday *claims* would not be removed, our philosophical attitude toward the everyday claims would leave us with a set of *beliefs* that are consistent. Thus we keep the full set of claims, the full content, contradictions and all, but adjust our attitude to avoid having to believe yet more impossible things before breakfast. We use more claims than we believe.

Science and Religion: The Usual Suspects

What now about science and religion? There are a number of familiar points of apparent tension between the claims of science and the claims of religion – you can provide your own list. For example, there are various tensions between scientific accounts of the development of the universe and of life in it on the one hand, and the accounts of these matters in Genesis on the other. There are tensions between a scientific view of the world and the miracles and wonders described for example in the book of Exodus. There are tensions between the results of the secular historical study of the origins of the Bible and what that text says about its own origins. And there are apparent tensions between what science and religion seem to tell us about the status and indeed the existence of God. (Although the only religious text I refer to by name in this essay is the Bible, my hope is that my discussion applies more widely.)

Before I consider how tensions of these sorts might be managed, I issue two health warnings. Both are in effect warnings against identifying the tension problem with the much broader topic of the relations between science and religion. First, although I am focusing on the apparent incompatibility between various religious and scientific claims, I do not want to encourage the common and primitive practice of presenting a picture of religious life that would reduce it to religious doctrine. My intention is closer to the opposite: I want to make more room for a religious form of life in the discussions of the relation between science and religion, and I do not suppose for a minute that religion is reducible to religious claims: there is much more to religion than that.

The second health warning is that although I am here focusing on tensions between science and religion, I would not wish to give the impression that the histories of science and religion have been histories dominated by conflict. That is another surprisingly common view but it too is fundamentally mistaken. The constantly retailed story about Galileo and the Church notwithstanding, science and religion have often been seen as complementary. Indeed a great deal of science has been driven by religious motivations and has performed essential religious functions. Thus science has been taken to reveal the majesty of creation and the will of God, to illuminate religious doctrine, and to provide the technologies to support religious observance by, for example, providing for more accurate chronology. Conversely, it has often been held that religion is indispensable for science, for example because it underwrites the reliability of scientific methods.

These extensive cooperative relations show that the tension problem is only one part of the much broader issue of the relations between science and religion. But it is the part that concerns me in this essay. How are we going to manage these tensions between science and religion, arising from incompatible content? Recall that the general choice I wish to discuss is between changing content and changing attitude. There are a number of familiar ways of managing the tension by changing content, and in particular by diminishing content. Let me begin by putting three such views to one side, with unseemly haste. First, one could take the view that religious discourse is through and through figurative or metaphorical, so for example talk about God is really just an oblique way of referring to nature. That will eliminate much of the tension between science and religion; but I do not find this route attractive. The problem with the metaphor view is not with the idea that a religious text might contain metaphor. Some of the writing in the Bible certainly does appear to be metaphorical. For example, when God is described in Exodus as liberating the Jews from Egypt with a mighty hand and an outstretched arm the text is not I think making an anatomical point. But nor is all of the text metaphorical, and in my view not enough of it is to solve the tension problem without extensive semantic violence. Thus the story in Exodus is of a personal God who liberated the Jews from slavery, fed them in the wilderness and gave them the Torah. This material seems clearly written as a literal narrative, not as a metaphor. Of course we can choose to read any text as a pervasive metaphor, but in the case of the Bible this would be to go against the plain meaning, and it would in my view so diminish the value of that text and of the religious traditions it supports that we should try to find a less disruptive way of resolving the tension.

A second route I will not follow is the value view. Instead of saying that science is literal and religion metaphorical, you might say the following. There can be no real tension between science and religion because science is in the fact business and religion is in the value business. They are in such different lines of work that there can be no incompatibility between them. Fact claims and value claims can bear no logical relations (the maxim is that one cannot derive an 'ought' from an 'is'), so they cannot contradict each other, so they cannot generate the tension problem.[3] But like the appeal to wholesale metaphor, the value view is unattractively diminishing, and for a parallel reason. Of course religious texts and traditions include value claims, but they make factual claims as well. To this one might add that the suggestion that science is a value-free zone is difficult to defend, and that the assumption that there is no logical contact possible between fact and value is dubitable. But my main objection to the value view is that it would force us to eliminate or ignore too much of the plain factual content of our religious texts. So the value solution is not for me.

Third, there is the selection view. On this view, science and religion both deliver factual claims and, taken together, these claims form a multiply inconsistent set. So we should weed out claims, until we have a consistent subset. The claims we remove should be those which we judge to have the weakest warrant, or anyway a weaker warrant than the claims they contradict. In some cases, this means the claim that goes is religious; in other cases it will be scientific: we have to decide on a case-by-case basis.[4] This selection view is epistemically responsible, but in my view it would leave far too many holes in the religious text.

The metaphor, value and selection views all would deal with contradictions by diminishing content. The metaphor view does this by eliminating the literal meaning of the religious text, the value view by eliminating the factual content of the religious text, and the selection view by removing claims both from religion and from science. The admirable motivation in all three cases is to avoid saddling ourselves with contradictory beliefs. If diminishing content were the only way to avoid contradictory beliefs, one of these three approaches might be our best option, at least for those who are not willing to give up on religion altogether. But diminishing content is not the only way: it is also possible to maintain content and adjust our attitude towards it.

Antirealism

Philosophers of science have explored several ways to keep content while adjusting attitude. The content in question for them is the content of scientific theories, but some of their proposals may be adaptable to religious discourse. That is the possibility I wish to explore. Scientific realists take a stand on both the question of content and the question of belief. They maintain that theories are to be interpreted literally – given their full content – and that the best ones should be believed to be at least approximately true. Some antirealists agree with realists about content, but disagree about belief. This may provide us with ways to relieve the tension between science and religion. We may preserve content, what a scientific theory says, because that content serves various valuable purposes, yet at the same time we can forbear believing that content to be revelatory of a mind-independent reality. In so doing, we can manage contradictions without dropping content.

---

3   Cf. Stephen Jay Gould, *Rocks of Ages: Science and Religion in the Fullness of Life* (New York: Ballantine Books, 1999).

4   Cf. Alvin Plantinga, 'When Faith and Reason Clash: Evolution and the Bible', in David L. Hull and Michael Ruse (eds), *The Philosophy of Biology* (Oxford: Oxford University Press, 1998), pp. 674–97.

Descartes provided a striking example of how this adjustment of attitude towards science is possible, and specifically in the context of the relation between science and religion:

> For there is no doubt that the world was created right from the start with all the perfection which it now has.... This is the doctrine of the Christian faith, and our natural reason convinces us that it was so.... Nevertheless, if we want to understand the nature of plants or of men, it is much better to consider how they can gradually grow from seeds than to consider how they were created by God at the very beginning of the world. Thus we may be able to think up certain very simple and easily known principles which can serve, as it were, as the seeds from which we can demonstrate that the stars, the earth and indeed everything we observe in this visible world could have sprung. For although we know for sure that they never did arise in this way, we shall be able to provide a much better explanation of their nature by this method than if we merely describe them as they now are or as we believe them to have been created.[5]

Was Descartes sincere, or was he just protecting himself from religious persecution? My own view is that he was sincere and that his religious belief ran very deep. If you do not really believe in God, you do not make him the lynchpin of your great philosophical system; but that is exactly what Descartes did. He was thus a realist about religion and an antirealist about certain parts of science, but he preserved the content of both realms. A scientific theory may be valuable even if we know it is false. Descartes took it that the theory of development from seeds must be false because it contradicted religious doctrine he knew to be true. Nevertheless, he maintained that the theory is valuable because it improves our understanding by providing a potential though not the actual explanation of how the world came about. That understanding requires that we take the scientific theory literally, but not that we believe it.

My own preference is the opposite of Descartes' – I want to consider how one might be a realist about science but an antirealist about religion – but like Descartes I want to be an antirealist who preserves literal content on both sides. And work on antirealism in the philosophy of science gives us a number of models for what such a position in religion might look like. There are two I would like to explore here, one associated with Thomas Kuhn,[6] the other with Bas van Fraassen.[7]

---

5   René Descartes, *Principles of Philosophy* (1644), in John Cottingham, Robert Stoothoff and Dugald Murdock (trans.), *The Philosophical Writings of Descartes*, Volume I (Cambridge: Cambridge University Press, 1985), p. 256.

6   Thomas Kuhn, *The Structure of Scientific Revolutions*, 2nd edition (Chicago: Chicago University Press, 1970).

7   Bas van Fraassen, *The Scientific Image* (Oxford: Oxford University Press, 1980).

The Many Worlds Solution

I understand Kuhn's antirealism through Immanuel Kant, as Kuhn himself sometimes did.[8] Kant held that the empirical world, the world that science investigates, is not even in its inanimate parts a world entirely independent of us.[9] Rather this 'phenomenal' world is a joint product of a 'noumenal' world – the things in themselves as they are entirely independent of us (but for that reason unknowable) – and the organizing activity of the human mind. According to Kant, the human contribution to the phenomenal world is very substantial, since it includes space, time and causation. It is only in virtue of the active contribution of the mind that we are able to experience or represent an external world at all, and we do this by creating a stage on which we can then view the appearances of the noumena, though not the noumena themselves.

Kuhn agrees with Kant that the world that scientific theories represent is not entirely independent of the scientists: it is a phenomenal world, a joint product of the things in themselves and the intellectual activities of the scientists. But there is an important difference. Kuhn is Kant on wheels. Whereas Kant thought that the human contribution that goes into the construction of the phenomenal world was generic and invariant, Kuhn maintained that the scientific contribution is quite specific and varies across the history of science. Scientific revolutions, on this view, are episodes where the human contribution to the world changes. One of the virtues of this interpretation of Kuhn as a dynamic Kantian is that it makes sense of his notorious claim that, after a scientific revolution, scientists work in a different world,[10] a claim that otherwise seems either trivial or crazy. If 'different world' just means different *beliefs* about the world, then the claim is trivial; if it means different *noumena*, so that the world as it is quite independently of us changes, then the claim is crazy. But we can make sense of the claim that the *phenomenal* world changes, because after a scientific revolution the scientists' contribution to that world has changed. On this view, scientific theories are to be construed literally, but what they describe is a world that is partially the scientists' own construction.

The semantic reflection of Kuhn's doctrine of multiple worlds appears in his development of the idea that theories on either side of a scientific revolution are 'incommensurable'. In his earlier work,[11] this was a blanket term for any feature that makes theory comparison complicated because scientists are not comparing like with like. Compare they must, but where there is incommensurability then intelligent and well-informed practitioners may disagree about the winner. The features that generate incommensurability extend from the relatively mundane fact that in a scientific revolution one is comparing achievement (the old theory) against promise (the new theory), all the way to the claim of different worlds that we have just

---

8   Thomas Kuhn, 'The Road since *Structure*', in his *The Road since Structure* (Chicago: Chicago University Press, 2000), pp. 90–104, esp. pp. 101–4.

9   Immanuel Kant, *Prolegomena to any Future Metaphysics* (1783) (Indianapolis: Hackett Publishing Company, 1977).

10   Kuhn, *Structure*, ch. X.

11   Kuhn, *Structure*, ch. IX.

considered. But in his later work[12] Kuhn came to focus on a different sense of the term: incommensurability as untranslatablility. Theories that are incommensurable in this semantic sense do not just conflict: the conceptual resources of the one do not even allow full expression of the claims of the other. One reason for this semantic disassociation, according to Kuhn, is that the two theories divide the world up in such different ways that they do not simply make conflicting claims about the same things, but are talking about different things. This is the way in which incommensurability ends up for Kuhn as the linguistic reflection of the metaphysical plurality of phenomenal worlds. One world cannot be characterized in the terms applied to the other.

Kuhn's multiple worlds and incommensurability have suggestive application to the relationship between science and religion. It might give us a way of reconciling literal interpretation with incompatible content by taking science and religion to be describing different phenomenal worlds in incommensurable languages. These worlds would share their noumenal component – the things in themselves are in common – but the human contribution would differ. Thus at one level the Kuhnian account suggests how science and religion, though incompatible, might in a sense be offering descriptions of a common world, the noumenal world. And at another level, it suggests how the incompatible descriptions could both be correct, since they describe different worlds, different phenomenal worlds. Each set of descriptions, the scientific and the religious, are to be taken literally. Those descriptions are in deep conflict: they do not simply make incompatible claims about the same things, since they are talking about fundamentally different things, and indeed the claims of the one cannot even be fully expressed in the language of the other. Nevertheless, although those sets of descriptions could not be jointly true of any one world, they might each be a more or less correct characterization of different worlds, worlds that are equally real and have noumena in common. Kuhn thus appears to offer everything some of us could want. We acknowledge the deep differences and incompatibilities between science and religion, we understand both discourses literally, and indeed we could even take both to be true of their respective worlds. We can retain the conflicting content without impossibly supposing that the world as it is in itself, independently of us, is somehow self-contradictory.

Would this appropriation of Kuhn's account of science in order to give an account of religion and its relationship to science do mortal violence to Kuhn's ideas? Certainly Kuhn would not endorse the wholesale application of his account of science to religion, because he held that science is a distinctive human activity and that his account helps to locate its distinctive features. But Kuhn does not find this in his claims about incommensurability and multiple phenomenal worlds. Rather, according to him, what is distinctive about science is the way it supports an empirical puzzle-solving tradition during periods of normal science between scientific revolutions.[13] This sort of puzzle solving may not have a close counterpart

---

12   Kuhn, 'Road since *Structure*'.

13   Thomas Kuhn, 'Logic of Discovery or Psychology of Research?', in Imre Lakatos and Alan Musgrave (eds), *Criticism and the Growth of Knowledge* (Cambridge: Cambridge University Press, 1970), pp. 1–23, esp. pp. 6–9.

in the case of religion, but nor do the notions of incommensurability and multiple worlds seem to depend on it. Indeed, although he does not himself seek to apply his account beyond science, Kuhn in effect acknowledges this broader applicability when for example he suggests that ordinary human languages (e.g. English and French) are incommensurable, on the grounds that the concepts they deploy carve up the world differently.[14]

Another obvious difference between Kuhn's account as applied to science alone and the attempt to extend it to apply to both science and religion concerns competition. When Kuhn talks about incommensurable theories, he is talking about problematic choices, choices where there is 'no common measure' and where intelligent and well informed investigators may disagree; but he is talking about cases where choices must be made. This is clearly different from the extension of Kuhn's ideas we are here exploring, since the point is not to analyse a forced choice between science and religion but rather to see how one could have them both, while yet admitting that they are in some ways incompatible. But here again Kuhn's willingness to apply his notion of incommensurability to different human languages suggests that the extension would be permissible. (Kuhn would I think also allow that certain non-competing scientific theories in different disciplines are incommensurable.) If this analysis were correct, one might expect there to be particular challenges in holding on simultaneously to both the scientific and religious worlds, but this is indeed what we find. Moreover, Kuhn makes an observation about incommensurability which suggests that the challenges, though real, need not be insuperable. He claims that although incommensurable theories or languages are untranslatable, this does not exclude bilingualism: you may be able to speak and understand both languages without being able to translate the claims of one into the claims of the other.[15]

Kuhn thus offers us a suggestive resource for a distinctive account of the nature of religious discourse and its relation to science, of particular interest to those who wish to have their cake and eat it, with literal interpretation and acknowledgement of conflict, yet no forced choice. At the same time, I do have reservations about this resolution of the tension problem between science and religion. One is a general ambivalence about the metaphysics of constructed worlds, whether in science or in religion. In what sense is a Kuhnian world really a world? As I have noted, 'different worlds' had better not reduce to 'different beliefs', lest we trivialize Kuhn's claims. Moreover, in the context of applying this view to the relationship between science and religion, such a reduction would undo my attempt to find a way to accept conflicting claims while avoiding conflicting beliefs. The promise that Kuhn's many worlds account offers is that, while my descriptions are incompatible, there is a sense in which my beliefs are not, because they are beliefs about different worlds. If 'different worlds' is just a hyperbolic expression for 'different beliefs', then we seem back to square one.

I can think of two philosophical models that might help us to articulate the nature of these phenomenal worlds. They only provide approximations to Kuhn's

---

14 Thomas Kuhn, 'Commensurability, Comparability, Communicability', in his *Road since Structure*, pp. 33–57, esp. pp. 48–9.

15 Kuhn, 'Road since *Structure*', p. 93.

metaphysics, but they may be helpful nevertheless. The first is the model of a traditional philosophical view of secondary qualities such as colours. According to this view, colours are dispositions of the surfaces of objects to cause certain sensations in us.[16] Thus colours are not simply sensations – they are properties of physical objects – but they are peculiarly anthropocentric properties, since they are dispositions defined in part in terms of our sensations. Colours are on this view phenomena, a joint product of the things in themselves (the surfaces of objects) and the nature of our mind. (Kant himself uses secondary qualities as a model for his view of the phenomena.[17]) And if we imagine people who react to the same electro-magnetic radiation reflected off surfaces with systematically different sensations, as in classic philosophical thought experiments about 'spectrum inversion', we capture a sense in which those people live in different worlds.

The second model is a kind of nominalism about the noumena.[18] On this view, in order to represent the world we must suppose it to consist of objects with various properties. But while the objects are out there independently of us, the properties are not: the world does not come pre-divided into kinds. So on this view the phenomenal world – which is the only world we can represent – includes properties, but these properties are our contribution, and indeed different people might divide up the world differently, might contribute different and incompatible properties. Here too we capture a sense in which the differences are not merely differences in belief but differences in the world, since unless we suppose them to be features of the phenomenal world we would not be able to see our beliefs about the world as representing anything, which would be to say that they are not beliefs.

Both these models help to make sense of how some feature could be both of the world and put there by our cognitive activity. And I think this leaves us with an approach to science and religion well worth developing. But now I must confess that I am not myself entirely happy with the application of the Kuhnian metaphysics either to science, or to religion, for pretty much opposite reasons in the two cases. The Kuhnian approach gives too little cognitive credit to science and too much cognitive credit to religion for my taste. On the science side, as I have already confessed, I hold out the hope for a realist model, according to which properties and natural kinds are not put there by us but are features of the noumenal world that science may disclose. Kuhn is unwilling to go this far. And if applied to religion, Kuhn's ideas seem to go too far. What is attractive about Kuhn's account of science is that Kuhn combines a kind of relativism with the insistence (even if this is not seen by all his readers) that science is empirically constrained. For Kuhn, the fact that scientists believe something does not make it so, even for 'their' world. Science is a game against nature, an attempt to meet the relentless constraints that observation and experiment impose. Indeed on Kuhn's view nature always wins, because every normal science tradition is eventually overthrown by an overload of recalcitrant anomalies.

---

16   John Locke, *An Essay Concerning Human Understanding* (1689) (Oxford: Oxford University Press, 1979), bk. II, ch. VIII.

17   Kant, *Prolegomena*, First Part, Remark II.

18   Ian Hacking, 'Working in a New World: The Taxonomic Solution', in Paul Horwich (ed.), *World Changes* (Cambridge, MA: MIT Press, 1993), pp. 275–310.

I do not see religion thus empirically constrained (though it may be constrained by our needs and desires). I see religious texts as human productions which, although obviously inspired by experience, have nothing like the close responsiveness to the nature of the natural world to which empirical science aspires. This does not absolutely rule out seeing those texts as providing descriptions of Kuhnian worlds. For God might exist, have created the world in a certain way, and then informed us about that creation. At the same time, it might be that, our intellects being what they are, we are unable to take information about the noumena straight, so God ladens the descriptions with a conceptual structure that both makes them comprehensible to us and generates a phenomenal world that is their subject. In other words, although the epistemology of religion might be non-empirical and thus radically different from the epistemology of science, what is required for a Kuhnian world is not that we know about it in a certain way, but that it includes the appropriate noumenal and conceptual components.

But I still cannot go this far. For me, religious texts are much more akin to imaginative writing than to scientific theories, different not only in their epistemology but in what they are about, and they do not in my view satisfy the noumenal constraints that a Kuhnian world requires. Novels do not create Kuhnian worlds; they create fictional worlds. Religious texts do purport to describe the actual world – they are not presented as fiction – but I maintain that the worlds they describe are significantly closer to imagined worlds than to the worlds of science. At the same time, I hold fast to the view that religious texts may have the deepest value, and that this is best understood by finding a way of giving them a literal interpretation. So I turn now to another antirealist model from the philosophy of science, to see whether it suggests a religious analogue that may be, for me anyway, more congenial.

The Immersion Solution

This approach to retaining the literal content of both science and religion is inspired by a position in the philosophy of science known as constructive empiricism, a position developed and championed by Bas van Fraassen.[19] Constructive empiricism has three core components: semantic, methodological and epistemic. The semantic component is that scientific theories are to be understood in the same way a scientific realist understands them. They are to be given a literal interpretation: they are not metaphors, and they are not shorthand for statements about observable states of affairs. If a theory seems to be talking about invisible subatomic particles, then it is talking about invisible subatomic particles. Moreover, these are descriptions of a possible noumenal world, of the things as they might be in themselves, not of a phenomenal world partially constituted by our concepts, as we have seen Kuhn to have it. So that is the first component: a literal semantics.

The second and methodological component of constructive empiricism is 'immersion'. To immerse oneself in a theory is to enter into the world of that theory and to work from within it. This is not to believe that the theory is true, but it is to enter

---

19 *The Scientific Image* (Oxford: Clarendon, 1980), esp. ch. 2.

imaginatively into its 'world'. In some ways this is like Eddington's familiar table. Even if as a physicist one does not believe that tables literally have the qualities of colour and solidity that commonsense attributes to them, one may immerse oneself in the world of the everyday table: for everyday purposes we think about the table as if it were as commonsense supposes it to be. Indeed we cannot help but do this. The constructive empiricist makes the parallel suggestion for the scientific table. Here we do have a choice, but the suggestion is that even though we are not to believe everything physics tells us about the table, we are to do our science from within that model, almost as if we did believe in those invisible atoms. Indeed one may wonder whether immersion is in the end distinct from belief. On behalf of van Fraassen's claim that it is, we might focus on incompatible models, such as Eddington's two tables. One may consistently immerse in both, but not consistently believe both. And incompatible models are common within science itself. Thus a fluid is sometimes modelled as a continuous liquid, sometimes as a collection of discrete particles, depending on which sorts of phenomena one is attempting to predict or explain. Those are incompatible models, but the scientist may well use both, in some context immersing (as it were) in the one and in other cases in the other, though she does not believe both.

Immersion is distinct from belief, and this is important, because the third, epistemic component of constructive empiricism is the suggestion that scientists do not believe even their best theories. Scientists should only 'accept' them. To accept a theory, in van Fraassen's neologistic sense, is not to believe that the theory is true but only that it is empirically adequate, that what the theory says about observable things is true. As for the balance of the content of the theory – all that talk about unobservable entities and processes – one is agnostic. So in accepting a theory one is believing only a part of it, and the suggestion is that acceptance is the strongest cognitive attitude one should take towards a scientific theory. There is neither warrant nor need to believe more than this. This brings out the contrast between the constructive empiricist and the realist, for while they share their literal semantics, the realist is willing to believe more, in some cases the entire content of the theory, even where that theory speaks of unobservable entities, properties and processes.

How much of a theory is one believing when one accepts it, in van Fraassen's sense? Along one dimension, a great deal, though still only a small part of the full content of a high-level theory. For to accept a theory is not only to believe the part of the theory that one has actually observed, but everything the theory says about what could in principle have been observed, whether it is ever actually observed or not. Thus in accepting a theory about dinosaurs one believes what it says about the skin colour of long dead dinosaurs, because skin colour is observable, though never observed by palaeontologists. At the same time, along another dimension the part of the theory one believes by accepting that theory is very limited, according to van Fraassen, because for him observable means naked-eye observable. A distant planet is observable, because although it may never be so observed, it would be visible by the naked eye if one were close enough. By contrast, a small amoeba is unobservable, because even though it may be 'seen' clearly through a powerful light microscope, it cannot be seen by our eyes without the instrumentation, however close we get to it.

What would it be to appropriate the ideas of constructive empiricism to religion? We may consider the three core ideas: literal interpretation, immersion and acceptance. First, literal interpretation. This would be to hold that the Bible means what the Bible says: it is not an entirely metaphorical document. Thus when the Bible says that God parted the Red Sea, what that means is that God parted the Red Sea. Second is immersion. The idea here is that just as a scientist may immerse herself in the world of the theory, so we may immerse ourselves in a religious text. But here we might go even further than in the scientific case. We might understand religious immersion as entering the form of life of religious practice and religious thought. It involves a kind of participation and a kind of commitment to action. It also involves a kind of identification and solidarity with co-religionists.

What about acceptance? This is the most difficult of the components to bring across to religion, and it will require modification along the way. The governing idea behind acceptance is the idea of partial belief, in the sense of believing some but not all the consequences of a claim and remaining agnostic about the rest. But as the immersion component of constructive empiricism makes clear, this is a committed agnosticism: scientists are to deploy the theory as a whole, not just those parts of it they believe. In the scientific case, the part of the theory to be believed is that part that makes claims about observable states of affairs. Could we say that same thing in the case of religious texts? Like scientific theories, religious texts seem to make claims both about observable and unobservable states of affairs, for example about the nature of an invisible God and about the observable consequences of God's will and activity. So we might attempt to keep the notion of acceptance constant as we carry it over from science to religion. On this view, we are enjoined not to believe that the Bible is true, but only that what it says about observable states of affairs is true.

This may be a coherent position, but from my point of view it is both too liberal and too strict. It is too liberal, because it would require belief in the observable factual content of miracles the Bible describes – for example a belief that the Red Sea did part, a conspicuously observable state of affairs – though not the supernatural aetiology. But I myself cannot believe that the miracles in the Bible occurred, whatever their supposed causes and even if described in purely observable terms. More importantly, this interpretation of acceptance would not solve the tension problem between science and religion, because I take it that the factual claims about some of the miracles contradict what our best science tells us about how the world has behaved. Thus acceptance of religion in this sense and belief or even just acceptance of science would still leave us with contradictory beliefs. That is why the observability criterion is too liberal for my purposes. It is also too strict, because it would remove from the believed part all the normative content of the Bible, since norms are not observable, yet some of these I do believe.

This suggests an alternative account of religious acceptance, which would be to mandate belief not in the observable content of the text, but rather in its normative content. But here too I think we would end up both with too much and too little. Too much, because I do not wish to endorse the entire normative content of the Bible; too little, because I want to take more, in terms of belief, from the Bible than its normative content. For example, I think that a religious text may be a powerful resource for working out what to believe about one's own nature and one's relations to other people, and these results seem to go well beyond the strictly normative content of the text.

To provide the epistemic flexibility I desire requires a third construal of acceptance, where the class of consequences to be believed is given an extrinsic characterization or, to avoid euphemism, where the characterization is more ad hoc. The reason this is necessary is because, for the most part, I take it that the warrant for those aspects of our religious text and tradition that we believe must come primarily from outside the religious text. I say 'for the most part' and 'primarily', because I give the text itself independent epistemic weight in certain areas, for example where it enjoins certain forms of ritual behaviour and where it in effect characterizes certain group values. The source of that weight requires no divine role: in choosing to identify with a religious tradition, I choose to give that tradition this weight. But for most of the claims of my tradition, belief must be earned largely from outside the text itself, and this includes most of the moral claims. That is, I do not accept that in general something is made the right thing to do because the Bible says it is the right thing to do; nor do I accept that the Bible has a moral authority (whatever the source of values) that automatically trumps independent reflection and evaluation.

Accepting a religious text thus means believing some but not all of its claims, but which claims we believe is largely externally determined, by moral reflection, and in some cases by science. So the epistemology of religious acceptance as I am construing this notion is importantly different from the epistemology of scientific acceptance as the constructive empiricist construes it. For in the case of a scientific theory, while we are only to believe its observable claims, we are to believe those (in cases where we have not actually made the observation) because they follow from the theory, which has itself been tested empirically. Here the warrant for the observable consequences flows from the warrant for the empirical adequacy of the theory, which flows from observation and experiment. By contrast, in religious acceptance, as I have ended up construing it, the warrant comes mostly from other places. We are thus moving quite far from van Fraassen's notion of acceptance. In at least one respect, I would move even farther, since 'agnosticism' does not describe my own cognitive attitude towards the supernatural claims of the Bible. For it is not just that I don't believe them true, I believe them false. Where they contradict scientific theories I believe, I have no choice; but even if there are some supernatural claims compatible with that science, my epistemic attitude towards those claims will be determined by what I take to be their warrant or lack of it. The question then must be whether I have now have left constructive empiricism so far behind as to make the analogy worthless.

I think not. In part that is because I wish to emphasize the other two components of constructive empiricism, the insistence on literal construal and the advice to immerse oneself in the world of the text. But the notion of acceptance also helps me to articulate the religious attitude I wish to adopt. It captures the idea that one may define an epistemic attitude of partial belief, involving the belief in some but not all the content of a text. But as I have already indicated *en passant*, there is more to acceptance than this, as Van Fraassen characterizes it, though the additional element is closely related to immersion. Acceptance is not just partial belief; it is also a kind of commitment to use the resources of the theory. In the scientific case, 'acceptance involves a commitment to confront any future phenomena by means of the conceptual resources of this theory'.[20]

The religious case is not quite the same, but what I have in mind is that in accepting a religious text we not only believe parts of it; we also commit ourselves to using the text as a tool for thought, as a way of thinking about our world. The scientist accepts her theory and her techniques and for van Fraassen that means she takes the stand of using the theory and the techniques as tools that help her to come to grips with the phenomena. Adapting constructive empiricism to religion yields a perspective from which religious people accept their tradition and their texts as tools for thinking through their lives, their projects, and their attitudes. For those inside the tradition, the Bible is good to think with and to grapple with, and not just in the parts of it that are antecedently believed. On this view, acceptance and immersion are not passive activities, nor are they matters of all or nothing. In my view one sometimes has to struggle with one's religious text, not just in order to understand it but in order to come to terms with its moral content. In some cases we may find this content morally unacceptable. As a progressive Jew this will sometimes lead me to reject clear moral content present in my religious text, but here too I would continue to preserve its literal meaning. Nor is rejection to be taken lightly if we are to preserve the constructive attitude of immersion in the text, but in my view the difficult material is there to be struggled with, not to be bowdlerized or ignored.

The signal advantage of the immersion solution over the metaphor, value and selection solutions is that it is preserves the integrity and hence the useful power of the religious text. Recall that the metaphor view would have us construe all religious claims in conflict with belief-worthy science figuratively, the value view would have us construe the religious claims as without descriptive content, and the selection view would have us excise whatever conflicts with the science. If a religious form of life is of no interest to you, this may not matter. But for those of us to do wish so to engage, the trouble with those three views is that they allow science to mangle the text, and this would deprive it of much of its value. On the immersion view, by contrast, we have the text to use in its full, unexpurgated form, the form in which I believe it can do us the most good as a tool for thinking and for living.

Conclusion: Religion without Belief

This completes my sketch of what it might look like to adapt constructive empiricism to religion. We construe our religious text literally, we believe only parts of it but we use all of it and we immerse ourselves in the world it describes. The point of exploring this approach is not to persuade those hostile to religious activity that they should repent, but to consider a way those who find themselves with a commitment both to a religion and to science might have it both ways. But while the immersion solution will clearly help relieve the tension of incompatible beliefs, are literalism, acceptance and immersion enough to do justice to religious commitment? The immersion solution involves no distinctive religious faith and

---

20 Van Fraassen, *Scientific Image*, p. 12.

no belief in supernatural power. Indeed isn't it tantamount to treating the Bible as a *novel*? After all, novels often invite literal interpretation, includes some claims the reader believes, and may support a kind of immersion into a fictional world. Richard Braithwaite, whose work has influenced my development of the immersion solution, bit the bullet. He thought of religious texts as stories with morals, where 'it is not necessary…for the asserter of a religious assertion to believe in the truth of the story involved in the assertions'.[21]

The immersion solution would have been enough for Braithwaite, but it is obviously not enough for everyone with religious commitments. Many religious people have difficulty seeing the point or value of religion without belief in God. If that is what you need, the immersion solution is not for you. But the immersion solution can provide a great deal, more than even the most enthusiastic book group. The religious story has its life in the context of ritual observance and more generally as part of a religious form of life. It is a story in which the reader herself is also a participant, and it may provide extraordinary support for communal identification and moral reflection. Consider the natural worldly benefits that religious activities provide for the religiously committed, benefits that can be characterized independently of the question of a supernatural source. The immersion solution will not support the belief that their source is in fact supernatural, but it may support the benefits themselves. For some religious people, the satisfaction they derive from their religion would evaporate if they ceased to believe in the existence and influence of God. But for others, it is not belief that is doing the work, but rather intense and communal engagement with religious text and with religious practice. For those people, the immersion solution may be enough.

On the immersion solution to the tension problem, religious commitment and religious identification flow from the contents of the texts of one's religion literally construed. Some of the claims of religion may conflict with the claims of science. The immersion solution does not aim to remove that inconsistency, but by distinguishing acceptance from belief it finds a way to achieve consistency of belief without effacing incompatibility of content. On this approach, we preserve content by adjusting our attitude towards it. We have literalism without fundamentalism; inconsistency without irrationality. There is conflict between some of the claims we invoke, but not in what we believe. To some this may smack of hypocrisy, but in the context of the relation between science and religion I myself think it is one route to personal and intellectual integrity, a route which tries to preserve as much as possible from both religion and science without ignoring the tensions between them.[22]

---

21   Richard Braithwaite, 'An Empiricist's View of the Nature of Religious Belief', The Eddington Lecture (Cambridge: Cambridge University Press, 1955), p. 25.

22   I am grateful to Lorenzo Bernasconi, Paul Dicken, Wang-Yen Lee, Peter Ochs and Andrew Pickin for comments on an earlier version of this essay.

Chapter 4

Religion and Ontology

Simon Blackburn

I

When theologians talk of ontology, I suspect they intend something very different from philosophers, or at least philosophers in the tradition I respect and represent. I suspect they often mean something along the lines of a 'Ground of Being', an attempt to see beyond the world of the senses and of natural science to an ultimate cause or final explanatory principle: the eternal light that streams out of the cosmos, the tortoise at the very bottom of things and on which all the elephants stand, the Atlas that holds up the world, the terminus of the cosmological argument, in fact. There is always a problem for theology in connecting this whatever-it-is to the hopes and aspirations of the ordinary believer in the pew. But if to the Timaeus, or Plotinus, we add a Heideggerian despair about the partedness of man and God, witnessed in the modern living that has driven us from the Garden and divorced us from the Primal Ground of Being, we get a potent mix indeed, as if the turmoil of the times (any time) bears direct witness to the accuracy of the metaphysics.

I shall have little to say about this kind of thought. I believe that Hume showed, in his widely-misunderstood *Dialogues Concerning Natural Religion* that any quest for this particular Holy Grail has no route to follow, no procedures to adopt, no conception of an endpoint, and no measure of whether it is getting closer or further away from it. It is like the quest for the snark, conducted with a blank chart on an empty ocean: no quest at all, but a self-deception about the limits of meaning. The Grail would have to be a 'necessary existent', a '*causa sui*' on which the request for explanation gets no purchase. And we are not capable of meaning anything by that. The predicate 'exists necessarily' might as well apply to the whole empirical cosmos as anything else. It is sometimes suggested that cardinal numbers form a counterexample, but these abstracta are doubtful candidates for existence at all.

A rather different legacy of phenomenology is use of the notion of Being in the description of consciousness and experience: the tradition that ruminates on the way in which consciousness is frequently consciousness of absence, as much as consciousness of existence, and that tries to parlay that into a message about death or about the hole left when God absconds. I find it difficult to imagine this at the centre of theology. Philosophers can and should respect Sartre's or Heidegger's insight that our capacity for awareness of what is not the case or what is missing, lacking, absconded, or absent is a salient feature of conscious life. But by itself this idea suggests no way of distinguishing good apprehension of a lack or an absence from a fanciful one, as when one imagines something absent that has either never been present or never could be present. The experience of a loss of God, while meaningful enough to many people, cannot be thought of as like experience of the loss of a favourite dog, when both the onetime presence and subsequent absence are real objects of memory and perception. It is, rather, the awareness that what was once credible is so no longer. It is awareness that there never was a dog. It is in fact tendentious to think of that as experience of loss, since if the loss is phenomenologically real — that is, the ensuing state is one of disbelief, then it cannot at the same time be held that the preceding state was one of genuine apprehension. It becomes revealed to have been one of delusion, and recovering from that is no loss at all but the beginning of health.

So in this paper, I am going to confine myself to philosophical approaches to ontology from another direction, and from the traditions I know best. I appreciate that this may be asking some readers to traverse some unfamiliar territory. But I deplore the compartmentalization of philosophy, as if one could have interesting views about religious ontology without having any views at all about numbers, possible worlds, values, mental events, or other categories whose titles to a place in the halls of Being are disputed. At the very least, it should be interesting to compare and contrast the twists and turns of more general debates with any questions specifically belonging to the philosophy of religion.

In fact, much modern philosophy has a no-nonsense way with ontology, or the question of what there is. Following the broad path blazed by W. V. Quine, it asks about the ontological commitments of a theory, or a discourse. It finds out these commitments by what seems like a very simple method. You find what the theory or discourse *says* there is. You find this out by laying out the logical structure of the theory, which in practice means putting it into a form in which the kinds of inference it allows are most easily detected. Once that is done, if the theory says that there are things of some kind, then it is ontologically committed to things of that kind. If it is your theory, then you are committed to things of that kind.

Finding the logical structure may involve an element of 'regimentation' or cleaning up. For example, nobody is going to urge that sociology is ontologically committed to the average person. The reason is that statements about the average person are reducible in content to statements about sums of magnitudes in aggregates of people. They involve only ordinary, empirically given people, not ordinary people and average people besides. It is hoped that this kind of regimentation can proceed without too much controversy, as in this example, although in practice this proves far from the case. We need only think how controversial it would be to suggest, for instance, that statements apparently involving mention of God can be paraphrased by ones that talk only of love, to see how one person's regimentation is to another person the elimination of everything distinctive about a discourse or theory. We return to this later.

Quine's approach survives indeterminacy over the strength of commitment, although that too has occupied a good deal of attention. If you think, for instance, that it is best not to believe a theory, but only to hold it *pro tem*, or as a speculation, then you may also think it best not to believe in the existence of things of the relevant kind, but only to hold that *pro tem* or as a speculation. If, like the empiricist philosopher of science Bas van Fraassen you think it often best only to hold that theories are empirically adequate, but not to take the further step of believing them, then you may equally think it best only to hold that the existence of the things talked of by the theory is an empirically adequate hypothesis, but that you should not take the further step of believing in them either.[1] You *could* hold some existence claims that are made by a theory with more conviction than you hold the rest of the theory, but only if they seem less contentious than the other parts of what the theory says, or if they get some support from elsewhere. But what you cannot do is hold the existence claims with any *lesser* conviction than that you attach to the theory that delivers them.

This deceptively simple methodology leaves the philosopher somewhere at the rear of the parade. The people who use the theory, or practice the discourse, direct the show. If the philosopher does not like their commitments, then so much the worse for the philosopher. If good mathematics tells us that there are sets of some size, or functions of some type, or if good science tells us that there are waves or particles or forces or fields, then who is the philosopher to pipe up otherwise? As David Lewis forcefully argued, the philosopher taking any such line is apt only to make himself look foolish. Considering the case of sets in mathematics, Lewis wrote:

> Mathematics is an established, going concern. Philosophy is as shaky as can be. To reject mathematics for philosophical reasons would be absurd…I'm moved to laughter at the thought of how *presumptuous* it would be to reject mathematics for philosophical reasons. How would *you* like the job of telling the mathematicians that they must change their ways, and abjure countless errors now that *philosophy* has discovered that there are no classes?

Philosophy simply has not got the track record of certainty, or utility, or progress, or unanimity, to mount any such high horse. If it is a question of philosophy versus physics, or philosophy versus maths, everyone knows which side to back.

It is a little unclear just which theories or bits of discourse get the protection of this argument, which has become known as Lewis's Credo argument. Suppose we look at ethics, and find plentiful talk of duties, obligations, and rights. Can we say:

> Ethics is an established, going concern. Philosophy is as shaky as can be. To reject ethics for philosophical reasons would be absurd…I'm moved to laughter at the thought of how *presumptuous* it would be to reject ethics for philosophical reasons. How would *you* like the job of telling the ethicists that they must change their ways, and abjure countless errors now that *philosophy* has discovered that there are no duties (etc.)?

Or how about this:

> Religion is an established, going concern. Philosophy is as shaky as can be. To reject religion for philosophical reasons would be absurd…I'm moved to laughter at the thought of how *presumptuous* it would be to reject religion for philosophical reasons. How would *you* like the job of telling the theologians that they must change their ways, and abjure countless errors now that *philosophy* has discovered that there are no gods (etc.)?

A lot of philosophers will pause at this last, since post-Enlightenment philosophy has typically felt rather proud of its role in undermining religious thought. Fortunately, there is a principled way of drawing the distinction between the first two applications

---

1   Bas van Fraassen, *The Scientific Image* (Oxford: Oxford University Press), 1980.

of Lewis's Credo and this last one. Mathematics and ethics, it can be said, are in themselves free of philosophical arguments. They are autonomous disciplines, standing only on their own feet. It takes a mathematical argument to prove or disprove a piece of mathematical reasoning, and an ethical argument to support or attack a piece of ethical reasoning. But religion is not in the same way autonomous. It constantly rubs up against philosophy. It purports to deliver philosophical results, for instance about the immortality of the soul, or the nature of free-will, or the notion of substance. And it may buttress itself by employing philosophical arguments, as the traditional arguments for the existence of God are supposed to be. When it does either of these things, it cannot at the same time claim immunity from philosophical criticism, if the purported results, or the purported arguments, fail to commend themselves. Actually, the original contrast with mathematics and ethics was slightly overdrawn, because the same is true of some branches of ethics. If, for instance a moral view depends upon some conception of responsibility and freedom, then it cannot claim immunity from philosophical criticism, since finding and defending such conceptions is a paradigmatic philosophical activity.

Before thinking further about that, however, I want to return to the approach of which the Credo argument is a part. And the question I want to raise is whether it really gives us a good way to think about ontology, either in mathematics, or science, or ethics or theology.

II

The reason for doubt is fairly obvious. Quine's approach makes it very easy to determine something called ontological commitment. But should it be so easy? And if so, what kind of commitment is in question, and what goes wrong if the commitment is awry?

Quine and his followers thought that ontology was important. You should keep your universe as little cluttered as possible, sharing his taste for desert landscapes. But what is this importance? We can understand people arguing about whether there are specific numbers – prime numbers between 17 and 23 for example. That's a mathematical question, soluble by mathematical means. We can understand people arguing about whether there are duties of some kind: that is the stock issue in many ethical debates, when one side supposes that moral perdition awaits the denial of some duty or another. But what other perdition is there? What risk is purified ontology supposed to guard against?

Consider a child learning elementary mathematics. Suppose the child says that there is a number between five and seven, how many ticks should she get? One for the arithmetic, clearly, but an additional one for the philosophy? Or might she get a tick from the mathematics teacher and a cross from the philosopher, on the grounds that her ontology has become over-inflated? After all, if there are two different things involved, then presumably they might come apart, so that one is going right and the other going wrong. But can one really believe in any such duality?

This way lies deflationism or minimalism, or what Paul Horwich felicitously calls a world without -isms altogether. The idea is that people used to argue about, say platonism versus nominalism in the philosophy of mathematics, or realism versus expressivism as a theory of ethics, or 'onto-theology' versus some postmodern construction of religious discourse. But perhaps there is no issue. We either accept the discourse, with as much conviction as we think it merits, in which case we find ourselves saying its 'there are....' claims, or we reject it in which case we do not find ourselves saying any such thing. Or, we may not know which way to jump. But those are the three alternatives. You may be religious or you may be an atheist, or you may sit on the fence and say that you just do not know. But there is no room to be either a postmodernist, or a specially robust 'onto' theologian. For such people are each trying to mount theory where there is no theory to be had. They are trying to jump outside their own skins, or stand on their own shoulders, or take up an illusory Archimedean or sideways point of view, a view from nowhere.

Deflationism has its home in the theory of truth. An increasing number of philosophers believe that there is simply no topic of truth: nothing to be said about it. This is not because the notion is sublime or ineffable, but because it is too small, as it were, to get a chapter to itself. Their idea is that we deceive ourselves when we think that Pilate had a good question.[2] When Pilate asks 'what is truth?' the right response is not to attempt some large philosophical story, taking sides with Plato against Protagoras, as it were. The right response is to say: what are you interested in? Once Pilate specifies an issue (for instance, whether the prisoner in front of him committed some specific act) then we can answer: it is true that the prisoner committed the act if, and only if, the prisoner committed the act. That is what you have to discover or judge to discover or judge the truth about this issue, on this occasion. Other issues would see you having to discover and judge different things of course. But once you locate the issue, the question of truth solves itself.

This is a disappointing answer, perhaps, but the deflationist point is that it is is the only kind of answer you can get. As to the utility of talking of truth, it lies in collecting and generalizing – bookkeeping rather than metaphysics.[3] For example, suppose we want to thump the table (together with writers such as Primo Levi, or George Orwell) and to insist that truth is important, that a pure worship of truth is one of humanity's greatest qualities, that the systematic degradation of truth is the Achilles heel of democratic politics, and so on. It might seem that if deflationism is right, these thoughts vanish. But this is wrong. According to the deflationist, these are not illusory or fantastic goals, the product of false philosophy, as is alleged by some postmodernists and perhaps most famously by Richard Rorty. Indeed, by making an issue of them and opposing them the postmodernists reveal themselves to be under just the same illusions as Platonists who cherish them as signs of the awful majesty of Truth. According to the deflationist the serious, Orwellian thoughts are perfectly in order, but we must be aware of what they mean. So, consider people who:

---

2   In my book *Truth: A Guide for the Perplexed* (London: Penguin, 2005) I call the section dealing with this, 'Down with Pilate'.

3   The best introduction to these issues has been Paul Horwich, *Truth* (Oxford: Blackwell, 1990). An overview is given in the introduction to the collection *Truth* edited by S. Blackburn and P. Simmons (Oxford: Oxford University Press, 1999), which also contains a selection of classic papers for and against deflationism.

believe and say that dogs bark if and only if dogs bark
believe and say that Labour is working if and only if Labour is working
believe and say that God will look after them if and only if God will look after them...

And so on for as many issues as you care to write down. Then the table-thumpers point is that it is better to be thus than to:

believe and say that dogs bark when they do not
believe and say that Labour is working when it isn't
believe and say that God will look after you when he won't...

Collecting and generalizing we can say that it is better to satisfy the schema

believing and saying that *p* if and only if *p*

as often as possible, than it is to satisfy the schema

believing and saying that *p* when not-*p*.

And that is all the worship of truth or fear of its declining lustre amounts to. Since the instances and the schema generalizing them make no mention of truth, they cannot be the subject of postmodernist scepticism or attack. This is why the polemic of philosophers such as Richard Rorty misfires so badly. A Tony Blair who believes and says that *p* pretty much regardless of whether not-*p* is as guilty in deflationist eyes as he is in those of anybody else.

Obviously one can elaborate on this by distinguishing important from trivial issues, or ones worth finding out about from others, or by distinguishing further, as Bernard Williams does, between the vice of inaccuracy (leading to believing what is not true) from that of insincerity (leading to saying what is not true). But the groundwork of any such further reflections is laid by the deflationism.

III

Deflationism about truth is widely supposed to give us the kind of thought expressed above: that there is no sideways perspective, no standing outside our own skins, no Archimedean point, from which to conduct philosophical reflection on the nature of a discourse. Our options shrink to the three mentioned: accept it, reject it, or sit on the fence.

An especially acute example of this deflationism in action comes from David Lewis's own special baby, realism about possible worlds.[4] Lewis records that when he started to go around saying that he believed in possible worlds, real 'concrete' worlds just like ours, only possible and not actual, he was met by an 'incredulous stare'. It did not bother him very much, for as he remarked, he did not know how to refute an incredulous stare. But now the question is whether those other philosophers really had anything to stare at. Here is Lewis, saying that there is a possible world unlike the actual world in containing talking donkeys. Since there is this one possible

---

4   See David Lewis, *The Plurality of Worlds* (Oxford: Blackwell, 1986).

but not actual world, there are possible but not actual worlds – and if it proves useful to do so, we can go on to discuss their properties and relations and number. You might not want to talk like this, but then you have to decide how much modal thought and talk you can tolerate. After all, is it not possible that there should have been a talking donkey? And then Lewis will push you towards saying things that are most elegantly said, or perhaps even only said, using full possible worlds' talk. What people wanted to stare at, after all, was not the utility of more or less complex modal idioms, but the *realism*: the awful image of the pluriverse, the reality of a dreadful infinity of worlds with their talking donkeys and kangaroos with no tails, and worse besides. And this, as well, is what Lewis fostered and regarded as a bold and powerful metaphysical position. But in the presence of deflationism both Lewis and his staring detractors suffered from the same illusion: the illusion that there was something called 'realism', a theory about the discourse as a whole, which was itself an object of surprise and wonder, or, if you prefer, incredulity.

Here is another way of putting the point. Lewis supposed that if you took commitments 'at face value' then you came to rest with his realism. This shifts the philosophical burden onto those who would call themselves 'anti-realists'. They face the task of 'reconstructing' the discourse, perhaps regimenting it in some devious and unobvious way, which usually goes wrong. For example, they might try to reconstruct mathematics as not about sets, but about symbols. Or they might try to reconstruct modal talk not as about possible worlds, but about inferences. The trouble is that these tasks are not easy to accomplish, and all the while the 'realist' is presenting himself as a bland, straightforward kind of chap, doing no more than taking things 'at face value'. Similar positions have been advanced by 'realists' in ethics, who first rest happy in our talk of duties, obligations, or values, secondly insist that no further philosophy is necessary or possible, and thence draw the conclusion that moral reality is a given – only deniable, in fact, by the immoral.

But in the presence of deflationism, this realist pose is shown to be hollow. The face value of 'there is a number between five and seven' is that there is a number between five and seven. You do not get two ticks, one for the arithmetic and another for giving the remark the right 'face value'. You might get a philosophical tick for eschewing the devious reconstructions, but you get no tick for positive doctrine, and if you think you deserve one then you get a philosophical cross instead, for thinking you have a theory when you don't. Similar remarks apply to ethics, when what are in essence deflationist arguments are suddenly, miraculously, supposed to deliver a theory called realism, again presented as a bland, straightforward, plain common-sense kind of doctrine. You cannot take advantage of deflationism to defend yourself as having a 'theory' where deflationism precisely says that there is no theory to be had.[5]

---

5   In other writings I have called this taking advantage of the horizontal nature of Ramsey's ladder to climb it, and then announcing a better view from the top. See *Ruling Passions* (Oxford: Oxford University Press 1998), p. 294.

IV

I believe that deflationism gets many things right, and one thing wrong. It is right that the child that says there is a number between five and seven deserves one tick, not two. It is right that there is no difference of levels between asserting the claims made inside a theory, and asserting the existential consequences of such claims. It is right that truth does not itself make up a topic. But it is wrong to try to take *everything*: that is, to deny that there is space to stand on from which to gain a philosophical perspective on a discourse, a perspective that might be 'realist' and ontologically robust or committing, but might equally be no such thing. And I shall argue that this space is one where there can be a debate between an 'onto-theologian' and a postmodernist opponent. Philosophy can flourish once again, rising from the ashes to which it is reduced by deflationism. I fear, however, that in theology, when there turns out to be such a debate, it also turns out not to be very interesting.

One reason philosophy or metatheory can continue is already latent in what we said about regimentation. Quine's ontological criterion is only to be wheeled up when the regimentation is satisfactorily complete, but we can expect a good deal of philosophical water to flow under the bridge before that happy day. However, I am not going to concentrate upon that in what follows. This is partly because the general mood in philosophy is sceptical of aggressive regimentations. Philosophers in general prefer to leave the content of theories alone. They say what they say: why expect there to be a better way of doing it? Mathematics appears to be about sets: why perversely see it as being about symbols, or anything else? Ethics is about values, duties and obligations: why expect there to be a way of moralizing that eschews moral language?

The other point of attack for philosophical theory is more Wittgensteinian. It is the *activities* associated with a use of language that come to the fore. The bland realism we have met so far tacitly assumes that all discourse is there in order to *represent* the way of the world. It is there to describe how things are, whether the things in question are sets, values, possibilities, or Gods. But this only has to be stated to seem doubtful. J. L. Austin is supposed to have estimated that there are between one thousand and ten thousand things to do with language. I think he expected to count them by listing so-called 'illocutionary' verbs: in saying something I may threaten, cajole, praise, sneer, rhapsodize, dismiss...and so on. This method of counting seems unnecessarily restrictive: if sneering is one thing, are not sneering out loud and sneering behind someone's back two further and different things, and then how finely are we to subdivide? In any case, since we clearly lack a settled principle for counting, anyone sensible will hold simply that there are a lot of things we do. Some of them include or imply representation, and they are only 'felicitous' if things stand as we say. Those will include more than bare descriptions. A warning of a bull in a field is felicitous only if there is a bull in the field. It is ontologically committing. A supercilious attitude to someone only begins to be appropriate if the belief that they know less or otherwise do less well than you do is true, and that is in itself a representation of one fact about them. But is this representative function there across the board?

The question will be whether language has a non-representative function, forms of words whose role is not to display how things stand, but to do other things instead (not, other things in addition, as in the bull in the field warning). Wittgenstein was an addict of this kind of thought. He thought that claims of necessity were not in the business of describing an alien part of the universe as well as the rest (the non-actual part as well as the actual part), but to lay down rules of description. He believed that mathematical remarks were not so much descriptions of a part of the world called numbers, as a kind of rule determining how to describe the (number-free) world. He thought that first-person remarks such as 'I believe' or 'I intend' were not self-descriptions of a shadowy sort, but avowals. He denied that there are ethical facts, or that ethics purported to describe such facts, seeing ethics instead in terms of commitment. He thought the activity of claiming and ascribing knowledge was essentially practical, an announcement of what has gone into the archive, or now forms the riverbed or the hinge around which enquiry can swing.[6]

Such views need a hearing. They are not to be dismissed by the bland assertion that *p* is true if and only if *p*. For Wittgenstein's views survive that point. All it brings to the table is the idea, which he himself supported, that talk of truth will not advance the discussion. It will not give us a key diagnostic to determine when we are in the business of representing things, and when we are not. All it will give us is a slightly longer statement 'it is true that *p*', with the same import as the original '*p*', and about which exactly the same questions can then be asked.

The deflationist will fight back. He will claim that Wittgenstein's position gains its identity by contrasting the other things we do with words with 'representation'. But, he will ask, why not go deflationist about representation? Just as 'it is true that *p*' and '*p*' come to the same thing, so do '*p* represents how things stand' and '*p*'. The former is a longer way of saying the same as the latter. Representation is not a substantive, philosophically particular kind of achievement, had by some claims and not by others. It is no more a robust 'metaphysical' notion than truth itself. So it cannot sustain a debate.

I find this unconvincing, and certainly less convincing than the parallel noises made about truth. The reason is that representation is a quite natural notion (not the preserve of philosophical specialists) tied in with quite common-sense understandings of how the world works. Its principal link is with *explanation* and its homeland are cases where the state of the representing device or medium is explained by some corresponding state of what is represented, and which can therefore be recaptured or read off from the former. Petrol gauges, timetables, and marks on charts are in this homeland. We understand the explanatory links, and we understand the symbols as a result. If we trust the instrument, we believe in the linkage. If we act upon the information presented, then the success of our actions is itself explained by the same thing: the state of things that was represented in whatever sign with which we were presented. Wittgenstein's cases are ones where it is reasonable to doubt any such explanatory linkage. We find it difficult to understand how our thoughts about possibilities could maintain good explanatory links with unactualized possible

---

6   I detail these claims in *Truth: A Guide for the Perplexed* (London: Penguin, 2005), chapter 5.

worlds, and therefore how they could represent them. Insofar as we find values, duties and obligations somehow alien to the natural world, we will find it hard to see how our ethics could be explained by their nature and being, and the same is true of sets and states of mind. And sure enough, those opposing Wittgenstein's non-representative account of these things have sought to play up their explanatory credentials, arguing that only a misconception of natural facts, or a misconception of values and the rest, or of sets or possibilities, generates an explanatory anxiety.

It is not my purpose in this paper to decide which position has the right of it here, and the debates about explanation can themselves take different shapes in the different areas. But the ground the contending parties have found to fight upon is, in my view, the only ground there is. If it did not remain dry above the rising waters, deflationism would drown everything.

V

How does all this affect theology? In the eighteenth century, David Hume noticed the 'somewhat unaccountable' state of mind of the religious believer, with its inevitable mixture of belief and lack of conviction. But if we bring in Wittgenstein, the unaccountability turns into a wider indeterminacy, for the question becomes what religious language *does*, and unfortunately the doings of religious sayings are legion. Persons indulging in religious practices, and that includes saying religious-sounding things, or using specifically religious language, may be doing any of many things. They may be calming down, or working themselves up. They may be taking a quiet moment out, sorting things out for themselves. They may be confronting their own sins, or those of others. They may be solemnizing births, marriages, or deaths, and we can see what they are doing in the light of social ritual. Perhaps we should see religion in the light of poetry, symbol, myth, practice, emotion and attitude, or in general a *stance* towards the ordinary world, the everyday world around us. Religion is not to be taken to describe *other* worlds, nor even past and future events in *this* world, but only to orientate us towards the here and now. Religious language is not representational, giving an account of disconnected parts of the cosmos, regions of space-time, or even of something like space and something like time, but in which all kinds of different things are going on. It is symbolic or expressive, orientating us towards each other, or towards ourselves, or towards our place in this world.

Let us call this interpretation of religious practice the expressive interpretation. Like other anti-realist or anti-representational theories, it could be offered in a number of different ways. It might be offered in the spirit I have here adopted, as a description of the 'somewhat unaccountable' state of mind of the ordinary practitioner in the pew. Or, it may be offered normatively: the people in the pew may think of themselves as representing mysterious regions of space and time, but they ought to see themselves as expressing stances. Following David Lewis we might call expressive theology the 'minimal unconfused revision' of the confused state of mind of the person in the pew.[7]

This would be the right way to develop the idea of theology without ontology. Is it to be embraced? Unhappily, I believe not, at least as things stand in the Vatican, or Belfast, Jerusalem or Riyadh or even Canterbury, although in this last the case is less clear. I do not think that a purely expressive theology can be used to interpret the ordinary believer in the pew, nor can it be suggested as a minimal unconfused revision of his 'somewhat unaccountable' state of mind. When theology without ontology came onto the scene in the United Kingdom, perhaps with John Robinson's *Honest to God*, some forty years ago, the general reaction was that churchmen embracing it were 'atheists in dog-collars' and I have to say that I believe there is something right about this reaction.

The reason is that for the person in the pew, religion typically offers not only practices, music, poetry, emotions, attitudes, and symbols, and symbolic expressions of them all, but also explanation and justification. 'We want your land' is a simple enough expression of a desire. 'Your land is our holy land' might function as a symbolic or poetic way of insisting on the desire. And 'God has ordained that your land is really ours' has an overlapping function, certainly. It expresses the want, and does so through a megaphone. But in the mind of the ordinary practitioner, it does more than that. It is what enables and activates the megaphone. It justifies the want, and it explains it. It functions exactly like an appeal to legal authority, even if the law court in question is supernatural and invisible.

I do not believe you can have this justification and grounding without ontology. Something must be true, there must be a way of things, a fact, even if a fact in heaven, to which appeal is being made. It is not a question of an orientation towards the world, but, in the mind of the believer, the explanation of an orientation. And explanation takes us into the orbit of representation, and therefore the orbit of ontology.

Is this right? One orientation can justify and explain another. A dismissive attitude to someone's question might be explained and even partly justified by pointing out that he gets on my nerves. And according to some philosophers of science, overt fictions, models and metaphors, can play a valuable and indeed essential role in explanatory theories. Can either of these interpretations be of help here?

I do not think so. If I want your land, what further stance am I drawing upon if I say that the reason I want your land is that God gave it to me? I am, as I said, repeating my demand, perhaps through a megaphone, or more accurately, in tones of the pulpit, tones of conviction and self-righteousness. But there is nothing else, for instance along the lines of 'I can make use of it and you cannot', which is thereby brought to the table. There is no further worldly orientation or worldly belief drawn into the discussion. It is not like, for example, justifying one policy by drawing on our approval for some neighbouring policy, which is of course a perfectly legitimate device in moral discussion. So I do not see the first suggestion as promising.

---

7   David Lewis, 'Quasi Realism is Fictionalism' in *Moral Fictionalism*, ed. Mark Kalderon (Oxford: Oxford University Press, 2005). I try to rebut Lewis's defence of moral fictionalism, in 'Quasi-Realism No Fictionalism' in the same volume.

The second may be more help. If it is legitimate, explanation-by-overt-fiction would allow the man in the pew both to cite the gift of God as an explanation and justification of his desire, in one breath, and in the next to admit that it is all a fiction, a myth or symbol or piece of poetry, with no worldly solidity, no ontological implications to which he need own up. But I do not think it is legitimate, and the two-faced nature of the position gives it away. Even in these postmodernist times, I cannot both say that I believe your baby was brought by the fairies, and I don't believe in fairies. I can play along with the fairy fiction, or I can explain the appearance of your baby by citing the doings of fairies, but I cannot consistently do both.

The scientific cases which bring some apparent credibility to the idea in fact deserve different treatment. Suppose I explain, say, the refractive behaviour of light by citing its wave composition, although I then go on to say that probably the theory describing this wave composition is a model, or metaphor or fiction. Surely the right interpretation is that I am confident that in its refractive behaviour light behaves 'as if' it is a wave. The theory is good for prediction: whether it is the final truth about the nature of light can be bracketed although we can also go ahead and use it. It might be more accurate to say that we have systematization rather than explanation. But in the theological case there is no parallel. I cannot cite an 'as if' in the same justificatory or explanatory role as the original appeal to the deity. I cannot amplify my demand for your land just by announcing that it is 'as if' God had given it to me, any more than I can expect to impress bystanders by saying that I shall henceforward behave as if I had a right to it, although I probably do not. That is the way thieves behave, and the rigmarole would be heard as no more than the shameless announcement of a theft.

A similar diagnosis would emerge if we consider the use of idealizations as fictions in science: frictionless planes, point masses and the rest. Idealizations are useful when our empirical systems approximate to the behaviour which we can calculate for them. But the idea of an 'approximation' to God having ordained the land for us makes no sense. Nobody could be content with the suggestion that something a bit like God has ordained the land more or less for us.

I believe, then, that expressivist theology cannot be true to the functions that religion centrally serves. There is no evading the fact that the person in the pew needs the ontological dimension. To repeat, this is for two reasons. The first is that the ontology alone gives the explanatory and justificatory thoughts that are integral to his or her understanding of what they are doing. The second is that the overt empirical payoff, the practical result of invoking the language, could not be sustained without it. If the talk of God did not function ontologically, it could not put the extra amplification, or the self-righteous timbre, into the megaphone.

What is true, certainly, is that one can imagine a purged and purified religious practice of which ontologically uncommitted theology was an adequate theory. This might leave the best parts: the social solidarity, the ritual, the confronting of human verities, the communions with the self, piety towards passed generations, resignation or humility in the face of the cosmos, the music and the poetry, celebrations of human reason and science, engagement in the here and now of human life and experience. Perhaps this is how Eastern religions are, or could be. All that would be lost would be superstition, such as the jealousy of the monotheistic gods, the distortions of morals in favour of anger and guilt, and in favour as well of the duty of sectarianism, the elevation of ignorance and unreasons, and ethically what would be lost would be the self-righteousness that comes from thinking of oneself as basking in the divine favour. It sounds an appealing direction in which to progress, but at the beginning of the twenty-first century, I am not holding my breath.

Chapter 5

Scientific and Theological Realism

Alexander Bird

1 Introduction

In this paper I shall explore the parallels and contrasts between scientific and theological realism. I shall start by providing an outline of the various aspects of scientific realism before looking at these in more detail and in comparison to theological realism. I hope that by this comparison with the well-developed debates between various species of scientific antirealists and realists, some light may be shed on debates concerning realism in theology.

The term 'scientific realism' covers a variety of related positions. These may roughly be divided into the metaphysical and the epistemological. The former concerns the subject matter of science. The realist and antirealist may disagree on the correct answer to the question, 'what is particle physics about?' Since such questions may be couched in terms of the reference of the key terms of science, we may regard many of the important debates concerning realism as debates about the semantics of scientific terms. Epistemological realists and their opponents take positions on what we can and do know in science or on whether our scientific beliefs are justified. A third area that links with both parts of the realism debate concerns the question, 'what is the aim of science?'

I shall briefly consider each of these three aspects of the scientific realism/ antirealism debate before looking at the parallels in the theological realism/antirealism debate. My conclusion will be that metaphysical antirealism faces many obstacles both in science and theology. If anything the obstacles are greater in theology, even though antirealism is a popular option among theologians. Epistemological antirealism (scepticism, agnosticism, atheism) is better grounded, but in science there are strong responses that do not have theological parallels. Consequently, the theological *metaphysical* realist is threatened by epistemological antirealism.

2 Metaphysical/Semantic Scientific Realism

I shall consider various claims that are typical of those made by scientific realists.

2.1 The World as Investigated by Science is Largely Mind-independent[1]

This claim is intended to rule out idealism. As such, this is a rather more general issue in metaphysical realism and antirealism than one limited to the philosophy of science.

---

1   Cf. R. Boyd, 'On the current status of scientific realism', in R. Boyd, P. Gasper and J. D. Trout (eds), *The Philosophy of Science* (Cambridge, Mass.: MIT Press), p. 195.

Nonetheless many scientific realists assert this claim, for two reasons. First, because general idealism is global it applies to the objects of scientific inquiry in particular. If, for example, one holds that any entity is just some congery of ideas in the subject's mind, then cells, atoms, magnetic fields and so on are also only congeries of ideas in the mind. This creates particular difficulties for entities the subject has not yet given any thought to, such as some as yet undiscovered subatomic particle. On this idealist view, since there is no idea corresponding to the undiscovered particle, that particle cannot exist. Consequently, discovery is not so much a matter of coming to know about something that previously existed but of whose existence one was previously unaware, but rather it is instead a matter of bringing something into existence by thinking about it.

It should be noted, however, that Berkeley's response to an analogous problem may cut the link between general idealism and scientific antirealism. If to exist is to be an idea in the mind of God, then the distinction between genuine existence and merely being thought to exist by a scientist (and between non-existence and ignorance of existence) can be maintained. The entities of science would be dependent not on the mind of any scientist or group of scientists but rather on the mind of an independent being, God. Thus there could be room for the other debates we shall consider to be live debates within a general idealist framework.

The second reason why scientific realists feel required to assert a rejection of idealism is that some writers in the 'science studies' tradition (though not any philosopher of science of note) seem to adopt an idealism concerning the subject matter of our most favoured scientific theories. According to social constructivists (or 'constructionists') cells, atoms, magnetic fields, etc., are 'social constructions' the work of scientific communities, rather than entities uncovered by those scientists. In this connection, Kuhn's comment that as a result of a scientific revolution the scientist's world changes also is often cited as an instance of this sort of view.[2] However, it is highly debatable whether Kuhn was saying anything that implies that such entities, while genuinely existing, are also brought into existence by the beliefs of the scientists. Paul Hoyningen-Huene gives a Kantian reading of Kuhn that perhaps comes closest to this. According to this view there is a world-in-itself that is unchanging but there is also a 'phenomenal world' the world of the scientists' perceptions and belief, that does change. The scientist is trapped within the latter and has scant if any access to the former. Another view, which to my mind better captures Kuhn's original intentions, is simply to regard the use of 'world' as metaphorical (just as it often is in everyday speech). A change of 'world' is a certain kind of psychological upheaval, not any change to the cells and atoms themselves. Similarly, it seems that when pressed the social constructivists may be just expressing in a misleadingly dramatic way the view that our theories respond rather less to the world than realists think and rather more to the social relations among scientists (or between science and the rest of society). That is, social constructivists may be taken to be making an epistemological point in metaphysical terms: what explains belief in, for example, neutrinos, is not an objectively rational response to the evidence but rather a set of social and political commitments that exist largely

---

2   See T. Kuhn, *The Structure of Scientific Revolutions* (Chicago: University of Chicago Press, 1962), p.150.

independently of any imperceptible micro-entities. In this epistemological guise I shall consider social constructivism again below.

2.2 Names of Scientific Kinds and Properties are Genuine Referring Terms[3]

Here the idea is that when we talk of electrons, as in, for example, 'electrons are negatively charged', we are talking about certain entities and ascribing a property to them. The contrasting view is that this apparent logical form is misleading and a proper analysis of the given sentence will reveal that it is not about such entities at all, at least not about imperceptibly tiny entities that a naive view will take 'electrons' to be. The function of the sentence is not to ascribe a property to entities but is rather to play a role in making predictions about the results of laboratory and other observations. Percy Bridgman's operationalism helps clarify this idea. According to operationalism to say 'the gas is at 1134 K' is to assert that the observed result of a properly conducted measurement using a thermometer of some specific type will be 1134 K. We can generalize this for all theoretical claims. Thus 'electrons are negatively charged' may be taken to assert something such as 'the bright spot on the phosphorescent screen of a cathode ray tube will deflect towards the anode, when an anode and cathode pair are placed across the cathode ray tube'.

In general, for the antirealist of this stripe, it is only terms that relate to observable entities and properties that refer. The terms of theoretical science, that superficially seem to refer to unobservable entities and properties, must be treated in a semantically distinct fashion. Thus we have, in effect two languages, a language of observational terms and a language of theoretical terms. As regards the latter, one possibility already considered is that it is analysable in terms of the former. And so all scientific sentences are about something, only the things they are about are all observable. An alternative, inspired partly by problems in implementing the first proposal, is that the theoretical language is irreducible. In which case a question is raised about the meanings of sentences employing theoretical terms. The answer given was that individual theoretical terms get their meanings in a holistic manner, via the roles they play within theories and that theories or groups of theories get their meaning via the (non-reductive) links they have with observational language.

2.3 Theoretical Assertions are Truth-apt

If, according to the antirealist we have just been considering, theoretical assertions are not about theoretical entities, and they are also not reducible to assertions about observable entities, what then makes the assertions true (or false)? One possibility is to adopt an holistic approach paralleling the holistic, theoretical-role view of meaning just considered; this would be coherentism about truth. But an alternative is simply to deny that strictly speaking theoretical claims have truth-values at all (to deny they are truth-apt). The function of truth-apt assertions is to describe, whereas the function of theoretical claims is not to describe but to provide a means of making accurate predictions. Theories may be adopted or rejected on the grounds of being

---

3   Cf. R. Boyd, 'On the current status of scientific realism', p. 195.

reliable instruments for prediction or unreliable. But acceptance is not acceptance as true, nor is rejection a matter of taking to be false.

Thus a realist rejecting this view will claim that theoretical assertions are either true or false. The realist may go further in asserting that truth for theoretical claims is the same as truth for observational claims, rejecting the view that the former should be given a coherentist account whereas the latter should be given some other account. More generally still, the realist will assert that the semantics for theoretical expressions and sentences containing them should not differ from the semantics for observational expressions and sentences. The realist's claim that scientific terms are referring terms (discussed above) may be seen as an instance of this (if it is held that observation terms are referring terms).

3 Epistemological Scientific Realism

We have briefly examined the debate between the realist and antirealist as regards the content of scientific, typically theoretical, claims. I shall now turn to epistemological matters. The term 'scientific antirealism' covers both metaphysical/semantic issues *and* epistemological ones. Epistemological antirealism is typically not called 'antirealism' outside of philosophy of science, but rather 'scepticism'. Nonetheless, as we shall see, there is an intimate relationship between metaphysical antirealism on the one hand and scepticism on the other, in such a way that it makes sense to regard them as different sides of the same coin.

The epistemological realist will want to say something positive about a ground for belief in our best theories, while the antirealist will take a more sceptical line. In such debates metaphysical/semantic (scientific) realism is typically assumed. For example, one might be sceptical about the theory of neutrinos because neutrinos, if they exist, are unobservable and very difficult to detect in other ways. But to assert such grounds for scepticism is to accept that the existence of neutrinos is independent of our beliefs, that claims about neutrinos are truth-apt and that 'neutrino' is a referring term.[4] Note that the dependence of scepticism on metaphysical/semantic realism provides a motivation for metaphysical/semantic antirealism. The metaphysical/semantic antirealist is able to claim that there is no problem in knowing the truth of theoretical assertions since (on one view) they are equivalent to observational assertions. Or (on another view) the problem of knowing just doesn't arise, since the assertions are not truth-apt (and knowledge or otherwise requires truth-aptness).

3.1 It is Possible for Science to Provide Good Reasons in Favour of Theories[5]

The above is a very general and reasonably weak expression of the epistemological optimism of the realist which can be strengthened or extended in various ways. Most obviously it can be supplemented by the claim that the possibility mentioned is actual, that as a matter of fact modern science does give us grounds for preferring some

---

4   Note that a term can be a referring term without succeeding in referring – for example, 'phlogiston'.

5   Cf. R. Boyd, 'On the current status of scientific realism', p. 195.

theories over others. A stronger claim is that our reasons can (and do) give us reasons for believing a theory, and yet stronger is the claim that these reasons can (and do) give us scientific knowledge.[6] A strengthening in another dimension is to claim that the theories that make the above assertions true include theories concerning unobservable entities.

Epistemological antirealism will reject in some measure some or all of the optimistic claims made above. Thus some kinds of antirealism may be sceptical as regards theories concerning the unobservable but not as regards the observable. The grounds for sceptical antirealism are many. I shall briefly mention the major ones.

3.1.1 Inductive scepticism   Those convinced by Hume's problem of induction will inevitably be sceptical as concerns pretty well any scientific theory, since almost all theories make assertions (so it seems to most philosophers) that go beyond the evidence in the sense that the theory is not deducible from the evidence. Popper was the most prominent advocate of inductive scepticism in the philosophy of science. Nonetheless he did not hold himself to be an antirealist; he believed that the some kind of epistemological optimism may be retained thanks to his falsificationism. The consensus now is that if induction is rejected, falsification cannot provide a basis for optimism.

3.1.2 Rejection of inference to the best explanation   Many philosophers of science hold that many of our most important inductive practices can be aptly described by the phrase 'Inference to the Best Explanation' (IBE). One reason why IBE is significant is that it appears to be the mechanism whereby we justify our beliefs in the existence of unobservable entities. For a long time physicists believed in the existence of neutrinos because they best explain mass and spin discrepancies in beta decay. There are various reasons why an antirealist might reject IBE: (i) why should 'better' explanations be more likely to be true?; (ii) the criteria of 'goodness' (for example, simplicity and elegance) are too subjective to be a reasonable basis for inferring the truth of a theory; (iii) it is unlikely that the true theory is among those we have considered – so choosing the best will typically be to choose a false theory.

3.1.3 Underdetermination of theory by evidence   The third complaint against IBE draws upon a more general problem advanced by antirealists. It is alleged that our theories are radically under-determined by the available evidence. That is, the evidence we actually have and could reasonably hope to have is such that many theories (infinitely many) are consistent with that evidence. Such a claim needs supplementation for it to have any sceptical consequences, for it needs to be shown that there are infinitely many hypotheses that explain the data equally well.

---

6   Arguably the last claim isn't stronger than its predecessor, if one holds that one should not believe something unless by believing one would know it.

3.1.4 Pessimistic (meta-)induction   Previously well-confirmed theories are typically rejected by later developments. Therefore we can expect our current (and future) best theories to be refuted in turn.[7]

3.1.5 Epistemological social constructivism   Science is merely a social construct, similar to the arts or a political system, differing primarily in that it makes a claim to have privileged access to an objective truth. But this claim is only a political manoeuvre to claim corresponding privileges for scientists. As in these other areas of activity, developments are explained by social and political forces, and are not the outcome of an impartial examination of an objective nature.

3.2

In favour of realism, many realists (but by no means all) subscribe to the No Miracle Argument (NMA): 'Realism ... is the only philosophy that does not make the success of science a miracle.'[8] The NMA can be understood as an instance of IBE. The only satisfactory explanation of the success of science is that science is an effective mechanism for getting to the truth. The various epistemological antirealist claims considered above can be read as attempts to undermine the NMA. Objections to IBE are objections to the form of inference employed by the NMA. Underdetermination raises the possibility that many false theories would be equally successful. In which case the truth of our best theories is not the best explanation of their success. Social constructivism alleges that the best explanation of the 'success' of science is that this so-called success is measured by the scientists themselves. For example, we are told that Quantum Mechanics is the predictively most successful theory of all time. But its predictions concern the behaviour, primarily, of sub-atomic particles. So the predictions are assessed by scientists on the basis of abstruse scientific theories. Thus the success of quantum mechanics is not independent of science but is itself part of science.

4 Realism and the Aim of Science

Another area where antirealists and realists disagree concerns the very aim of science. Realists will typically claim that science aims at the truth, hoping to achieve at least increasing nearness to the truth. Realists may even claim that science aims at producing knowledge. Antirealists may claim that science aims at less than truth. Thus van Fraassen takes the aim of science to be empirical adequacy – the theories of science should have only true observable consequences (science does not aim to assert truths concerning the unobservable).[9] This reflects a long-standing empiricist and positivist tradition. Others such as Laudan and Kuhn take science to

    7   Psillos discusses and rejects the pessimistic induction; see S. Psillos, *Scientific Realism: How Science Tracks Truth* (London: Routledge, 1999), pp. 101–14.
    8   H. Putnam, *Mathematics, Matter, and Method: Philosophical Papers Vol.1* (Cambridge: Cambridge University Press, 1975), p. 73.
    9   See B. van Fraassen, *The Scientific Image* (Oxford: Oxford University Press, 1980).

be in the business of solving scientific puzzles.[10] Note that they do not require that a puzzle-solution be true to be an adequate solution, only that it fit in with the current practice of science. Lastly, social constructivists will claim that the aim of science is the perpetuation of science itself (or, more bluntly, the scientists themselves and whatever class or other political interests they have).

5 Metaphysical Realism in Science and Theology

The scientific realist takes the scientific claim 'electrons are subatomic entities too small to be perceived that are negatively charged and are constituents of atoms' at face-value. 'At face-value' means that the sentence should be understood as on a par with 'pips are the parts of an apple that may grow into a tree' or more generally that the semantics of that claim and other scientific claims should not differ from the semantics of the bulk of non-scientific claims. Thus, taking it for granted that 'apple' refers to a kind of tree or its fruit, then 'electron' refers to a kind of subatomic particle. In each case we do not think that what it is for entities belonging to the kind to exist is dependent on human thought. Correspondingly the theological realist will take claims about God's existence, nature, and actions at face value. Thus when the Nicene creed opens, 'We believe in one God, the Father Almighty, Maker of Heaven and Earth, and of all things visible and invisible', the realist holds that the belief in question is a belief about God and the belief is true only if God did make Heaven and Earth, in just the same sense as when some one says, 'I believe that Phidias carved the Elgin marbles', that statement is about Phidias and is true only if he did indeed carve those marbles. The metaphysical realist, qua metaphysical realist, is not strictly committed to the truth of such assertions, but is rather committed, primarily to claims made about what would make the assertions true. In this sense most atheists are metaphysical theological realists. They agree that what would make the assertion 'God made Heaven and Earth' true is the existence of a divine creator amongst whose works are Heaven and Earth – they just deny the existence of such a creator. For this reason the relevant kind of realism is best expressed in semantic terms. Theological claims should not receive a special kind of semantic analysis just in virtue of being theological. Theological language is not distinct in this sense from the rest of our language.

5.1 Projectivism

Metaphysical social constructivism in science is difficult to take seriously. But a theological parallel has influential support. Non-theism (a version of which is Contemporary Christian Humanism) takes God to be the Sum of our Highest Ideals. Such a proposal originates with Feuerbach.[11] More generally, religious projectivism proposes that God and other elements of theology are projections of some human or social entity.

---

10 See T. Kuhn, *Structure of Scientific Revolutions* and L. Laudan, *Progress and its Problems: Towards a Theory of Scientific Growth* (London: Routledge and Kegan Paul, 1977).

11 See L. Feuerbach, *Ludwig Feuerbach's Sämmtliche Werke* (Leipzig: Otto Wigand 1846–1866).

Broadly speaking projectivism can be taken in two ways, an epistemological or causal way and an ontological way. The epistemological/causal way takes the 'God is X' equation as shorthand for a causal explanation of religious beliefs and activities. Thus, if it is proposed, in this way, that God is the Sum of Our Highest Ideals, then it is being suggested that the psychological importance of our ideals causes a belief in God. Or, as in another of Feuerbach's proposed projections, God is the projection of the human longing for significance. This is consistent with a literal, semantically realistic view of the content of what is believed. A religious, Christian belief in God has the *content* that an all-good person created the world, loves us, and so forth. This epistemological projectivist view is nonetheless epistemologically antirealist because it follows that, since the cause of the beliefs is a human/social cause rather than a supernatural cause, the beliefs cannot amount to knowledge.[12]

The nearest to projectivism in the philosophy of science is Comte's account of the metaphysical stage of the development of knowledge.[13] According to Comte's 'law of three stages', human knowledge starts with a theological stage, whose explanations are religious. This gives way to the second, metaphysical stage, whose explanations are in terms of essences and imperceptible entities, such as forces. The third and final stage is the positive stage, which concerns only correlations among what is observed. Note that Comte's view concerns not all science but only certain parts of science or ways of doing science (those which invoke the unobservable). According to Comte, the projection that is a belief in unobservable entities is not simply analogous to the projection that is a belief in God, but is a hangover from it. While the unseen supernatural causes have been eliminated they have been replaced by unseen natural causes. Whether Comte's account is strictly projectivist is perhaps a moot point. For it is not clear where projectivism ends and a socio-psychological account of belief allied with an error theory begins.[14] Karl Marx's account of religion falls more obviously into the latter category. Marx also suggested that Darwin's theory of evolution through natural selection owed its origins to Victorian capitalism. Although the suggestion was not developed by Marx himself, subsequent social constructivists have sought political and other social and psychological explanations not only of the origins of scientific ideas but also for the acceptance of those ideas.

The metaphysically projectivist reading of 'God is X' takes that statement to assert a genuine identity (where X = the sum of our highest ideals, etc.). Consequently some religious beliefs will come out to be true – for example 'God exists' (because there is a sum of our highest ideals). Some reductive versions of empiricism provide an analogue to this view. If we have a positive view of scientific enquiry we may hold that the cause of a scientist's beliefs is the observational evidence she has. So one way of making science reasonable without invoking unobservable entities is

---

12   Strictly one could have such religious beliefs caused in this way that turned out to be true, and so such views commit one to agnosticism. But the position is a natural one for an atheist to adopt, and it is natural to call such an account an 'error-theory' of religious belief.

13   See A. Comte, *Cours de philosophie positive* (Paris: Société Positiviste, 1892).

14   The distinction I have in mind is this. The cause of the belief in the projectivist case is something inner, an individual's own psychology, whereas in the social constructivist case the cause is something outer, for example, something political or social.

to equate the observational and the theoretical. Optimally we would have identities of the form 'electrons = X' where 'X' is an expression employing only vocabulary that describes observable things and properties. This would be parallel to the idealist claim that physical objects are congeries of ideas. Thus any claim about electrons would be really a claim about observable things and qualities. The gap between the causes of our scientific theories (our evidence) and the theories themselves would not be a gap between the observed and the unobservable, but rather, at most, a gap between the actually observed and some generalization thereof (which may cover the unobserv*ed* but nonetheless observ*able*). Operationalism, we saw, expressed this view with respect to theoretical quantities, regarding them as identical to the outcomes of measuring operations. Such proposals run into difficulties when we attempt to work them out in detail. For example, there are many distinct ways of measuring temperature (mercury thermometer, gas thermometer, Galileo thermometer, resistance thermometer, as well as various spectroscopic ways of measuring temperature, among others). So strictly there should be, according to operationalism, not just 'temperature' but a variety of different kinds of temperature, one for each mode of measurement. Furthermore, theoretical ideas do not relate directly to observational ones. A statement about electrons doesn't have any direct observable consequences. It has such consequences only in conjunction with other scientific propositions which will typically themselves involve further theoretical concepts. Thus a claim about the mass of an electron will typically require supplementation by an auxiliary hypothesis about its charge (and much else besides) before it has an observable consequence, because what one measures is the ratio e/m of the charge to the mass of the electron. The relation between theory and observation is not piecemeal but is holistic. For this reason there is no hope of making an equation of the form 'electrons = X' for an observational X. More generally theoretical claims are not reducible (equivalent) to observational ones.

5.2 The Meaning of Scientific and Religious Language

One might adopt one of two responses to the problems mentioned, both invoking a distinction between theoretical language and observational language and their semantics. According to the first option, a strict instrumentalism, sentences involving theoretical terms are strictly meaningless. Theories function solely to produce accurate empirical predictions (predictions concerning the observed), so the literal meaninglessness of theories is of no significance. However, the literal meaninglessness of theoretical language is difficult to square with both the phenomenology of science (the language seems meaningful) and the fact that the language is treated as more than gobbledegook when drawing inferences from theories to observational consequences. Thus the second option, the double language model, countenances a more liberal approach to semantics, allowing a different kind of semantics for theoretical terms. Observational terms get their meaning via a direct correlation with observable things and properties. Theoretical terms get their meaning holistically via their theoretical relations with one another and via connections with observational propositions.

Let us now return to the theological case. The proposal we were considering was some equation of the form 'God = X'. In the scientific case we found that either (as for operationalism) a multiplicity of such proposals each of which had a legitimate claim to translate 'temperature' (hence requiring a multiplicity of kinds of temperature), or we found that no plausible equivalence is available because of the holistic nature of scientific theory. The first of these problems has an analogue. The different kinds of thermometer each explain our temperature judgements. Correspondingly we might regard our belief in God as explained by our possessing ideals or having a capacity or need for love or a desire to be at one with the world and nature. In which case there is a multiplicity of proposals for X in 'God = X' (God is the Sum of our Ideals, God is Love, God is Nature). That seems to imply a multiplicity of Gods if there is more than one source of religiosity. The extent to which the second problem, the failure to find any reduction, arises in the theological case depends on the extent to which theological doctrines are bound up with one another. There are other theological concepts that need to be dealt with – not just God – such as, in Christianity, sin and the Trinity. If there are relatively few such concepts and the relevant doctrines are not too complex and interwoven, then it might be possible to find reductions for the other theological concepts too. Even so, the task looks daunting. The doctrine of the Trinity tells us that God is threefold and that one of the parts of God was killed for the remission of our sins. If we take, for example, God = Nature, this requires us to find three aspects of nature, to regard one as 'sacrificed' to redeem our sins, where 'sin' (and 'redemption') are given appropriate reductions also.

A rather different third kind of problem arises for the theological case. The antirealist's task is to reduce language T to language O. 'T' might be 'theological' and 'O' 'ordinary', or 'T' might be 'theoretical' and 'O' 'observational'. Some sentences will be pure T sentences, using only T terms (plus perhaps logical and mathematical language). Some sentences will be mixed sentences, and some will be pure 'O' sentences. A successful reduction must reduce not only the pure 'T' sentences but also the mixed sentences. The mixed sentences are a potential cause of particular trouble because the 'O' components of mixed sentences do not get reduced. Thus when we reduce the T terms their reductions must fit with the O terms in such a way that the mixed sentences, with the T terms replaced by their reductions, continue to make sense. This is not an especial obstacle for scientific antirealism but is a serious problem for theological antirealism.

Let us look at the scientific case first. Here the proposed reduction draws on the fact that good theories should successfully explain and predict the observable facts. At the same time the mixed statements of science are themselves concerned with explanatory, predictive and causal relations between theoretical and observable states of affairs. So one should expect the proposed reductions to fit well with the mixed statements. Thus a proposed reduction of electron might be 'trace of kind E in a cloud chamber' and a mixed statement might be 'electrons are correlated with phosphorescence in a cathode ray tube'. The combination of the two 'traces of kind E in a cloud chamber are correlated with phosphorescence in a cathode ray tube' is not especially problematic.

Many religious claims are also mixed – indeed there are clearly more mixed propositions in the Bible than purely theological propositions. Of the mixed claims many concern the actions and attitudes of God. However, the bases of the proposed reductions, that is the motivations for religious belief (ideals, love, need for significance) do not directly relate to the non-theological components of mixed sentences ('… made the Earth'). Thus there is a mismatch between the proposed reductions of the theological components and the non-theological components in mixed sentences as can be seen by considering 'the Sum of our Highest Ideals made the Earth'. Indeed, because so many of the mixed sentences in the theological case concern actions and attitudes, no reduction will be satisfactory that reduces 'God' to anything other than a person-like entity. For even 'Love loves us' is a nonsense.

While atheists may welcome such a conclusion, metaphysical/semantic antirealists are typically motivated by a desire to make religious and theological claims come out, by and large, as reasonable. Consequently, if, for example, the Nicene creed is to make sense and even be reasonable (without returning to realism), the antirealist must take one of two courses: (i) retain the suggested reductions (or one of them) and maintain that ordinary, non-religious language, when employed in a religious context, may be being used without its normal semantics; (ii) reject the reductions suggested and regard theological language as having its own semantics, not reducible to non-theological language, but not semantically realist either. I shall consider these two responses in the subsequent subsections.

5.3 Metaphor

As regards (i), the most obvious way of taking the non-religious language used in religious context to have a non-standard semantics is to regard such talk as metaphorical. In metaphorical talk the same terms are being used as one finds in literal talk, but the propositions expressed are not the propositions expressed when the same sentence is used literally. The view that some talk in religious contexts is metaphorical is a familiar one. An early step in this direction was Aquinas' doctrine of analogy whereby certain ordinary terms when applied in theological contexts do not have exactly their ordinary meanings but rather some analogical extension of those meanings. Even in Aquinas' day it was not held that every claim of the Bible must be interpreted literally. (Later, the inconsistency of Galileo's discoveries with the literal truth of certain Biblical passages was not, as is commonly supposed, an insuperable obstacle to the acceptance of his theories by the Church.) We may also note that apophatic theology is founded on a related doctrine, that of the *via negativa* – the only literally true statements about God are all negative, telling us what God is not.

However, the view we are considering goes beyond the limited medieval application of analogy and metaphor. Because mixed claims are ubiquitous in religion, it requires that pretty well all religious statements are metaphorical. And this is full-on metaphor rather than analogy. For Aquinas requires an analogical use of 'good' to apply to the perfectly benevolent creator, but it remains analogical because God is still person-like. But once 'God' is reduced to a non-person, analogy can no longer play a role.

The mixed nature of so much religious talk and the need to treat all of it metaphorically are major differences with antirealism in science. However there are some views about science that are not all that far from this. One might maintain that for various reasons we cannot really understand the world. For example, one might maintain in a Kantian vein that our conception of the world is so filtered through our unavoidably human or even cultural categories and concepts that the resulting image cannot be held to be a picture of a human-independent world. Or one might reflect on the fact that science shows that nature is ultimately quantum in nature and that the paradoxes of quantum theory show that we just are unable to understand quantum reality. Or one might argue that because our language is unavoidably vague but that reality cannot be vague, our language cannot adequately express the way reality is. These views might lead one to Kantian idealism: science is not about human-independent nature but is about our conception of nature. A different though related response is to regard science as consisting of models. Models are not intended as pictures of reality. Models may in some respects correspond to reality, but it is not possible to say how. Rather the function of models is to organize our scientific thinking. In this sense models are akin to metaphors. A good metaphor may be informative, but it is difficult or even impossible to say how. It is certainly not descriptive. The thought that religious talk is metaphorical may be inspired by roughly similar reasons. The transcendence of God may mean that it is impossible to say much that is a true description of the way God really is. Aquinas' doctrine of analogy starts from this position and the metaphorical account of religious language may be seen as an extension of it.

5.4 Non-realist Semantics

The second option, (ii), regards theological terms as irreducible and having their own, non-realist semantics. The work of Paul Tillich and Don Cupitt may be seen as instances where projectivism has led to a non-realist understanding of religious language.[15]

One extreme is to regard religious terms as having no semantics at all. We have considered the version of instrumentalism that maintains the same for scientific language. It is worth noting that an historically key motivation for both views is the same, *viz.* the verification principle that the meaning of a statement is its method of verification. Even theoretical statements of science cannot be directly verified and there is clearly no direct verification for theological statements. Whether science and religion can survive this depends on finding a function for science and religion that does not depend on the language they employ being meaningful. Such functions must be noncognitive – they must not involve the contents of scientific/religious statements being the object of propositional attitudes (such as belief), because the meaninglessness of the language means that such statements have no contents. In the case of science the function is prediction with respect to observables. It is questionable whether science could fulfil this function with a strictly meaningless language.

---

15 See P. Tillich, *Dynamics of Faith* (London: Allen and Unwin, 1957) and D. Cupitt, *Taking Leave of God* (London: SCM Press, 1980).

In the case of religion it may be different. It would not be much different if one thought that the point of religion was also explanatory, as Frazer and other early anthropologists have maintained. For then it is proto-science. Whereas if one maintains that the purpose of religion is expressive then the verificationist claim that religious language is strictly meaningless may not be so damaging. A. J. Ayer gives an account of ethical language in expressive terms and one may extend the account to religion also.[16] Ayer himself notes that many theists may be willing to accept the conclusion that religious statements are strictly meaningless.[17]

Verificationism is no longer regarded as tenable. So the less extreme option is to regard religious language as having some semantics, only not the same semantics as, say, talk about ordinary people and their actions. Such a view is expressed among Wittgensteinians by saying that the grammar of religious language is different from the grammar of everyday language and that the superficial similarity between the two is misleading (and the source of philosophical problems), and is supported by the claim that grammar is related to forms of life and the religious and everyday forms of life are clearly very different.[18] A key claim of this form is that 'God' is not a singular term. That is, 'God' should not be understood as the sort of term whose function is to refer. (It could have that function yet fail to refer, as does 'phlogiston' in science.) In particular, therefore, 'God' does not refer to any supernatural person; an utterance of 'I believe that God exists' by a religious person should not be construed as analogous to 'I believe that Princess Anastasia is alive' uttered by an historian. One problem for the double-language model in the philosophy of science is that it is not possible to draw a sharp dividing line between the observable and the unobservable, and hence there is no corresponding sharp dividing line between observational and non-observational/theoretical language. However, the claim that there is a distinct semantics for the non-observational requires a sharp division. Either a term refers or not; there is no halfway house. A similar problem arises in the religious case. There is good reason to suppose that Jesus of Nazareth and his disciple Simon (also known as Peter) as well Saul of Tarsus (also known as Paul) actually existed. At the very least one can ask that question in a purely historical, non-religious sense. So, clearly, 'Jesus', 'St Peter', and 'St Paul' are singular terms. Christians will assert the following: 'Jesus is the Son of God'. If 'Jesus' is a singular term, then so is 'the Son of God'. Similarly a pious Catholic will pray to God, the angels, and saints in a similar way, and possibly to all in the same prayer. Indeed the phrase 'all the angels and saints' is a common one in Catholic liturgy. It is difficult to see how the semantics of 'saints' and 'angels' could differ such that the first is a general term covering certain kinds of person and the latter is not, especially as the proposition

---

16 See A. J. Ayer, *Language, Truth and Logic* (Harmondsworth: Pelican, 1971), pp. 142–4.

17 See *Language, Truth and Logic*, pp. 152–3. Tillich's account (in *Dynamics of Faith*) of religious language as symbolic may be regarded as falling into the same category of expressivist accounts of language.

18 Cf. D. Z. Phillips, 'Searle on language-games and religion' and 'On really believing' in his *Wittgenstein and Religion* (London: Macmillan), pp. 22–55. For a response to Philips, see M. Scott and A. Moore, 'Can theological realism be refuted?' in *Religious Studies* 33 (1997), pp. 401–18.

'some angels are saints' is supposed to be true for Catholics. Note, however, that a distinct reason for supposing that we cannot divide observational from theoretical language is the claim that observation terms are theory-laden. That is, observational terms are themselves partly theoretical in that applying them implies the acceptance of some theory (if only a rather low level theory). It seems less plausible to claim that the bulk of our everyday language is in part implicitly religious also.

5.5 The Current Status of Metaphysical and Semantic Antirealism

Metaphysical and semantic antirealism are no longer popular options among the bulk of mainstream philosophers of science. Most accept that the semantics for scientific language is not different in kind from that for the remainder of our descriptive talk, that scientific claims are therefore truth-apt, and that if those claims are true then there exist entities and properties that are not perceptible. Not all these philosophers are ready to accept that all our most warranted scientific claims should be regarded as true. For many, some kind of epistemological antirealism is tenable. Metaphysical/ semantic theological antirealism is less unpopular than its scientific counterpart. One reason, I suspect, is that the corresponding arguments have not been explored with the same degree of analytic rigour as in the scientific case. A rather different reason is the existence of a trade-off between metaphysical and epistemological antirealism. Let us say that in a certain domain of discourse many people wish to make claims of the form 'there are Xs', 'Xs are thus and so' for some specific 'X'. Let it be that it is widely thought that if we take the semantics of 'X-speak' in a face-value, realist way, there are reasons to be sceptical concerning our ability to know such claims to be true – the evidence for Xs is poor, there are *a priori* reasons why we could not know about Xs even if they did exist, there may even be evidence against Xs. It would seem therefore that we should hold that those who assert 'there are Xs' and 'Xs are thus and so' are not entitled to make such assertions and we should not make them ourselves. However, the following move is left open to those who do not wish to reject the widely-made assertions. One may deny that the utterances in question should be given a realist semantics at all. Once given some alternative semantics (or metaphysics) it may turn out that the sceptical problems fall away, for example because 'Xs' are, given this semantics/metaphysics, much easier to know about, or even because this semantics suggests that it is a mistake to think that X-talk is cognitive at all (it is not truth- or knowledge-apt).[19] Berkeley's strategy is explicitly of this kind. He acknowledges that Locke's philosophy leads to scepticism if 'corporeal body' is understood in a materialist fashion. And so in order to avoid such scepticism Berkeley declares that corporeal bodies are not material but are ideas. Thus one strong motivation for metaphysical antirealism is the avoidance of scepticism that would otherwise arise. However, in the philosophy of science it is highly debatable whether any sceptical problem arises even on a realist metaphysics. On the face of it, many scientific theories are extremely well supported by the evidence, and so

---

19   In my view much of the motivation for Cupitt's antirealism comes from a desire to retain a commitment to orthodox theological claims. Cf. S. Ross White, *Don Cupitt and the Future of Christian Doctrine* (London: SCM Press, 1994), p. 20.

supporters of scientific realism as regards both metaphysics and epistemology think that they are on firm ground. The theological case is somewhat different. For here the strength of the evidence would appear, *prima facie*, to be rather weaker. There is considerable room for reasoned denial of the existence of God. Consequently there is a correspondingly greater motivation to avoid scepticism (i.e. agnosticism or atheism) by resorting to a metaphysical or semantic antirealism. In the next section I examine whether the appearance of greater epistemological strength in the case of science as opposed to religion is genuine.

6 Epistemological Antirealism in Science and Theology

In the above I did not distinguish between religion and theology, because in so far as both involve propositions, the subject matter of the propositions largely overlaps and thus the metaphysical questions are the same for both. However, now we are discussing epistemology, it will be useful to remember that the two are distinct, in that a religion is a set of practices, normally institutionalized, of which, as typically understood, beliefs form a part but only a part. It is not an essential part of religion that it seeks to justify, add to, or even explain its beliefs. Theology, however, is a form of enquiry. Its concern is to understand the subject matter of religious belief, to subject those beliefs to scrutiny, usually with the intention of justifying them. In the process it aims to add to our understanding of God, heaven, sin, or whatever it is that may be the subject matter of religion. Thus the epistemological questions that may be aimed at theology are not necessarily the same as those aimed at religion, although they do overlap.

6.1 Inference to the Best Explanation

Several of the antirealist objections to claims for scientific knowledge focus on the forms of inference employed – primarily enumerative induction and Inference to the Best Explanation. We can put the problem of induction aside since it concerns inferences to universal generalizations. While there are theological generalizations of interest ('all humans have souls') the most significant theological and religious claims are existential: that there is a God, with certain properties. Of greater interest are objections to Inference to the Best Explanation (IBE), for one of the classic arguments for the existence of God, the Argument from Design, takes precisely this form. It is worth noting, however, that while objections to IBE in the case of science are general, casting doubt on the ability of IBE to give us knowledge on any occasion, or on any occasion where the conclusion concerns the unobserved, in the theological case the objections are more specific. Thus Hume did not object to IBE in general; rather he complained that the particular inference, from perceived order in the world to a perfectly good and powerful creator, is a weak one. It is a weak one because the proposed explanation is a poor explanation of the evidence – or at least far from being the best one. Thus, if Hume is right, the Argument from Design fails even by the standards of those who do accept IBE as a route to knowledge.

Nonetheless, there are analogies between the general rejection of IBE by scientific antirealists and Hume's rejection of the particular application of it. Hume cites other explanatory hypotheses that would explain the data equally well, including hypotheses that are original to Hume. The general complaint against IBE is that however many explanations we have considered there will always be others we have not considered, and that among these will be explanations that are just as good as our preferred explanation. Another general complaint against IBE was that 'goodness' is too subjective a notion to be a sound basis for inference to truth. Again, one may employ a particular version of this complaint without necessarily subscribing to the general version. Thus it may be objected that the theological hypothesis favoured by the Argument from Design is likely to seem to be a good one only to those with strong religious inclinations to start with.

6.2 The No Miracles Argument and the Pessimistic Meta-induction

In favour of scientific realism some philosophers have raised the No Miracles Argument, that the success of science would be a miracle (i.e. implausible) if our best scientific theories were not largely true or near to the truth. This is a generalized version of Inference to the Best Explanation that sees science as more-or-less unified and as generally very successful in making predictions (including predictions about how pieces of science-based technology will behave). The best explanation for this success, so this argument goes, is that the processes of science lead us to the truth. In particular, science is a process of inquiry that continues to generate ever more successful theories. Thus the NMA can be seen as an argument to the effect that the method or methods of science are reliable and thus that its theories are likely to be true or nearly so. Since religion is not a form of enquiry one would not expect the NMA to have an analogue. However, since theology is a form of enquiry, there could be an analogue to the NMA. The problem here, however, is that the argument would not have the same immediate plausibility that it has in science, for the simple reason that theology does not have spectacular successes to point to. Of course this may be debated and we may ask, what counts as success? After all, most scientific predictions are those than can be assessed only by scientists employing other scientific theories, and it may be argued that by theologians' own criteria theology has been successful also. One difference, however, is science-based technology, for here the successes can be judged by the layman. It doesn't take a scientist to verify that radios can receive signals, that nuclear power stations produce electricity, that computers compute, that we have put a man on the moon and got him back again, and so forth.

Arguing in the opposite direction to the NMA, the pessimistic meta-induction (PMI) is a general argument against the inference from the success of theories to their truth on the ground that in the past successful theories have often been falsified in due course. One way of appreciating the PMI is this. Either our current most successful theories are false or they are true. If false, then success in science does not yield truth. Now consider the position if they are true. Such theories will typically have replaced successful predecessor theories. These older theories and their current replacements are inconsistent, hence if the current theories are true then the successful theories of the past are false. Thus again we have an example of successful but false theories. Either way we can see that the success of a theory does not show it to be true. Again, any analogous argument would be directed against theology rather than religion. The PMI could be mounted most straightforwardly against theology if we can see an historical succession of theological theories (positions, view, etc.) that (i) are each regarded as successful in their time, and (ii) are mutually inconsistent. Finding sequences such that (ii) holds is perhaps not difficult. For example, the antirealist and non-theistic theologies of many contemporary theologians are clearly inconsistent with the realist theologies of the past. In Protestant countries the Reformation was an exchange of one theology for another inconsistent with it. And even within the various Protestant traditions (and to an extent in the Catholic traditions) there have been changes of view over time. It needs also to be shown that (i) is true, that the relevant theories were regarded as successful by theological lights in their own time. This is perhaps more difficult to ascertain. One might measure success by general acceptance – but over how wide a range of theologians? Nonetheless, this may not matter for the theological sceptic. For if we cannot identify any theological view as successful, then that itself constitutes a reason for rejecting the capacity of theology to lead to the truth. In effect one can mount a synchronic PMI: at any time there are a variety of mutually inconsistent theological views on offer. None has a much greater claim to success than any other. Consequently the relevant degree of success achieved cannot be a sign of truth. This is just a more formal way of putting an often made complaint. There are many religions and even more theologies on offer. If we ignore fringe religions and theologies, we have no good reason to favour any one of the remaining well-established, widely supported and intellectually well-developed theologies as opposed to the alternatives.

Note that such a synchronic PMI does not have a significant scientific counterpart. Most scientists and philosophers of science would agree that where an analogous situation arises, the right response is a suspension of belief. Where there are well-developed rival theories each successful to some degree but none more successful than the other, the right attitude to take is that one should not believe any one of them to be true. Thus, for a while at least, it would have been proper not to take a view on whether the demise of the dinosaurs was caused by (i) meteor impact, (ii) volcanic explosion, (iii) Darwinian superseding by better adapted mammalian species. But for much of science there are theories that are almost universally accepted and which are far more successful than their (now moribund) rivals. In such cases a synchronic PMI cannot get off the ground. In this connection the cultural difference between science and religion/theology is often noted. The favoured theories of science are almost universal amongst well or even moderately developed societies. But this is far from being the case with theological theories. It is sometimes countered that the ubiquity of scientific agreement is just an aspect of western cultural imperialism. But this would not explain (i) why there is widespread agreement on which theories are successful, and (ii) why there is religious difference despite cultural imperialism. (Many imperialists tried harder to impose Christianity through missions than they did to impose western science.)

Not all realists subscribe to the NMA. One reason is that it treats science as a unified whole, whose method or methods are shared across all disciplines. But if that is not the case, it would be misleading to argue from the widespread success of science to the reliability of the methods of science and thence to the truth of its theories. And many naturalistically inclined philosophers of science believe that there is no unique scientific method but rather a plurality of methods some of which may be fairly specific to a particular discipline. This view, while it prevents the realist from deploying the NMA nonetheless also protects her from the PMI. The fact that we can find some sequences that show that success is not correlated with truth, is no reason to deny that success is ever a guide to truth, if we think that in different areas of science the methods of theory justification are different. Plausibly a parallel move could be made with respect to the application of the PMI to theology. Is theology a unified discipline that employs the same methods whether in Catholic or Protestant theology, whether in Christian or Muslim theology and so forth? Arguably not, and if one denies the unity of theology, then the disagreement between theologians of different traditions is not a strong reason to reject all theology.

6.3 Social Constructivism

The diversity of religious and theological beliefs, in contrast to the relative agreement on much of science, suggests that a social constructivist view of religion and theology might be better supported than a social constructivist view of science. In both cases the constructivist will appeal to social or political reasons in explaining the existence of the institutions and indeed of their particular practices and beliefs. The implication is that such explanations show that religion and theology are not responses to the existence of God and that science is not a mechanism for uncovering objective truths about nature. After all, if theology were a reliable way of coming to know about God, why is there such widespread disagreement? That disagreement is best explained by the existence of cultural diversity. The social constructivist has a more difficult time accounting for the remarkable cross-cultural agreement on scientific matters. Even if there are disagreements about the newest theories there is usually near-universal acceptance of better-established theories, and about techniques and instruments. As mentioned, the efficacy of the objection from religious and theological diversity does seem to depend on the assumption that cognitive methods of religion/theology are shared by the differing religions and their theologies. It also depends upon the divergences being significant. So as regards religion, some may argue that Jews, Christians, Muslims and perhaps others are indeed worshipping the same God and that to focus on differences in detail ignores the widespread existence of religion and 'spirituality' which can, allegedly, be seen as evidence for the existence of a supernatural being. The social constructivist critique does not necessarily depend on diversity of practice and belief, for even a widespread consensus can have a social explanation. When faced with the NMA, the social constructivist can point to the fact that much of the so-called predictive success of science is itself success only by the standards of science itself. For this reason realists will point to the technological success of science as providing external evidence of success. The problem for theology is that there is little that can fill the analogous function to technology. If prayer were provably efficacious in bringing about the prayed-for outcome, or if believers were protected from disasters that afflict non-believers, that might be analogous evidence. But there is little such evidence beyond suggestions that believers are on average slightly healthier and happier than non-believers.[20]

7 The Aims of Religion, Theology and Science

Scientific realists regard the aim of science as being the truth, or increasing nearness to the truth, or even knowledge. Antirealists may diverge from this by rejecting this claim to some degree or other. Theological antirealists may make a parallel move with respect to religion, although the matter is little discussed with respect to theology itself. Science and religion are however clearly different in this respect, even as far as the realist is concerned. While, on the face of it, science is primarily in the truth business, religion deals with a lot else besides. The main purpose is not the acquisition or inculcation of beliefs but is the worship of God in liturgy, communication with God through prayer, doing God's work on Earth, and so forth. Even so, it is clear that this perspective requires a core of belief in religion, that God exists, that He wants us to worship in such and such ways, that He wants us to act in certain ways. Theology, at least in its origin, may be seen as a systematic attempt to get such beliefs right.

Those kinds of semantic antirealism that deny that sentences of scientific or religious language are truth-apt will require us to deny that science or religion, as the case may be, are in the truth business at all. That would seem to be a consequence of the views of Tillich and the Wittegnsteinians. However, one might still hold that science and/or religion do not aim at truth, even if the claims are truth-apt. But if the claims of scientists and religious people do not aim at truth, then those claims cannot be held to be the expressions of belief. Thus van Fraassen thinks that scientists do not believe their favoured theories, they merely accept them.[21] Even so, acceptance has some connection with belief – it implies the belief that the theory in question is empirically adequate. Thus a scientist may well believe that the observable predictions of her theories are true. However, since religion is not in the prediction business, this kind of substitute for belief is not available. Thus the point of religion must be expressed in terms that are not cognitive at all (they may be expressivist, for example). The fact that religion involves so much liturgy and other kinds of individual and social practices that do not directly require belief makes it relatively easy to think that propositional elements of religion are not beliefs at all.

One problem facing such views is that many of the individuals concerned will declare that their attitude is one of belief or some related attitude that is also truth-apt or cognitive (e.g. faith, or partial belief). It is difficult to deny that Christianity is concerned with belief given the central role of the creed in its liturgy. In van Fraassen's case he can claim that the individuals in question have just confused the cognitive attitude they do have, acceptance, with a related one they do not have, belief. That may be a difficult enough position to maintain, but it is more difficult to

---

20 But they are also more likely to be overweight; see K. F. Ferraro, 'Firm believers? Religion, Body Weight, and Well-being' in *Review of Religious Research* 39 (1998), pp. 224–44. There may be many explanations for what is a marginal effect.

21 See B. van Fraassen, *The Scientific Image*.

hold that a traditional Christian is mistaken in holding that they really do believe (in an everyday sense) in God and that their attitude is in fact one of expressing some kind of need or desire or is in fact some kind of *sui generis* mental attitude specific to religion and bound up with engaging in religion as a practice (à la Wittgenstein).

One may make a distinction between the aim of science/religion as socially embedded practices and the attitudes of its practitioners. So scientists and religious people do believe in the truth of their theories and in the existence of God. But the aims of science and religion are not concerned with the truth of those beliefs but rather, for example, with the maintenance of the social position of the relevant elites. This need not show that those beliefs are false. One may admit that technology aims at the production of objects and techniques useful for certain purposes. Nonetheless, insofar as technological research does involve beliefs, those beliefs had better be true if technology is to achieve its aim of giving us effective products. Similarly the social position of scientists may also depend on their producing true theories. The role those theories play in technology is one reason why this is so. The internally critical nature of science is another. New ideas are subject to scrutiny at various stages that will weed out at least the most egregiously false ones. And since careers depend on successful problem solving, old ideas, even if long-standing, will be rejected if they impede that process. Thus the scientific realist may be able to concede that science is in the business of promoting the interests of (leading) scientists without admitting that this casts any doubt on the ability of science to produce true theories. For the ability of science to produce truth is part of what promotes the interests of successful scientists. On the other hand there are few analogous mechanisms in the case of religion that would link the social position of priests and others benefiting from religion (for example, aristocracies and governments) to the truth of religious belief. It is true that in some religions priests are supposed to help win wars, cure diseases, and ensure good harvests. But the links are sufficiently indirect that failure could often be explained away. And modern religions reject the thought that they have any role in changing the world in that way. Thus religion is more vulnerable than science to claims that its function is not concerned with or even related to the truth.

8 Conclusion

Many of the same themes crop up in debates between realism and antirealism whether in the philosophy of science or in the philosophy of religion. There are nonetheless various asymmetries. In both cases metaphysical and semantic antirealism faces serious difficulties, but these difficulties are more severe in the case of theology than science. Nonetheless, it seems that metaphysical/semantic antirealism is largely an historical phenomenon in philosophy of science, maintained by few serious philosophers of science today, whereas that kind of antirealism is fairly widely favoured among theologians.

There are two explanations for this apparently paradoxical state of affairs. First, the relevant issues have been explored more deeply and for a longer time in science than in theology and consequently the obstacles are more keenly felt. The second explanation lies in the trade-off between metaphysical/semantic antirealism on the one hand and epistemological antirealism on the other. As discussed, one way of avoiding scepticism about Xs is to re-construe what Xs are or what 'X' refers to. We have seen that there are quite general grounds for epistemological antirealism in the philosophy of science, some of which would carry over into theology (e.g. rejecting IBE in general would undermine not only belief in scientific theories but also the Design Argument). However, theology suffers from quite particular grounds for doubt as well. So even if one does not object to IBE in general one might agree with Hume that the Design Argument is a poor inference. One might think that even if not all theories are radically underdetermined by the data, the claim that God exists and has such and such properties is one that is badly lacking in evidence to support it strongly let alone convincingly. Since doubt and even disbelief are clearly reasonable and perhaps well-grounded options in religion, even without recourse to sophisticated philosophical arguments, the claims of scepticism are especially pressing in the case of religion. Consequently there is a greater pressure in theology to accept the trade-off between the two kinds of antirealism and to evade the pull of agnosticism or atheism by resorting to metaphysical or semantic antirealism. Berkeley made just this trade-off because he believed that metaphysical realism in the form of materialism leads to scepticism about physical ('corporeal') entities which in turn would lead to doubts concerning God's existence. But if there are quite independent doubts about God's existence one might have to extend the metaphysically antirealist manoeuvre to God himself.

Chapter 6

Prescriptive Realism

John Hare

In the first part of this paper I am going to discuss the position I have previously called 'prescriptive realism', and then in the second part I am going to describe one way of relating the position to theism. This is an ambitious project for a single paper, and I will sometimes have to rely on promissory notes rather than worked-out theory.[1]

In the first section of my book *God's Call* I tried to give a historical account of the dispute over the last century between realism and expressivism, taking central characters in sequence and labelling their theories, G. E. Moore ('platonism'), A. J. Ayer ('emotivism'), R. M. Hare ('prescriptivism'), Iris Murdoch ('humble platonism'), J. L. Mackie ('error theory'), John McDowell ('disposition theory'), David Brink ('new-wave realism'), and Allan Gibbard ('norm expressivism').[2] I could have chosen other exemplars, including some of the contributors to the present volume, but the purpose was not to be exhaustive but to illustrate what I saw as a convergence, as the two sides to the dispute progressively conceded points to each other. I proposed 'prescriptive realism' as a name for a view that combines the merits of each side that emerge from this history. In the present paper I am not going to describe this history, but the position in its own terms. My aim is to show in what sense the theory is expressivist and in what sense it is realist.[3]

1a. The Expressivism of Prescriptive Realism

Prescriptive realism is expressivist because it holds that one central function of value judgement is to express some motivational or 'orectic' state.[4] The orectic state that is expressed in the judgement is itself standardly complex. In cases where we respond affectively to some situation, we can then respond to that response, either by

---

1   I am writing a book that will cover these matters at greater length, but it is still in process.

2   John Hare, *God's Call* (Grand Rapids, MI: Eerdmans, 2001).

3   Two recent attempts to perform a similar synthesis are Linda Zagzebski, *Divine Motivation Theory* (Cambridge: Cambridge University Press, 2004), and David Copp, in 'Realist-Expressivism: A Neglected Option for Moral Realism', *Social Philosophy and Policy* 18: 2 (2001), pp. 1–43, especially p. 38. See also his 'Milk, Honey, and the Good Life on Moral Twin Earth', *Synthese* 124 (2000), pp. 113–37. I have reviewed Zagzebski's book in *Notre Dame Philosophical Reviews*, February 2005. My chief difference with David Copp is that he wants to deny that he is any kind of internalist except what he calls a 'discourse internalist', which is restricted to what I call 'conventional expression'.

4   In *God's Call* (p. viii) I used the term 'orectic', from the Greek *orexis*, which has a broader scope than any English term, and covers emotion, desire, and will.

accepting it or by refusing to accept it. Our acceptance can be normed, in the sense that we acknowledge that the initial response is permitted by the norms that we also accept. If a value judgement expresses this kind of normed acceptance, we can call it an 'endorsement'.[5] If I endorse the fear for my job, I give myself permission to act on the fear. For another example, to endorse the feeling that what one has done is morally reprehensible is to express one's acceptance of the norms that impartially prescribe guilt for the agent of such action and resentment for the recipient of it. The two terms 'express' and 'acceptance' need more discussion.[6] I will talk at some length about the first, and then more briefly about the second.

We need to distinguish between what I will call 'conventional expression' and 'effusive expression' (from the Latin *effundo*, I pour out). The OED gives, as one (rare) sense of 'effusive', 'that has the function of giving outlet to emotion'. The term is not ideal for what I have in mind, both because 'effusive' normally carries with it the connotation of *demonstrative* expression and because the kind of expression I am interested in is not always the expression of *emotion*. But I will use the term because I have not found a better one. The difference between the two kinds of expression is best seen in an example. If I apologize to you by saying 'I am sorry', I have expressed regret. But if this is conventional expression, I may not have any regret myself. I have still apologized to you, though not whole-heartedly. In this way apologizing is like promising and asserting. If I promise without the relevant intention, or assert without the relevant belief, I have still made the promise or the assertion. Saying 'I am sorry' counts as an apology to you because of the conventions accepted within the language community to which you and I belong. But if, when I apologize, this is effusive expression, then I must actually have the regret that I express. Effusive expression is a species of what we might call 'causal expression', which does not require utterance at all. In the original sense of 'pressing out', a lactating woman can express her milk, and this means that the milk has to go from being inside her to being outside her. More loosely, my careless dressing for a party can causally express my contempt for the people I am going to be with, whether or not I intend to communicate this contempt, but only if I have the contempt which is being expressed.

It is tempting to think that effusive expression is the same as sincere expression, but that is not quite right. There are different kinds of case here. An apology can be sincere even if the person making the apology is not at the moment feeling the regret. When I step on someone's foot in the bus as we shuffle past each other,

---

5   I mean here to be repeating Allan Gibbard's account in *Wise Choices, Apt Feelings* (Cambridge: Harvard University Press, 1990), pp. 6–7. He says that to endorse a feeling is to say that it is 'rational', or 'makes sense', and this means accepting the feeling as permitted by the norms that one accepts. I have discussed some disagreements with Gibbard in *The Moral Gap* (Oxford: Clarendon Press, 1996), pp. 182–88. The most important disagreement for present purposes is that I do not see that the expressivism I am defending requires the rejection of the kind of realism that Gibbard rejects.

6   I am influenced in this discussion by Richard Joyce, 'Expressivism and Motivational Internalism', *Analysis* 62: 4 (2002), pp. 336–44.

I may murmur to her, 'I'm sorry', and not have any *feeling* of regret at all.[7] But we would not say that the apology is insincere, though it might be perfunctory. There is perhaps, though I am not sure about this, a dispositional requirement here. If she were to stop me and ask, 'Are you really sorry?', I would probably first feel irritation. But perhaps if I were able to repeat the apology, I would have to have the feeling at *that* point if the apology were to be sincere. Perhaps sincere assertion similarly does not require occurrent belief, but a disposition to have an occurrent belief. I will not go further into this here.

The kind of expressivism I want to maintain holds that one central function of value judgement is to make effusive and not merely conventional expression of the normed acceptance of one's initial feeling about some situation. The term 'function' is tricky here. I am using it in the same way we can talk about the function of an artefact, such as a chisel. We have chisels so that we can make fine cuts in wood, and a good chisel is one that does this well. The term 'function' can also be used without this evaluative implication, so that we could talk about a chisel functioning to take out a screw, as a screwdriver does. But in the sense of 'function' I am using, this would be a misuse of the chisel, a failure to use it in accord with its 'function'. So the claim I am making is that one central point of having value judgement is so that people can make an effusive expression of their normed acceptance of their initial feelings. What I mean by 'acceptance' I will come to next. Purely conventional expression is parasitic upon the effusive expression. Saying 'I am sorry' where there is no regret only works to express conventionally an apology because standardly that form of words accomplishes an effusive expression of regret. This is like the case of promising. The conventional expression of a promise only succeeds in making a promise because we have the institution of promise-making. And we only have the institution of promise-making because we want to be able to make believable commitments on the basis of intentions we actually have.

There is a useful set of distinctions made here by R. M. Hare, deriving from a technical device invented by Frege and Russell.[8] Frege introduced the assertion sign and Russell took it over in order to explain how the p and q which enter into the proposition 'p implies q' are not strictly the same as the p or the q which are separate propositions. R. M. Hare distinguishes between the 'neustic' (from the Greek *neuo*, I nod assent) which is the sign of subscription to an assertion or other speech act, the 'tropic' which is the sign of mood and distinguishes, for example, imperative from indicative, and the 'phrastic' which is common to sentences with different tropics. So 'The door is shut' and 'Shut the door' share a phrastic, and not a tropic. But what I am interested in for present purposes is the neustic. It is a convention that when a person gives philosophical examples, as in the two sentences quoted within the previous sentence, he is not subscribing to them. I was not telling you, my reader,

---

7   This is similar to a case mentioned by Richard Joyce, in which Fred and Carol have to leave the dinner party unexpectedly, and, as they rush out of the door, dragging on their coats, they call out 'Thanks!'.

8   R. M. Hare, 'Meaning and Speech Acts', first published in *Philosophical Review* 79 (1970) pp. 3–24, and republished in *Practical Inferences* (London: Macmillan, 1971), pp. 74–99 especially pp. 89–93.

to shut some door, or telling you that some door is shut. By contrast, when a person gives historical examples, the convention is that he is subscribing to the claim that these historical examples occurred. There are various other conventions for neustic withdrawal, like the conventions that enable us to recognize a play on stage. An actor who wants to communicate with the audience that there really is a fire in the theatre has to explicitly cancel these conventions. In the absence of some such special convention, we assume that utterances or written sentences (as in this paper) do have neustics attached to them. Discerning the tropic in a sentence does not by itself, however, tell us whether the person uttering the sentence has attached a neustic to it. It is part of R. M. Hare's prescriptivist theory that in value judgements there are other speech acts involved and not merely assertion. But, he adds,

> the fact that other tropics may figure in the analysis of ['good'] besides the indicative tropic, and that therefore sentences containing it cannot be described without qualification as assertions, but have to be explained in terms of the more complex speech act of commending, is no bar to the appearance of the word in contexts where commending is not taking place, providing that the relation of these contexts to those in which it is taking place can be explained.[9]

On this view we need to distinguish two questions about the use of a term like 'good' in a judgement. One question is about the tropic, whether there is commending going on. The other is about the neustic, whether, if there is commending going on, it is being subscribed to. If there is not commending going on, then there will not be subscription to commending; but there can be commending without subscription. An example (but only one kind of example) where there is not commending going on, even though the word 'good' is being used, is the 'inverted commas use', where the person using the expression means not to commend, but to report some general commendation that she does not share. For example, 'She's a very *good* woman' (in a sarcastic tone of voice) can mean that she is insufferably self-righteous. An example where there is commending going on, but not a neustic, is where I say to you, 'He's very good company', when in fact I think he is tedious but I want to persuade you to spend time with him so that I can escape.

Value judgement can fail to accomplish effusive expression in these two ways, and in many others. There is a multitude of different kinds of case, of value judgement

---

9   Note that R. M. Hare is not denying the indicative tropic. He did deny several times that he was a 'non-cognitivist', though he is often described that way in the secondary literature (for example in the article by Joyce I have just referred to). For example, 'I hope [I have] shown how little grasp of these issues those people have who think (as many beginner students are taught to think) that it is sufficient to distinguish between what they call cognitivist and non-cognitivist theories by saying that they give opposing answers to the question 'Can moral statements be true or false?' The answer to this question is that they can, but that the important issue between descriptivists and non-descriptivists is not settled thereby', *Sorting Out Ethics* (Oxford: Clarendon Press, 1997), p. 56. I am not, however, claiming that R. M. Hare is a prescriptive realist. He is, rather, what Simon Blackburn calls a 'quietist', holding that 'no real issue can be built around the objectivity or otherwise of moral values', see 'Errors and the Phenomenology of Value', in Blackburn, *Essays in Quasi-Realism* (Oxford: Oxford University Press, 1993), p. 153.

in the presence of multiple kinds of weakness and self-deception and listlessness and disingenuousness. What they all have in common is that there is something second-rate or defective in them *qua* value judgements, some failure in what I called a central function. It would be instructive, though I am not going to try to do it here, to distinguish in these various cases where we have tropic failure and where we have neustic failure. In any case, any good moral theory should acknowledge that there is something problematic in these various cases, and it is a merit of expressivist theories that they can do this. They display, for example, what is horrible about the case of a person who can no longer subscribe to the judgements she makes, or cannot endorse her affective responses (in the sense I am going to describe). Such a person is excluded from the human enterprise of sharing with others through our language our deepest commitments about how to respond to what is happening to us. Saying that there is a failure of function, and tying this to a failure of effusive expression, means that prescriptive realism is a kind of internalism. But the term 'internalism' has been used so variously that it is not much help. According to prescriptive realism, a person who makes a value judgement is not accomplishing all the central functions of value judgement unless she accomplishes an effusive expression of her normed acceptance.

I will confine myself here to listing five features of this kind of acceptance, without trying to give a comprehensive account. I will also confine myself to the acceptance of affective response, even though acceptance itself is not so confined. A typical example of an affective response is an emotion (though not all affective responses are emotions), and for present purposes we can borrow Robert Roberts's account of an emotion as a concern-based construal.[10] If I fear my job is in jeopardy because I have failed to carry out some task, I take up my concern for my job into the construal of my situation as dangerous.

1. There are, however, different levels or stages of accepting and endorsing an affective response, and these can be understood as different stages of reflective distance. In *The Moral Gap*, I distinguished acknowledging a response, identifying with it, and endorsing it.[11] For example, I can forgive someone while still believing that the anger I felt against her was appropriate to the cruelty of what she did; but I decide that I no longer want to be angry, and I want to seek reconciliation. Or a young surgeon can feel fear at the danger to the patients under his knife, but still be grateful for the gradual numbing of such fear that accompanies extensive professional practice; he refuses to endorse the fear. There are many different types of examples here.
2. Acceptance and the endorsement which expresses it are places where we can properly talk of autonomy. Emotions are characteristically not directly chosen, but experienced as responses to the situation encountered. But endorsement means judging that the response is fitting, or that the situation calls for it or deserves it. The expressivism I am defending (which departs here from Gibbard) allows that there can be an external value property (e.g. cruelty)

---

10 Robert Roberts, *Emotions* (Cambridge: Cambridge University Press, 2003), chapter 2.
11 *The Moral Gap*, pp. 118–28.

to which my emotion is a response, and which I autonomously judge to be fittingly responded to in this way. Even though the emotion is not chosen, and the norms by which I judge it appropriate are standardly not created by me, there is still autonomy in my submitting to these norms in my judgement of the appropriateness of the emotion. I have argued in various places that Kant's notion of autonomy is consistent with this kind of submission.[12]

3. Acceptance and endorsement need not be relativistic about value. I may be embedded in a culture, and in the 'thick' value terms used by that culture. For example, I may have grown up using the term 'gentleman', within a whole set of practices and institutions surrounding that term. But I am not constrained in my endorsement by that set of practices and institutions. It may be true that only someone who has grown up within them can understand the whole flavour of the term. But I can decide when I grow up that I reject the British class system, and then I will no longer use the term with the same effusive expression that characterizes its use by people who still accept those norms. There are two types of disentangling here that need to be distinguished. The first is the disentangling of evaluation and description within the emotion (which may not be completely achievable), and the second is the disentangling of emotion (which involves both) and acceptance or endorsement. Given the first point above about different levels or stages, the ease of this second disentangling will depend on the level of the acceptance and endorsement.

4. Normed acceptance (and so endorsement) is not just a particular response to a particular situation, but requires similar response to similar situations. Beyond this, since rationality aims at consistency, endorsement has a tendency towards a normative system in which different norms for different kinds of response are integrated with each other. We can think about such a system as an attempt to track our values that we hope are themselves coherent. Iris Murdoch talks about a 'magnetic centre', which unifies all our fragmentary experiences of value into a whole that transcends us.[13] Her guiding image is Plato's picture of the sun in the *Republic*, but Plato also has the analogy of a magnet attracting a set of iron rings, which transmit the attraction to each other, and eventually to us (the final ring).[14] The expressivism I am defending allows that the norms I use in evaluating my affective responses can make reference to such a magnetic centre. In terms of the analogy I will endorse a feeling to the extent that I believe that the magnetic attraction to which it responds is itself transmitting attraction from the magnetic centre. I will give more detail about one way to apply this analogy in the second half of the paper.

5. Finally, acceptance and endorsement not only allow but require some kind of moral realism. I have given the argument elsewhere both for the case of moral judgement and for the case of prudential judgement.[15] Roughly, the point is

---

12   E.g. *God's Call*, pp. 92–7.

13   Iris Murdoch, *The Sovereignty of Good* (New York: Routledge, 1970), p. 100.

14   Plato, *Ion* 536a.

15   The argument in the case of morality is in *The Moral Gap*, chapter 3, and in the case of prudence it is in *God's Call*, 40–46. Only the first is explicitly linked with Gibbard.

that if a person is going to endorse an affective response, she must believe that the norms she is accepting are consistent with her own happiness (in the case of prudence) or with the happiness of all (in the case of morality). Kant's argument in the *Critique of Practical Reason* (and elsewhere) is that in order to sustain such a belief in the case of morality, the agent must postulate a governance of the world in which virtue is consistent with happiness in the long run. Her commitment to morality would otherwise be rationally unstable. But this view of providence is itself a kind of moral realism (though not yet a kind of theism; that would take a further argument). The good that the agent believes is going to prevail in the long run is not a good projected onto the universe by the agent herself. If it were projected in this way, it could not do the job of making her commitment rationally stable in the way the argument requires.

1b. The Realism of Prescriptive Realism

In the next section of this paper I want to talk about the sense in which prescriptive realism is a form of realism. The theory is realist because it holds that when we judge something evaluatively we are picking out a value property that we attribute to the thing, which is no less a property than a descriptive property like 'red', and the judgement is objectively true when the thing has the property and false when it does not. The main difficulties in explaining this view come with the notions of 'property' and 'objective truth'. I am going to try to show in the second part of the paper a way to see the value properties as constituted by relations of various kinds to God, but prescriptive realism does not require this. Very roughly, there are two families of value properties that are involved in ethical evaluation, the family of attraction and repulsion (including 'thin' terms like 'good' and 'bad' and 'thick' terms like 'beautiful' and 'nauseating') and the family of permission and proscription (including 'thin' terms like 'right' and 'wrong' and 'thick' terms like 'polite' and 'murder'). But dichotomies fail both at the level of distinguishing the two families (which are not exhaustive of the class of value properties, since many of the virtue terms do not fit well in either family) and at the level of distinguishing within each family between the positive and the negative. In the present section I will focus on the term 'good' and use an analogy between 'good' and 'water'. This analogy has become familiar in recent discussions, and I want to use it but also to point out some ways in which it fails.[16] In the second part of the paper I will compare the relation of water and its chemical constitution to the relation of the value properties and God's constitution of them in the various ways I will discuss.

In the previous section I said that value judgement has effusive expression as <u>one</u> of its central functions. I am coming now to a second function, namely picking out these properties. The difficulty here is that people differ significantly in what things they call 'good' and in their account of what goodness is. This makes it hard to believe that there is one set of properties being picked out. We can see the difficulty

---

16 See H. Putnam, 'The Meaning of "Meaning"' in K. Gunderson (ed.), *Minnesota Studies in the Philosophy of Science* 7 (Minneapolis: University of Minnesota press, 1975), pp. 131–93.

even in the case of the term 'water'. Does the term pick out the property of being H_2O? Webster's Dictionary gives, as the first definition, 'a colourless transparent liquid, etc.' but then goes on to give the chemical definition. Probably millions of people who use the term have 'H_2O' in mind as part of what they mean, and equally probably millions of people do not. Certainly the second part of this is true if we consider the people who used the term 'water' to talk about what they drank and washed in and what filled the rivers and lakes and seas, before our present chemical analysis was discovered. Nonetheless we can say that the use of the term 'water' aimed at picking out the property even if most users of the term did not know what the property was. The same is true with 'good'. Suppose Robert Adams is right that goodness is constituted by resemblance to God.[17] Many religious believers link God and the two families of evaluative terms so intimately that they include that link in what they mean by the terms.[18] But they share a large number of evaluative practices with people who do not include such a link in the meaning. For example, both groups commend and advise and warn and proscribe. I am going to return to this matter when I discuss the difficulties about 'moral twin earth' after making some remarks about objectivity.[19] At the moment all I need to say is that value judgement has these two central functions, one of which is effusive expression, and one of which is to pick out properties whose nature may not be known to the people making the judgements. According to the theory outlined in the second part of the paper the value properties are constituted by a relation to God of a certain kind. This may not be known to the users of the value terms, who are nonetheless aiming to pick out the value properties, whatever they turn out to be. The thought experiment about moral twin earth will help us be clearer about the relation between these two functions.

I will assume that objectivity is desirable in a value judgement. Some thinkers who want to insist on the embodied character of human life find the notion 'objectivity' oppressive.[20] This paper is already covering too much, however, and I cannot enter into this part of the problem. In the history of the expressivism-realism debate, objectivity was seen to be threatened by emotivism, which seemed to reduce moral judgement to the expression of emotion. R. M. Hare responded by articulating an expressivist account of objectivity along roughly Kantian lines (though Kant should not be considered an opponent of moral realism). The idea is that the person making the moral judgement is required by the logic of the moral words to abstract from any improper partiality towards herself, by eliminating all essential reference to individuals, including herself, from the judgement. This kind of objectivity is what we would want in a Little League umpire, for example, who refuses to discriminate

17   Robert Adams, *Finite and Infinite Goods* (Oxford: Oxford University Press), 1999.

18   See Robert Adams, 'A Modified Divine Command Theory of Ethical Wrongness' in *The Virtue of Faith* (New York: Oxford University Press, 1987), pp. 97–122.

19   The thought experiment was suggested by Terence Horgan and Mark Timmons in 'New-Wave Moral Realism Meets Moral Twin Earth', in *Rationality, Morality and Self-Interest*, ed. J. Heil (Savage, MD.: Rowman & Littlefield, 1993), pp. 115–33. See also Mark Timmons, 'On the Epistemic Status of Considered Moral Judgments,' *Southern Journal of Philosophy* 29 (Spindel Conference Supplement, 1990), pp. 97–129.

20   See Emily Townes, *In a Blaze of Glory: Womanist Spirituality as Social Witness* (Nashville, TN: Abingdon Press, 1995).

in favour of one team even if his own child is on it. Objectivity in this sense is not an issue between expressivists and realists. But the kind of realism I am defending requires more than this. It requires that the value properties that are judged to hold of something hold of that thing independently of the person making the judgement. To take an example of a realist theory, an action is wrong for a person if God commands her not to do it, and God's proscribing the action does not depend on her making the judgement that the action is wrong.

A qualification needs to be made to this second account of objectivity. A realist does not have to see values as real independently of general human capacities to respond to them in a certain way in appropriate circumstances.[21] There is an analogy between value and colour, though the analogy also fails in a way I am going to mention. An object's being red should be understood as its having the disposition to look red to us in appropriate circumstances. We could correctly call colour, on this view, both subjective and objective. It is subjective in the sense that it is understood relative to the capacities of subjects. It is objective in the sense that its existence does not depend on reception by any particular subject. Values are subjective and objective in the same way. But there is also a disanalogy between value and colour. McDowell insists on the essential contestability of value judgement. We should never be unreflectively content, he says, with the current state of our judgements as an undistorted perception of the relevant value aspect of reality.[22] On the theist account I am going to give, the situation is worse than this. We are not only fallible about value, but we have an in-built tendency to distortion. This means that we cannot, as in the case of colour, say that the property is correlative to *our dispositions* to respond, since our dispositions are (on my theory) radically unreliable. Nonetheless it is true that the value properties are correlative to our *capacities* to discern them (though we still need an account of these capacities).

One account of objective truth makes use of the notion of a property: a judgement about a thing is true when the thing has the property that the judgement attributes to it.[23] I said that according to prescriptive realism the property picked out in a value judgement is no less a property than a descriptive property like 'red'. I put it this way because I do not want to commit myself to any particular account of the necessary and sufficient conditions for properties. Suppose we restrict ourselves to causal properties, reference to which is required for any full causal explanation of events. So we might say that any full causal explanation of the events of Hitler's life requires reference to his moral depravity.[24] The point I want to make is that evaluative language does have the function of picking out these properties, but

21 I am relying here on some distinctions made by John McDowell in a series of papers, and in *Mind and World* (Cambridge: Harvard University Press, 1994).

22 McDowell, 'Values and Secondary Qualities', in *Morality and Objectivity*, ed. Ted Honderich (London: Routledge & Kegan Paul, 1985), p. 120. I am rejecting here Simon Blackburn's claim that the secondary quality analogy simply adds unwarranted complexity, see 'How to be an Ethical Antirealist' in *Essays on Quasi-Realism*, pp. 110–11.

23 See Geoffrey Sayre-McCord's extended introduction to *Essays on Moral Realism* (Ithaca: Cornell University Press, 1988), pp. 1–23.

24 I take the example from Nicholas Sturgeon, 'Moral Explanations', in *Essays on Moral Realism*, pp. 229–55.

does not have *only* this function. The typical mistake of 'descriptivism' or what Austin called 'the descriptive fallacy' is to ignore the different ways in which value language and descriptive language operate, 'It has come to be commonly held that many utterances which look like statements are either not intended at all, *or only intended in part*, to record or impart straightforward information about the facts'.[25] A person who is sensitive to this fallacy need not deny that there are causal properties that are picked out by the value terms, but will want to insist that the value judgment does more than simply picking them out.

We can now return to the case of moral twin-earth. Putnam, in the article I have referred to already, gave us the thought experiment of another earth very like this one, including the use on both planets of the term 'water', except that on twin-earth the stuff in which people wash, and what they drink, and what is in their rivers and lakes and seas, is constituted chemically not by H_2O but by XYZ. He says that we should conclude that when we disagree with the inhabitants of twin-earth about whether something is water, we are talking past each other. There are simply two different properties, and 'water' rigidly designates one of them on earth and the other on twin-earth. But now suppose we imagine a moral twin-earth very like this one, including the use on both planets of the term 'good', except that on earth (let us say) the property that people pick out when they commend and advise and warn and proscribe is constituted by some relation between actions or human lives and God, and on moral twin-earth it is constituted (let us say) by some utilitarian relation between actions or lives and the general happiness. The question is whether when we disagree with the inhabitants of moral twin-earth we are talking past each other in the same way as in Putnam's thought experiment we were talking past each other when we talked with the inhabitants of twin-earth about water.

It seems clear that we should *not* say this. If we are talking about lying in some situation, for example, we can have a genuine disagreement about whether it is wrong (because always or almost always forbidden by God) or permissible (because always or almost always conducive to everybody's happiness). The disagreement seems genuine because value judgement has the same role for both communities in carrying out the central function of the effusive expression of normed acceptance. This role is independent of the question of what constitutes the properties ascribed to things when both groups commend and advise and warn and proscribe. But does this show that the realist analysis of the value property is wrong? I think it does not. This is because there is a second kind of overlap between the two earths. The second overlap is between what actions or lives are actually commended or proscribed etc. by the two groups. God, on the theory we are supposing true on earth, cares about human happiness, and when God attracts us by a quasi-magnetic attraction through intermediate rings (to return to Plato's picture) we are being attracted by things that will make us happy. Since God cares for humans equally, this attraction will be to things that are consistent with every human's welfare. There will still be differences between the value judgements of the two groups, since on earth the lives of its inhabitants continue (on the theist theory) past physical death and on moral twin-

---

    25   J. L. Austin, *How to Do Things with Words* (Oxford: Oxford University Press, 1965), p. 3, emphasis added.

earth, let us assume, they do not, and this will affect what kinds of sacrifices it is rational for each group to make during this life.[26] There will also be values on earth, such as gratitude for divine revelation, which will not be values on moral twin-earth. But the second kind of overlap means that both groups are trying to pick out the value properties that explain why roughly the same class of actions and lives are evaluated in roughly the same way. This second kind of overlap makes the thought experiment about moral twin-earth quite different from the thought experiment about twin-earth. For once the difference between H_2O and XYZ is understood, the groups will realize that they are talking about different stuff. But the inhabitants of earth and moral twin-earth will realize (after the differences are revealed) that they are talking about by-and-large the *same* 'stuff', though their analysis of this 'stuff' is different.[27]

The second kind of overlap is not a product simply of the example I have chosen of the moral theory on moral twin-earth.[28] Suppose that on moral twin-earth the prevailing theory is not consequentialist but deontological. Still there will be the same kind of overlap, because the rules that the deontologist proposes as normative will most probably be rules that God prescribes to us. There is no accident in this. These various moral theories all start historically from theism. They can all be seen as abstractions in two stages. The first stage is to abstract one part of God's relation to us as especially important for morality. The second stage (historically within the last two centuries) is to remove that part of God's role in the theory as well.[29] This is why the second kind of overlap between the theist ethics I am proposing and either consequentialism or deontology is greater than the overlap between the two offshoots. A theory can focus on God's commandments, and use them to structure the moral life, or it can focus on God's love, transcending the commandments, and on our freedom to respond to this love, or it can focus on the character that God wants us to have and the virtues that constitute that character. When the theist premises in each of the original versions of the various types of theory get dropped, this has effects on the rest of the theory (though different effects on the different theories). The non-theist versions end up more different from each other than any one of them is different from the original theism. But I think the overlap is still sufficient to legitimate the same reply about moral twin-earth.[30] The deontologist and the consequentialist are talking about roughly the same class of endorsed lives and actions, though there will

---

26 In order to make this thought-experiment work, we have to assume that it is possible for God to create a world in which God does not want its inhabitants to be attracted to or to be obedient to God, and this assumption is problematic from a theist point of view.

27 I have put 'stuff' in inverted commas because of the disanalogy between the cases. 'Water' is a stuff term, and 'Good' is not.

28 Horgan and Timmons, in their original thought experiment, proposed a deontological theory and a teleological theory as the two competitors.

29 John Hare, *God and Morality A Philosophical History* (Oxford: Blackwell, 2007). The argument requires sustained investigation of a number of founding texts, and I cannot do this here. In the book I compare a theist and a non-theist example of each of what I take to be the four main types of ethical theory in Western thought.

30 I am influenced here by David Merli, 'Return to Moral Twin Earth', *Canadian Journal of Philosophy*, 32: 2 (2002) pp. 207–40.

be some differences, whereas the classes of stuff-tokens referred to as 'water' on earth and twin-earth are totally different (and necessarily different).

2a. Theist Prescriptive Realism and the Good

In the second part of this paper I want to describe one way of relating prescriptive realism to theism. I am not attempting in this section to persuade non-theists of the merits of theism, but simply to lay out a coherent possibility. Non-theists, even if they find it coherent, will no doubt find it preposterous. I said that there were very roughly two families of value properties that are involved in ethical evaluation, the family of attraction and repulsion (including 'good' and 'bad') and the family of permission and constraint (including 'right' and 'wrong'). I will take the first family first, and I will talk about the relation between the two families later.

Robert Adams has an account of 'good' that I have already referred to, according to which God is the Good itself, or the transcendent good, and everything else that is good is good by imitating or resembling God. The structure of this account is Platonic, with God replacing the Form of the Good in Plato's theory. I want to mention two hesitations I have about this account. The first is with the notion of imitation. I am repeating Aristotle's objection that the things that are good are too different from each other for an account to be helpful which gives a single exemplar which is imitated by all of them. How does a good cup of tea or a good game of basketball imitate God? Aristotle's own answer was to point to a similar relation that all good things have to the type they belong to, so that a good cup of tea does well what cups of tea are *for*, and a good game of basketball does well what games of basketball are *for*, even though there may be no non-relational descriptive characteristic that the good cup of tea and the good game of basketball have in common that makes each one of them good. Aristotle may be right about artefacts, but I doubt that his account works for everything we call good. Beauty is good, for example, and pleasure is good, but it is hard to see that either of them is good because it fulfils the function of some type to which it belongs. Adams replies that excellence in cooking can resemble God, even though God does not cook, because it resembles God's creativity, and that a gourmet dinner can resemble God, because the Psalmist says 'Taste and see that the Lord is good'.[31] But the problem is that what makes the cooking and the dinner good ought to be something more specific than general creativity and less metaphorical than the good 'flavour' of God in religious experience.

The second difficulty is that Adams's account seems too static. I think our experience of goodness is an experience of being drawn towards God, not simply of seeing a resemblance to God. This sense of motion is not inconsistent with what Adams says, since he makes use also of Plato's account of *eros*. But the emphasis is different if we think of the good as primarily what draws us rather than as what resembles some exemplar, and I will try to show that this emphasis will enable us to overcome the difficulty mentioned in the previous paragraph.

---

31   Adams, *Finite and Infinite Goods*, p. 30. He adds that we can think about dinners as sacramental.

The good, then, is what draws us and what deserves to so draw us. We need to add the second clause, unless we are willing to take the alternative position that everything that draws us is good. This alternative is a possible line to take, even about examples like sadistic pleasure, if we can sort out the good in each case that is drawing us but is ranked wrongly (ranking our own pleasure greater than the other's pain). But it is not the line I am going to take, and instead I will add the second clause. This has its own difficulty, however, that the term 'deserves' is already evaluative, so that it looks as though the second clause has to presuppose an account of the good at the same time as modifying such an account. Prescriptive realism, being a kind of expressivism, is stuck with this kind of irreducible circularity, and interprets Moore's open question argument as showing that no reductive account of value terms to non-evaluative terms can succeed. So if we say that what deserves to draw us is finally God, we are not escaping the feature that such a judgement, if it fulfils all the central functions of value judgement, is an effusive expression of some motivational state. But the realist character of prescriptive realism is also manifested in the analysis of what is good as what draws us to God. To explain what I mean by 'drawing us to God', I will appeal to three features of what I take to be the ethical theory of John Duns Scotus.[32]

Scotus prefers, as his term for our moral status, the term 'pilgrims' (*viatores*). We are, as Peter Singer puts it, journeying on life's uncertain voyage.[33] The journey we are on is a journey towards our final good, which Scotus takes to be that we become 'co-lovers' of God (*condiligentes*), entering into the love that the three persons of the Trinity have for each other. The chief condition for our reaching this good is that we achieve the right ranking of two affections, the affection for justice (*affectio justitiae*) and the affection for advantage (*affectio commodi*).[34] The second of these is a love of what is good for *us* (especially our own happiness and perfection), with essential reference to us, and the first of these is a love of what is good in itself, independently of its relation to us. The primary object of the affection for justice is God. We cannot achieve the right ranking of these two affections without God's assistance.

All of this is highly abstract. To explain what it means that the good is what draws us to God, I will give four examples of different kinds of things that draw us in different ways. The first kind of thing is what resembles God, and this kind of thing fits Adams's account well. For example, if we see a person who is faithful to her covenant relations with other people, we can see that she resembles God's faithfulness to us and the unchanging love that the persons of the Trinity have for each other. This is the character of God's love into which we enter by becoming co-lovers. I think it is a common experience that when we meet a person like this, we experience a sense of being drawn to something larger than just that person. A non-theist can say that we are being drawn to some abstract value like faithfulness. But a

---

32   I have given a fuller account of this theory in the second section of *God's Call*, which is a version of 'Duns Scotus on Morality and Nature', *Medieval Philosophy and Theology*, 9: 1 (2000) pp. 15–38.

33   Peter Singer. '"Life's Uncertain Voyage"', in *Metaphysics and Morality*, eds Philip Pettit, Richard Sylvan and Jean Norman (Oxford: Basil Blackwell, 1987), pp. 154–72.

34   Scotus, *Ordinatio* II, dist. 6, q.2.

theist will say that we are being drawn to God who is faithful, and she will suppose that God uses and is delighted by human exemplars of divine virtues in this way.

A second kind of case is where we are drawn by something that does not resemble God, or at least resembles God too generally for the resemblance to be a good account of the goodness of what is drawing us. For example, we see fire-fighters go up into a burning skyscraper, and we admire their bravery. But it does not make sense to say that God is brave, because God is not in our situation in the relevant respects. It does not make much sense, either, to say that bravery is a virtue that God would have if God were in our situation.[35] The bravery is, to be sure, a form of benevolence, since the fire-fighters intend the benefit of the people they rescue; and it does make sense to talk of God's benevolence. But the bravery is good more specifically, not merely good *qua* benevolence or love. It is better to say that bravery is a *human* virtue, and that humans who are brave are (whether they know it or not) preparing themselves in this specific way for the relation of being co-lovers of God. It takes courage for pilgrims to relate themselves in this life to God, because of the disproportion between God's holiness and our impurity. Moses was told he could not see the face of God without being destroyed. Bravery is something that prepares us for union with God.

A third case is what we might call 'created integrity', and things that have this character appropriately draw us to God because we are grateful to God for them.[36] We can see in some things the goodness of how they were created to be, and we see in them God's creative act. This is not the same as admiring something because it resembles God. It is not in general true that we admire an artist for her work because it resembles her. Perhaps we admire, in a good cup of tea, the essence of tea, and we are drawn in gratitude to God not because the tea resembles God but because God made it. As far as I can see, gratitude to the creator for created integrity is not affected significantly by believing in evolution, for theistic evolutionists see evolution as God's vehicle and instrument.[37]

A fourth case is where we are drawn by our own happiness. The first three cases have all involved what Scotus calls the affection for justice. The fourth case is what he calls the affection for advantage. Putting it this way shows the overlap with a non-theist consequentialist account or a virtue account, like Aristotle's, that ties virtue to happiness. Aquinas revises Aristotle by distinguishing between two kinds of happiness, one in this life (where he thinks Aristotle's account is approximately right), which is only a preparation for the one in the next life (which is the beatific vision). But Scotus objects to the eudaimonism that is still implicit in the Thomist account.[38] Our final happiness draws us in a way that ranks the affection for

---

35   This is a difficulty for Linda Zagzebski's position in *Divine Motivation Theory*, p. 226. She thinks that appealing to the Incarnation helps, but on most views of the Incarnation this tells us what a truly good *human* fears, not what God would fear if God were human.

36   Gratitude is not the only emotion relevant to created integrity. Awe and reverence are different, and different from each other. See Roberts, *Emotions*, pp. 268–70.

37   See Richard Swinburne. 'The Argument from Design', *Philosophy* 43 (1968), pp. 199–212.

38   Thomas Aquinas, *Summa Theologiae* IaIIae, q.1. art.5.

advantage above the affection for justice, as long as we love God for the sake of our happiness and not for God's own sake. This distinction is made most vivid by a counterfactual thought experiment, which is repeated by Jonathan Edwards and by generations of Presbyterian ministers at their ordination services, who said that they would be willing to be damned for the sake of the glory of God.[39] There is nothing wrong in itself, as Scotus sees it, with the affection for advantage, as long as it is ranked rightly. But if the ranking is wrong, as it was for Lucifer, the desire for our happiness no longer draws us towards God but away from God. If the ranking is right, our happiness and pleasure in this life are a foretaste of the happiness involved in being co-lovers with God. I think it is true to experience, at least to the experience of religious believers, that the sense of happiness here is always incomplete, and pointing beyond itself to something better but, so to speak, in the same direction.

The next step would be to give an account of the different ways in which what is bad draws us away from God, or (to use the magnetic analogy again) repels us. And then the account should talk about the many value properties that are not exactly kinds of good or bad. But I am going to leave this topic, and go on to the second family of properties, including 'right' and 'wrong' or permission and constraint.

2b. Theist Prescriptive Realism and the Right

We can see the relation of the second family of properties to God in terms of what God commands and forbids. The question of priority between the two families of properties is complicated by the different kinds of priority that might be involved in answering the question. One way to take the question, for example, is to ask, 'Is one set of concepts the source of the other, so that the second needs to be tied to the first in any final explanation?' An example of this sort of priority is when Linda Zagzebski says, 'We can understand all the principal concepts of interest to ethics by reference to the concept of a good emotion: a virtue, a right act, a virtuous act, an obligation, a good outcome, and the good for human beings.'[40] A different way to take the question is to ask, 'Does one set have veto over the other, so that the second is, so to speak, trumped by the first?' An example of this trumping relation would be the principle stated in the Hippocratic Oath, 'The first thing is not to harm' (*primum non nocere*). This does not mean that refraining from harm is the source of every medical good, or that every medical good must be explained finally in terms of refraining from harm. Rather, the principle prescribes that where different medical goods are in competition, not harming takes precedence (as diamonds might win over hearts in a game of Whist, if diamonds are trumps). Obligation has this second kind of priority, but not, in my view, the first.

This priority that it has is not alien to the attractive power of the good. Rather, the right is determined by whether some particular good fits with the good of the

---

39 Scotus, *Ordinatio* II, dist. 6, q.2. Jonathan Edwards, *Religious Affections*, III, x. See Exodus 32: 32, and Romans 9: 3, where Moses and Paul say they would be willing to be blotted out of the book of life, or to become a curse.

40 Zagzebski, *Divine Motivation Theory*, p. 385. I am not endorsing this account, but using it as an example of the first kind of priority.

whole, seen in terms of the equal and unique value of each person. In Kant's terms, the moral law tells us what the king of the kingdom of ends prescribes or forbids, and we have to recognize our duties as God's commands.[41] In the *Groundwork* Kant distinguishes between ordinary members of the kingdom of ends, who are all legislators of the moral law and also subject to it, and the sovereign of the kingdom, who is the unique legislator not subject to the will of any other. The position of sovereign here requires that 'he is a completely independent being without needs and with unlimited power adequate to his will'.[42] We can elaborate the role of the sovereign by pointing out that we should prescribe in a way that is consistent with sharing (making our own) the morally permitted ends of all the parties affected by our decisions.[43] Achieving this consistency is helped by willing in accordance with the prescription of the sovereign, for three reasons.[44] Because 'the dear self' is always discoverable in our own willing, we have to worry about our tendency to prefer our own interests to those of others and the distortion this produces in how we perceive the situation; only an independent and holy being is reliable as a source. Moreover, even if we were not partial to our own interests in this way, we would not know the ends of all the affected parties, and only the sovereign who 'sees our hearts' is reliable as a guide. Moreover, even if we did know all these ends, and could will them impartially, we would not be able (because of our limited power) to coordinate the achievement of these ends in such a way as to make them consistent with each other. For these reasons, the commands of the sovereign take precedence over the attraction we feel from other non-commanded goods, and this attraction has to be constrained by our checking whether it is consistent with these commands. This does not mean that a virtuous person needs to be constantly anxious about whether she is meeting her obligations, but she will want to check her obligations, rather as a good driver checks the rear-view mirror of her car to make sure that the direction she wants to go and the speed she wants to go are consistent with the intentions of the other drivers on the road.

I have been talking in Kant's terms about obligation, but I need to return for a moment to Scotus. A divine command theorist will want to deny, as Scotus does, that our obligations are deducible from human nature. If we could deduce the laws about how we ought to live from our nature, then even God would be bound to command those laws to creatures with our nature (if we hold, as we should, that deduction requires broadly logical necessity, and this necessity applies to God). Scotus distinguishes between the first table of the ten commandments (which has to do with our relation to God) and which he thinks is strictly necessary (so that even God has to command it) and the second table (which has to do with our relations to each other) and which he

---

41   This view is pervasive in Kant, e.g. *Religion within the Boundaries of Mere Reason*, 6: 154.

42   *Groundwork of the Metaphysic of Morals* 4: 434. Kant uses gendered language for God, but we do not have to follow him in this, and the term 'sovereign' is not gendered.

43   This is the way Kant explains the 'formula of the end-in-itself' in *Groundwork of the Metaphysics of Morals* 4: 430.

44   I am influenced here by Thomas Carson, *Value and the Good Life* (South Bend, IN: University of Notre Dame Press, 2000). See my *Why Bother Being Good?* (Downers Grove, IL: InterVarsity Press, 2002), chapter 8.

thinks is contingent.[45] This means that God can command differently with respect to the second table, and Scotus thinks God sometimes does give 'dispensations', though we are not allowed to argue for such a dispensation on our own authority. To take the case of the prohibition on theft, for example, Scotus holds that human beings are not essentially propertied, so that the prohibition on theft is also not essential. Before the Fall, at Pentecost, in Heaven, (and even, he might have added, in certain long-lasting human societies) there is no institution of private property. Moreover, at the Exodus God commanded the 'despoiling of the Egyptians', and Scotus does not find it necessary (as Aquinas does) to argue that God transferred ownership of the gold to the Israelites first, so that it was not really theft.

In other work, I have suggested the analogy of a progressive treasure hunt, according to which God's commands about our obligations should be seen as being within God's discretion (as a mother can choose where to put the clues).[46] The point can be explained by using the idea about the different kinds of priority mentioned earlier. There are all sorts of goods attracting us to God, and God, as sovereign, has discretion over which of these goods to require and which evils to forbid. A divine command theorist will trust that God knows when goods are so important for all of us that they need to be protected by the special requirements and prohibitions that are the source of our obligations (even if there is no unique set of such goods).

There is one more topic I want to take up briefly, again with reference to Scotus. Are the commands that God gives general, for all human beings, or are they unique to each individual? Or are they both? Scotus has the notion of an individual essence possessed by each substance, and he holds that this essence is a perfection of the common essence possessed by each member of the species.[47] To love a human being is thus to love the individual essence which is unique to her, but not in such a way as to fail to love her humanity which she holds in common with all human beings. Scotus also holds that the natural inclination of the will is towards something particular and not something universal, and so towards a particular happiness rather than happiness in general.[48] Since our happiness consists in becoming co-lovers of God, the particular happiness must be in the different relation between each of us individually and the God whom we all love. Scotus does not say this, but it is consistent with his view to hold that God, besides giving common commands to all human beings, gives commands to the individual that are a route to that individual (unique) way of loving God. Perhaps the divine dispensations from the common commands are best understood like this, but these are extraordinary cases.

---

45 Scotus, *Ordinatio* III, suppl., dist. 37. The exception in the first table is the instruction about the 'seventh day', which Scotus does not think is necessary, though regular periodicity may be.

46 *God's Call*, pp. 69–75, also in 'Duns Scotus on Morality and Nature'.

47 Scotus, *Lectura* II, d.3, qq. 1–6. See Allan B, Wolter, *The Philosophical Theology of John Duns Scotus* (Ithaca: Cornell University Press, 1990), pp. 68–97.

48 Scotus, *Ordinatio* IV, suppl., dist 49, qq. 9–10. There is a biblical picture (Revelation 2: 17) of this in the individual name given to each of us in heaven on a white stone, which tells us who we are in God's eyes (like 'Peter', meaning 'rock', the name which Jesus gave to Cephas, Matthew 16: 18).

More usually, the particular commands to individuals will be consistent with the common commands, and will fit the common essence.

Robert Adams uses the term 'vocation' to discuss the question of whether God gives particular commands to individuals.[49] He describes the case of Bonhoeffer who felt he was 'called' to return to Hitler's Germany, 'even though God does not call everyone to martyrdom'. Adams understands the basic notion of vocation to be a matter of 'what goods are given to us to love'. In my terms we can make a distinction between the two families of value properties I have been talking about. There will be different good things that are salient to different individuals, in the way that one person can be indifferent to a good cup of tea and another can be indifferent to a good game of basketball. But there will also be different obligations, deriving from the individual's unique character and circumstances. In *The Moral Gap* I defended the notion of what I called 'particular obligations' while at the same time denying the truth of what I called 'extreme particularism'.[50] I distinguished between different positions in a value judgement (the addressee position, the agent position, the action position, and the recipient position), and I claimed that moral judgements require universalizability only of the term in the action position. I will not repeat the argument here. The relation to the theistic form of prescriptive realism is that if we allow that God can address commands to individuals, the term in the addressee position (which will usually, though not always, be also the term in the agent position) may not always be replaceable in principle by some universal term. For example, God can address the house of Israel, without the implication that the command applies to anyone who is like Israel in the relevant respects, though in some cases no doubt it does and in some cases it does not.[51] And the same is true with the term in the recipient position. For example, there can be a universal obligation to love God, without the implication that there is a universal obligation to love anyone who is like God in the relevant respects.

It is time to sum up. The paper has had two parts, each of which is divided itself into two. The first part was an account of prescriptive realism, which is a theory that contains no essential reference to God, but which aims to combine the merits of both expressivism and realism. I tried to explain in what sense the theory is expressivist (discussing especially the notions of 'expression' and 'acceptance') and in what sense it is realist (discussing especially the notion of 'objective truth' and the thought experiment of moral twin-earth). The second part of the paper was an account of a theist version of prescriptive realism, and I tried to explain how this version accounts for the different relations to God of the two main families of value terms, one including 'good' and 'bad', and the other including 'right' and 'wrong'. My intention was that the two parts of the paper would be roughly independent, so that it would be possible (for a non-theist, for example) to accept the first and reject the second. However, the second is intended to be a coherent model for how endorsement might work given a particular normative theory about how to determine what is 'good' and 'right'. I have not attempted what Robert Adams calls a 'moral

---

49   Adams, *Finite and Infinite Goods*, pp. 292–317.
50   *The Moral Gap*, pp. 150–69.
51   See Amos 5: 1–15, a set of commands which seems to be a combination of the two.

epistemology' for this normative theory, namely to discuss how God reveals 'good' and 'bad' and 'right' and 'wrong' to us and how we might distinguish when God is doing so and when God is not.[52] But I have tried to show how God's drawing us by means of the good is different from God's selecting the requirements for the route by which, as Scotus would say, pilgrims are to become co-lovers.

---

52 Adams, *Finite and Infinite Goods*, pp. 353–89.

Chapter 7

Religious Language Games

Graham Oppy and Nick Trakakis

Alan Keightley, in *Wittgenstein, Grammar and God*, identifies a group of 'devout Wittgensteinians' including some of Wittgenstein's students, such as Rush Rhees and Norman Malcolm, and some of those who have been closely associated with the work of Wittgenstein's pupils, including Peter Winch and D. Z. Phillips.[1] These and like-minded thinkers have come to form what might be called 'the Wittgensteinian school of philosophy of religion'. One feature of the writings of members of this 'school' is that they make use of a *theoretical* vocabulary that is derived from the writings – and, in particular, the later writings – of Wittgenstein: 'language game', 'form of life', 'grammatical observation', 'philosophical grammar', 'depth grammar', and the like. While there are differences in the views of the members of the 'school', there are also many important similarities. In particular, members of the 'school' are agreed that religion constitutes a 'form of life', and that 'the religious language game' has a unique 'grammar' that is utterly misrepresented in standard philosophical discussions of religion and religious belief.

Critics of 'the Wittgensteinian school of philosophy of religion' are apt to complain that the crucial theoretical vocabulary involved in these formulations is, at best, 'obscure and ambiguous'.[2] While the key terms are undeniably *theoretical* – they are, after all, the *terms of art* of a particular philosophical movement – there is nowhere that they have ever been given a satisfactory explication. Moreover, and perhaps more importantly, even if we suppose that we can give sufficient sense to this theoretical vocabulary, it seems clear that there are competing theories, couched in terms of alternative vocabularies, that should be preferred because of their greater explanatory scope, explanatory power, advancement of understanding, and so forth.

The force of this complaint is perhaps best brought out by consideration of examples. Take the relationship between knowledge and belief as a test case. Many philosophers have supposed that knowledge entails belief: one can only know that *p* if one believes that *p*. Against this, members of 'the Wittgensteinian school of philosophy of religion' object that this remark misconstrues 'the grammar of our language': for, in circumstances in which it is true that someone knows that *p*,

---

1   Alan Keightley, *Wittgenstein, Grammar and God* (London: Epworth Press, 1976), p. 12. D. Z. Phillips provides a short list of works influenced by Wittgenstein in the philosophy of religion, in *Belief, Change and Forms of Life* (Basingstoke: Macmillan, 1986), pp. 131–3.

2   See, for example, Anthony Kenny's criticisms in 'In Defence of God', *Times Literary Supplement*, 7 February 1975, p. 145; quoted in Richard Messer, *Does God's Existence Need Proof?* (Oxford: Clarendon Press, 1993), p. 61.

it would be entirely inappropriate to say that that person believes that p, whence it follows that it is just a mistake to suppose that knowledge entails belief.

There is, of course, at least one well-known response to this 'grammatical' objection. As Grice pointed out, it is plainly true that there are various 'conversational maxims' to which we are enjoined to conform, and which we can exploit in order to achieve conversational ends.[3] One of these maxims is that, other things being equal, one ought to make one's conversational contribution such that one conveys all of the relevant information that one has at one's disposal. Applied to the case at hand, this means that if one is in a position to say that someone knows that p, then one ought not only to make the weaker claim that that person believes that p – because, in the circumstances, one's failure to say that the person knows that p will then be taken as an indication that the person does not know that p, but rather *only* believes that p.

Once we see that we can have conversational reasons for refraining from the assertion of claims that we nonetheless take to be true, we also see that the 'grammatical observation' made by members of 'the Wittgensteinian school of philosophy of religion' can only establish the claim that knowledge does not entail belief *if* there are reasons to prefer the theoretical apparatus invoked by the members of 'the Wittgensteinian school of philosophy of religion' to the Gricean theory of conversational implicature. Moreover, when we think about the relative merits of the competing theoretical accounts, it seems clear that it is the Gricean theory that ought to be preferred. After all, only the Gricean theory issues in clear predictions that are verified in case after case; and only the Gricean theory can be plausibly incorporated into a plausible broader theory of linguistic and conversational competence. While genuine philosophical understanding issues from the Gricean theory, the Wittgensteinian talk of 'grammatical observations' is theoretically sterile, and resists incorporation into broader theories of linguistic and conversational competence.

There are strands of thought in 'the Wittgensteinian school of philosophy of religion' that have been more widely adopted in recent times. In particular, there are clear affinities between the theoretical apparatus of 'language games' and 'forms of life', and the theoretical apparatus of 'domains of discourse' adopted by Crispin Wright.[4] Each of these cases is characterized by espousal of a theoretical *pluralism* about central vocabulary. For Wright, the crucial case is truth: his claim is that truth is *formally* uniform – in the sense determined by satisfaction of various key platitudes concerning truth – but that its *constitution* may vary depending on the type of statement and subject-matter concerned. This theoretical pluralism about truth seems to be central to the thought of 'the Wittgensteinian school of philosophy of religion', but, in this case, the theoretical pluralism is also extended to the full family of transcendental notions: *identity*, *existence*, *object*, *being*, and so forth.

---

3   See Paul Grice, *Studies in the Way of Words* (Cambridge, MA: Harvard University Press, 1989), esp. ch. 2.

4   See Crispin Wright, *Truth and Objectivity* (Cambridge, MA: Harvard University Press, 1992).

Wright's argument for pluralism about truth depends upon an analogy with identity. In that latter case, it seems quite plausible to claim that, while the formal properties of identity are invariant across the full range of discourses, the constitution of identity varies according to the subject-matter under consideration: material objects, numbers, directions, people, and so forth. However, there is a central disanalogy which threatens to cripple Wright's argument at this point, namely that, while there are considerations about 'identity under a sortal' that make it plausible to claim that there is diverse constitution of identity, there are no similar considerations about 'truth under a sortal'. We can sensibly ask whether this is the same cow/number/person/etc. as the one we encountered previously. But there is no corresponding formulation – no corresponding thought – in the case of truth. A plausible consequence here is that, Wright's protests to the contrary notwithstanding, his pluralism about truth is defeated by considerations concerning 'mixed' discourses and 'mixed' inferences.

Consider, for example, the inference from 'He lives in a beautiful Edwardian house' to 'He lives in an Edwardian house'. This inference moves from a sentence that contains an evaluative predicate – and hence which, plausibly, belongs to evaluative discourse – to a sentence that contains no evaluative predicates, and which, plausibly, belongs to straightforward fact-stating discourse. If we suppose that there really are distinct truth predicates that are appropriate to evaluative (aesthetic) and non-evaluative discourse, then it is very hard to see how the inference in question could be justified. Multiplication of examples such as this one strongly suggests that pluralism about truth is simply a mistake (and, if we give up on pluralism about truth, then, very plausibly, pluralism about at least some of the other transcendental notions must also be relinquished).

The above pair of criticisms of the members of 'the Wittgensteinian school of philosophy of religion' – *viz.*, that they are committed to an indefensible pluralism about truth and at least some other transcendental notions, and that their central method of argumentation is vitiated by a refusal to attend to the evident consequences of Grice's work on conversational implicature – proceed at a highly theoretical level, and are not directly concerned with what these philosophers have to say about *religion*. However, as our subsequent discussion of the work of D. Z. Phillips indicates, disagreements between the members of 'the Wittgensteinian school of philosophy of religion' and their opponents typically turn on these kinds of highly theoretical disagreements, even when there are other kinds of less highly theoretical disagreements – particularly concerning matters specific to religion and religious belief – in play. It is therefore important to remember that the vocabulary of 'language games', 'forms of life', 'grammatical observations', 'philosophical grammar', 'depth grammar', 'world views', and the like, is the vocabulary of a highly controversial philosophical theory; it does not constitute an incontestable framework within which discussion of questions about religion can straightforwardly proceed.

D. Z. Phillips and the Metaphysical Reality of God

> God Grant the Philosopher Insight into What Lies in Front of
> Everyone's Eyes.[5]
> – Wittgenstein

The most prominent member of 'the Wittgensteinian school of philosophy of religion' is undoubtedly D. Z. Phillips. In what follows, we examine two important and related aspects of his perspective on religious language. We begin with Phillips's critique of the traditional philosophical understanding of God as a 'metaphysically real' or 'independently existing' being. We then consider his reasons for rejecting views of religious language which hold that such language is in some important respects 'fact-stating'.

Phillips strikes many as a perplexing figure. In a large body of work from the early 1960s, he has repeatedly argued in support of a conception of religious belief that is, in the eyes of most contemporary analytic philosophers of religion, downright mistaken. The following comments from Richard Swinburne typify this kind of response:

> Phillips's account of religious language is subtle and coherently developed, reflecting Wittgenstein's immense sensitivity to the different uses of language. It seems, however, to me to be in essence plainly false as an account of what the vast majority of normal users of religious language during the past two millennia have meant by the words and sentences which they have uttered.[6]

Indeed, it is a mystery to many how Phillips could continue to advocate his conception of religious belief when the case against it appears to be so overwhelmingly strong. Phillips's view of religious language, sometimes described as 'non-realist' or 'anti-realist',[7] can be approached from a variety of directions, but one obvious entry point is to look at his critique of the traditional way philosophers have conceptualized God, that is to say, the God of the Abrahamic faiths.

Although philosophical conceptions of God vary widely, something approximating a consensus has emerged – at least within analytic philosophy of religion – that God is best thought of as *a perfect being*, where to be perfect is to be *the greatest being possible* or, to borrow Anselm's well-known phrase, *the being than which none*

---

5   Wittgenstein, *Culture and Value*, transl. Peter Winch (Oxford: Basil Blackwell, 1980), p. 63. Although Phillips is fond of this quote, we will argue that he himself misses 'what lies in front of everyone's eyes', *viz.*, that religious beliefs do purport to state facts and to answer to metaphysical realities.

6   Swinburne, *The Coherence of Theism* (Oxford: Clarendon Press, 1977), p. 92.

7   Phillips, however, does not think of himself as a non-realist or anti-realist, for in his view 'theological non-realism is as empty as theological realism' ('On Really Believing' in Joseph Runzo (ed.), *Is God Real?* New York: St. Martin's Press, 1993, p. 87). But see Andrew Moore, *Realism and Christian Faith: God, Grammar, and Meaning* (Cambridge: Cambridge University Press, 2003), pp. 80–92, where Moore argues that, despite Phillips's disavowal of non-realism in his more recent writings, Phillips 'never quite succeeds in being a realist' (p. 91).

greater can be conceived.[8] Such a conception of God forms the starting-point in what has come to be known as 'perfect being theology'.[9] On this view, one begins with the idea of God as maximally great or absolutely perfect, and then from this conception of deity one deduces all of God's core or essential attributes – i.e., those attributes which are constitutive of God's nature, so that he could not at the same time exist and lack any of these attributes. The claim, then, is that God can only be the greatest being possible in virtue of possessing every great-making quality or perfection to an unlimited degree,[10] where a quality may be said to be great-making insofar as it increases the degree to which the object to which it applies is worthy of worship and moral admiration.[11] But to have all the great-making properties and to have them to an unlimited extent is to possess such attributes as maximal power (omnipotence), maximal knowledge (omniscience), and maximal or perfect goodness, as well as whatever attributes are entailed by these great-making qualities. It is therefore thought that God's essential attributes can be distilled solely from the notion of God as an absolutely perfect being. These essential attributes include: omnipotence, omniscience, perfect goodness, aseity, incorporeality, eternity, omnipresence, perfect freedom, and creator and sustainer of all contingent things.

Various criticisms have been levelled against perfect being theology. It is sometimes objected, for example, that such a theology is liable to yield divergent conceptions of

---

8   See chapter 2 of Anselm's *Proslogion*, in *Saint Anselm: Basic Writings*, 2nd ed., trans. S. W. Deane (La Salle, IL: Open Court Publishing, 1962), pp. 7–8. To be sure, the idea here is that God does not just happen to be the greatest conceivable being, but that this is a property he has essentially.

9   The foremost contemporary defender of perfect being theology is undoubtedly Thomas Morris – see his 'Perfect Being Theology' *Noûs* 21 (1987): 19–30; 'Introduction' in Morris (ed.), *The Concept of God* (Oxford: Oxford University Press, 1987), pp. 6–10; *Anselmian Explorations: Essays in Philosophical Theology* (Notre Dame, IN: University of Notre Dame Press, 1987), ch. 1; and *Our Idea of God: An Introduction to Philosophical Theology* (Downers Grove, IL: InterVarsity Press, 1991), esp. ch. 2. See also George N. Schlesinger, *New Perspectives on Old-time Religion* (Oxford: Clarendon Press, 1988), ch. 1, esp. pp. 16–21; Katherin A. Rogers, *Perfect Being Theology* (Edinburgh: Edinburgh University Press, 2000), esp. chs 1 and 2, and Daniel J. Hill, *Divinity and Maximal Greatness* (London: Routledge, 2005).

10   This is not entirely accurate. As Schlesinger points out, 'God's perfection cannot amount to His having each perfection-making attribute to the highest degree, since the maximization of some desirable qualities is incompatible with the maximization of others. Divine super-excellence is to be understood as the possession of each enhancing attribute to the precise degree required so that in combination they contribute to the maximum sum total of magnificence' (*New Perspectives on Old-time Religion*, p. 1).

11   We borrow here from Joshua Hoffman and Gary S. Rosenkrantz, *The Divine Attributes* (Oxford: Blackwell, 2002), pp. 14–16, who take great-making to be a function of worship-worthiness and moral admirability. Morris, on the other hand, suggests that worship-worthiness 'can be held to supervene upon, or to consist in, some of the properties ingredient in perfection' ('Perfect Being Theology', p. 24). He then goes on to make perfection or greatness supervenient on intrinsic goodness or value, so that a great-making property is defined as one which is intrinsically good to have, and intrinsic goodness is in turn made a function of metaphysical status or stature ('Perfect Being Theology', p. 26).

God when there is a clash of intuitions over which properties are great-making or over what is and is not a perfection.[12] Phillips, on the other hand, objects to the idea of God as a perfect being on far more radical grounds. In particular, he takes issue with the very presupposition that God is a 'metaphysical reality', that is to say, a 'pure consciousness' that exists over and above all human consciousnesses.

Let's backtrack a little, to 1975, to a conference organized by the Royal Institute of Philosophy at the University of Lancaster.[13] Hick, Swinburne and Phillips were charged with discussing the problem of evil, and in the light of Phillips's response to Swinburne, Hick states that the differences between the two run quite deep. It is not simply that Swinburne advocates the construction of theodicies in the face of the world's evils while Phillips's rejects the project of theodicy-building. More importantly, they differ on the question of the very reality of God:

> For reading Phillips' paper, in the light of his other writings, I take it that he denies the existence of an all-powerful and limitlessly loving God. I take it, that is, that he denies that in addition to all the many human consciousnesses there is another consciousness which is the consciousness of God, and that this God is the creator of the universe and is both all-powerful and limitlessly loving. I take it that he rejects this belief as a crude misunderstanding of religious language and holds that, rightly understood, the 'existence of God' consists in man's use of theistic language within the context of a pattern of religious life.[14]

Phillips's response to the question of whether 'in addition to all the many human consciousnesses there is another consciousness which is the consciousness of God' is revealing:

> I can only reply, with Charles Hartshorne, in words that could have come equally from Wittgenstein: 'Confusion in the posing of a question generates confusion in the answering of it'. In speaking of 'consciousness' in the way he does, Hick not only reifies an idea, an accusation Feuerbach might have made of him, but reifies a confused idea. So I do not deny it; it is not intelligible enough to deny.[15]

Remarks such as these have given Phillips a reputation for evasiveness and obscurity. Stephen Davis, for example, writes in exasperation:

---

12 See Brian Leftow, 'God, Concepts of', in E. Craig (ed.), *Routledge Encyclopedia of Philosophy*, vol. 2, p. 97, and William J. Wainwright, 'Worship, Intuitions and Perfect Being Theology', *Noûs* 21 (1987), pp. 31–2. To be fair to Morris, however, he does not think of intuition as an infallible guide in this respect, but rather thinks that our intuitions on these matters may need to be reinforced or corrected by the data of revelation in conjunction with other methods for arriving at a religiously adequate conception of deity (see Morris, *Our Idea of God*, pp. 41–5). Other criticisms of perfect being theology are addressed by Morris, 'The God of Abraham, Isaac, and Anselm', in *Anselmian Explorations*, pp. 13–25, and Schlesinger, *New Perspectives on Old-time Religion*, pp. 16–21.

13 The proceedings of this conference are published in Stuart C. Brown (ed.), *Reason and Religion* (Ithaca, NY: Cornell University Press, 1977).

14 Hick, 'Remarks', in Brown (ed.), *Reason and Religion*, p. 122.

15 Phillips, 'Theism without Theodicy', in Stephen T. Davis (ed.), *Encountering Evil: Live Options in Theodicy*, 2nd ed. (Louisville, KY: Westminster John Knox Press, 2001), p. 153.

I simply want to insist that Phillips knows good and well what Hick was driving at – as I do and as everybody else does – and that Hick's question deserves a straight answer.[16]

Phillips's reply is again revealing:

Really? I do not think Hick can say what he means. And how can Davis, since he does not 'deny that there are conceptual problems' with talk of the consciousness of God. Conceptual problems are problems of intelligibility. Davis says that I say 'somewhat petulantly that [Hick's] statement "is not intelligible enough to deny"'. But that statement is the conclusion to arguments. Davis ignores them…[17]

Phillips's view, then, is that the traditional philosophical understanding of God – one might say the 'realist' view of theistic discourse – according to which God is an incorporeal person-like being who exists objectively or independently of any creature, is committed to the notion of God as a pure consciousness, a notion that ought to be rejected as conceptually confused. How, then, does Phillips reach this conclusion?

In a recent discussion of Wittgensteinianism in the philosophy of religion, Phillips notes that the twentieth century witnessed a revolution in philosophy led largely by Ludwig Wittgenstein.[18] On Phillips's account, the revolution was sparked by Wittgenstein's critique of Descartes's epistemological legacy, a legacy which – Phillips adds – most contemporary philosophers of religion have uncritically inherited. According to Phillips, a crucial element of the Cartesian legacy is the gap it opens up between consciousness – or thought, or ideas, or mind – and a mind-independent reality. What worried Descartes, in Phillips's view, is: How, from *inside* my consciousness, can I make contact with a reality *outside* it?[19] On Phillips's account of the Cartesian view, this gap between consciousness and reality is reflected in the idea of God as a metaphysical reality existing beyond all human consciousnesses.

---

16   Davis, 'Critique [of Phillips's 'Theism without Theodicy']', in Davis (ed.), *Encountering Evil*, p. 168. Phillips's refusal to supply 'a straight answer' has led some to suspect that he is 'deep down' an atheist. Consider, for example, the following humorous gloss on the exchange between Phillips and Hick:

Hick wants to say Phillips can't get away with claiming to believe in God. 'You can't fool us Phillips', I hear Hick saying, 'when you talk about God moving upon the face of the waters. You don't believe in God, you only believe in your feelings aroused by the view of Swansea Bay from your study window'. Phillips asks: well then, what must I do to be believed that I believe? You must admit 'God exists' is a proposition, Hick says, and accept the responsibility for proving it. (Alfred Louch, 'Saying is Believing', in Runzo (ed.), *Is God Real?* p. 110).

17   Phillips, 'Rejoinder', in Davis (ed.), *Encountering Evil*, p. 176. See also Phillips, *The Problem of Evil and the Problem of God* (London: SCM Press, 2004), p. 152.

18   Phillips, 'Wittgensteinianism: Logic, Reality, and God', in William J. Wainwright (ed.), *The Oxford Handbook of Philosophy of Religion* (Oxford: Oxford University Press, 2005), pp. 447–71. Much of this material is included in ch. 2 of Phillips's *Religion and Friendly Fire: Examining Assumptions in Contemporary Philosophy of Religion* (Aldershot: Ashgate, 2004).

19   Phillips, 'Wittgensteinianism', p. 450.

Phillips argues, however, that the import of the Wittgensteinian revolution is that such an idea of God must be deemed unintelligible, the product of confusion.

Phillips subjects the metaphysically real God to a fourfold critique. His *first* objection emerges from a critique of 'the empiricist notion of ideas', i.e., the view that we are not immediately acquainted with the world, but rather are only ever immediately acquainted with our ideas. Phillips writes:

> God as a pure consciousness, pre-existing all things, is said to have ideas and to entertain thoughts. But what makes these ideas and thoughts what they are? The logical difficulties inherent in the empiricist notion of 'ideas' reemerge, difficulties encapsulated in Wittgenstein's arguments against a logically private language.[20]

The reference to the private language argument advanced by Wittgenstein in the *Philosophical Investigations* may seem puzzling at first, for that argument is directed against the idea of an *essentially* private language. Wittgenstein describes such a language in the following terms:

> The individual words of this language are to refer to what can only be known to the person speaking; to his immediate private sensations. So another cannot understand the language.[21]

What Wittengenstein is describing here is a language which is in principle incomprehensible to everyone other than the user of the language in question, and its comprehensibility is limited in this way because the meanings of its putative signs are inaccessible to everyone bar the individual language-user. But the ideas and thoughts of God, considered as a metaphysically or mind-independently real subject, need not be inaccessible *in principle* to others. Indeed, theists commonly speak of God as revealing his plans, intentions and commands to his creatures, and it would make no sense to speak of God in this way unless it was assumed that God's plans, intentions and commands could be *understood* by his creatures. Phillips, however, is aware of this sort of reply, and counters it as follows:

> Nor will it do to say that God's thoughts and ideas need be only potentially shareable, not actually shared, since this will not secure the essential distinction between 'following a rule' and 'thinking one is following a rule', between 'getting it right' and 'thinking one has got it right'... For the idea that the rule is intelligible prior to its having a common use, would require the rule to provide, without such mediation, its own application. To postulate a rule for the use of the rule would leave us with the same problem, plus the prospect of an infinite regress. To know whether an individual is following a rule correctly, there must be a context other than the individual user in which a distinction between correct and incorrect has a purchase.[22]

---

20   Ibid., p. 456.

21   Wittgenstein, *Philosophical Investigations*, trans. G. E. M. Anscombe (Oxford: Blackwell, 1958), §243.

22   Phillips, 'Wittgensteinianism', pp. 456–7.

Phillips is here endorsing the so-called 'Community View' espoused by – among others – Rush Rhees[23] and Norman Malcolm,[24] according to which the concept of following a rule presupposes a community in which there is agreement as to whether doing such-and-such counts as following a particular rule. On this view, as Malcolm explains, 'to follow the rules for the use of an expression is nothing other than to use the expression as it is ordinarily used – which is to say, as it is used by those many people who take part in the activities in which the expression is embedded'.[25] Rule-following therefore makes sense only against the background of a shared linguistic practice, so that one can be judged to be correctly following a rule with respect to one's use of language only if one's linguistic usage conforms to the prevailing pattern of use as exemplified by one's fellow language-users. If, for example, I never participate in a communal linguistic practice, so that I 'make up the rules as I go along', then the crucial distinction between my following a rule and my *thinking* I am following a rule would be lost. As Wittengenstein points out in a related context, 'in the present case I have no criterion of correctness. One would like to say: whatever is going to seem right to me is right. And that only means that here we can't talk about "right"'.[26] Thus, to secure the objectivity of my judgements regarding what words or sentences mean, linguistic rules and meanings must be *independent* of me, or of any particular person.[27]

The implication Phillips draws from this is that God, conceived of as a solitary pure consciousness pre-existing all other consciousnesses, cannot intelligibly be thought of as having thoughts and ideas, or perhaps any mental life at all. According to Phillips, not even God could know what is expressed by God's own ideas and thoughts. Given that God is a solitary rule-follower and not a member of a community of language-users who act in accordance with rules, there can be no fact of the matter as to what the internal vehicles of God's musings signify. But what exactly are the internal vehicles of God's musings? It would be grossly anthropomorphic to think of God as literally using words or speaking in some human language. (This is not to say that God cannot inspire people to express his intentions or commands in human language, but this is not the same as saying that God himself uses human language.) God may, nevertheless, have ideas or thoughts, but here too Phillips would stress the logical dependency of thoughts on communal practices: just as we need to defer to community practices in order to individuate linguistic rules and meanings, so too the very possibility of having an 'inner life' of ideas and thoughts depends on there being shared activities and a language which people have in common. It is precisely for this reason that Phillips, in *Death and Immortality*, rejects the view that to survive death is just to survive as a disembodied soul. This view, Phillips states, rests on a conception of the self as an inner thinking and necessarily private

---

23   See Rush Rhees, 'Can There Be a Private Language?' *Proceedings of the Aristotelian Society*, suppl. vol. 28 (1954), pp. 77–94.

24   See Norman Malcolm, *Nothing is Hidden: Wittgenstein's Criticism of his Early Thought* (Oxford: Blackwell, 1986), ch. 9, and 'Wittgenstein on Language and Rules', *Philosophy* 64 (1989): pp. 5–28.

25   Malcolm, 'Wittgenstein on Language and Rules', p. 22.

26   Wittgenstein, *Philosophical Investigations*, §258; cf. §202.

27   See Malcolm, 'Wittgenstein on Language and Rules', p. 22.

substance (*viz.*, the soul). But private experiences and thoughts are logically parasitic on public meanings, and so the former cannot be divorced from the latter.[28]

The Community View, however, is not the only game in town. There are other, and perhaps more plausible, options, in particular the position advocated by G. P. Baker and P. M. S. Hacker.[29] Taking their cues from Wittgenstein himself, Baker and Hacker argue that language does not presuppose a community. Their position, more precisely, is that language does not require a shared, community practice, but only a *shareable* one: 'concept-possession, following a rule, mastery of a language presuppose not that these are shared with other people, but rather that they *can be shared*, that is must *make sense* for others to understand, agree on what counts as doing the same relative to a rule, follow the rule in the same way'.[30] On this view, whether one is correctly following a rule with respect to one's use of language is not determined by the extent to which one's usage agrees with shared community practice, but is rather determined by the rules themselves: 'It is rules (charts, signposts, etc.) that are *called* 'standards of correctness', and it is they, and not some other thing, that are used as such'.[31] But if it is not a shared social practice, but the rule itself, which determines what counts as following a rule, then will the distinction between 'following a rule' and 'thinking one is following a rule' be jeopardized? Malcolm, and Phillips after him, holds that this distinction would have no application unless the rules are in fact shared, that is, actually held in common amongst some community of speakers. But as Baker and Hacker note, it makes sense to say that a Robinson Crusoe, who – unlike Defoe's character – was stranded from birth till death on a deserted island, could invent a new card game and play it, where this includes making various mistakes in following the – unshared – rules of the game and subsequently noticing these mistakes and correcting himself.[32] As long as the *possibility* of sharing one's understanding of the rules is maintained, there seems to be no logical objection to the idea of solitary rule-following.[33]

---

28   See Phillips, *Death and Immortality* (London: Macmillan, 1970), pp. 2–10.

29   See G. P. Baker and P. M. S. Hacker, *Scepticism, Rules and Language* (Oxford: Blackwell, 1984), *Wittgenstein: Rules, Grammar and Necessity. An Analytical Commentary on the 'Philosophical Investigations', volume 2* (Oxford: Blackwell, 1985), pp. 169–79, and 'Malcolm on Language and Rules', *Philosophy* 65 (1990), pp. 167–79. See also John V. Canfield, 'The Community View', *Philosophical Review* 105 (1996), pp. 469–88, which attempts to reconcile the Community View (that language is essentially communal) with the opposing Baker-Hacker view (that it is conceptually possible for a Crusoe isolated from birth to speak or follow rules). In fn. 2 of his paper, Canfield also helpfully provides a short bibliography of publications relating to this controversy.

30   Baker and Hacker, 'Malcolm on Language and Rules', p. 171, emphases in the original.

31   Ibid., p. 170, emphasis in the original.

32   Ibid., p. 178.

33   It may be objected that even the Baker-Hacker view causes trouble for the philosophical theist who is intent on holding onto a 'metaphysically real' God. For if one's language, concepts and thoughts must be shareable on pain of being unintelligible, what is the theist to say of those concepts and thoughts entertained by God which are so complex that they are, in principle, unshareable (i.e., they cannot be understood by anyone who is less than omniscient)? One possible response is to reject shareability as a constraint for the meaningful use of language, and although this might seem a quite radical response to the Community View, we are not convinced that such a response is entirely lacking in plausibility – for an

Phillips's *second* objection to the idea of God as a pure consciousness relates to issues of identity and individuation:

> 'Consciousness' cannot yield the identity of its possessor. Consciousness cannot tell me who I am. If it is supposed to pick me out, I'd need to experience a number of consciousnesses, which is absurd... I am who I am in a human neighborhood, as *this* person, not *that* one. But God has no neighbors.[34]

To have an identity, on this view, one must exist within a community. It is not entirely clear why Phillips thinks this, but the idea seems to be that any description we give that uniquely identifies some person, say, Socrates, must refer to properties that Socrates has and that all *other people* lack – and so reference, if only implicit, to others in the community cannot be avoided. However, the only properties that could play this role would be properties that belong to Socrates *essentially*, where Socrates's essential properties may include such properties as *being Socrates, having been born on such-and-such day to such-and-such parents, having had a biography of such-and-such sort*, and so on. Socrates, therefore, can know who he is by knowing what his essential properties are. But then God too can know who he is, and be uniquely identified by us, by knowing what his essential properties are. And while there may be some plausibility in the view that a human person's essential properties must make reference to other people – consider, for example, the essential origins thesis – there is no reason to think that God's essential properties must make reference to other beings, whether they be of the same – divine – or different kind. Indeed, what are normally taken to be God's essential properties – e.g., omnipotence, omniscience, perfect goodness – can be understood without reference to any other beings.

Phillips's *third* objection runs as follows:

> The divine consciousness is supposed to be the source of the reality of all things, but...this metaphysical space is an intellectual aberration. Consider such a space in the Pythagorean claim that numbers entail the existence of ultimate units, which are supposed to account

---

early defence of this view, see A. J. Ayer, 'Can There Be a Private Language?' *Proceedings of the Aristotelian Society*, suppl. vol. 28 (1954): 63–76. But even if shareability were accepted, one may propose to define 'shareability' in a species-relative way, so that one's language, concepts and thoughts need only be shareable by other (possible or actual) members of one's species. In the case of God, his thoughts would then need to be shareable only with other (possible or actual) divine beings – say, another member of the Holy Trinity, or a fictional god who happens to be omniscient.

34   Phillips, 'Wittgensteinianism', p. 457, emphases in the original. A further difficulty with this passage, in addition to the one we go on to mention in the main text, resides with the assumption that the defining feature of personal agency is consciousness. With this assumption in the background, Phillips states that, 'If consciousness is the essence of a person, one would expect it, at the very least, to be the guarantor of that person's identity. But consciousness cannot tell me who I am' (*The Problem of Evil and the Problem of God*, p. 152). However, it is far from clear that consciousness is the only essential property of personhood (persons, according to many, must also be capable of exhibiting a variety of mental states and be capable of acting intentionally). Further, Phillips is conflating the general question of what it is to be a person with the more specific question of what it is to be the particular person that I am.

for our actual arithmetical configurations. Granting that the units are mathematical, they cannot fulfill this metaphysical role, since arithmetic does not spring from the units like shoots from a bulb...[35] It is not the units that give sense to the arithmetic, but the arithmetic that gives sense to the units... Similarly, it is not 'consciousness', metaphysically conceived, that shows us what is meant by 'the mind of God', but the religious practice in which that notion has its application.[36]

Just as the ultimate Pythagorean units were thought to account for – explain, give sense to – arithmetic, so the existence of God is thought to account for the reality of all things. For Phillips, however, this is all back to front: it is arithmetic that gives sense to the units, and it is everyday realities as expressed in our religious practices that give sense to our God-talk. There is no denying that we must often attend to the practices – and, in particular, the utterances – of religious believers if we are to properly understand their beliefs. But when believers profess that God is 'the source of the reality of all things', their words are not mysterious or an 'intellectual aberration'. It is, in fact, relatively easy to understand what they mean: the existence of the physical world and everything therein is ultimately dependent upon God, in the sense that God brought the world into being and conserves it in being at every moment. It is far from clear, *contra* what Wittgensteinians often say, that once we look to the believers' 'form of life' or religious practices, a very different account of 'God is the source of the reality of all things' will emerge.

The *final* criticism Phillips makes against the idea of God as a pure consciousness is that such an idea is explanatorily idle:

> God's consciousness is often associated with the notion of a divine plan which is supposed to explain all things, but no actual explanation is advanced. If I say that something has happened in accordance with a plan, I can check to see whether what happened deviates from the plan. But if *whatever* happens is said to be in accordance with a plan, reference to a plan becomes superfluous, an idle wheel.[37]

But are theists – of the traditional philosophical sort – committed to the view that 'no matter what happens in the world, it can be said to be in accordance with God's plan'? Some theists, to be sure, do talk in this way, but there is no reason why they must. Consider, for example, the response given by many theists to Flew's infamous falsification challenge, the challenge of specifying circumstances which, had they obtained, would constitute compelling evidence against the existence of God.[38] In response to this challenge, Colin Brown conceded that theism – or at least Christian theism – would be false if

---

35 Phillips here refers to an essay by Rush Rhees, 'On Continuity: Wittgenstein's Ideas, 1938', in Rhees's *Discussions of Wittgenstein* (London: Routledge & Kegan Paul, 1970), pp. 104–57, where similar sentiments are expressed, see esp. p. 114.

36 Phillips, 'Wittgensteinianism', p. 457.

37 Ibid., p. 457.

38 See Antony Flew, 'Theology and Falsification', in Antony Flew and Alasdair MacIntyre (eds), *New Essays in Philosophical Theology* (London: SCM Press, 1955), pp. 96–9.

suffering never proved to be a blessing in disguise. It would be false if adversity was never a means of finding a deeper meaning in life. It would be false if people had no experience of God working out a higher purpose in life. It would be false if adversity never offered others the opportunity of service and self-giving. It would be false if God had consigned all men to condemnation and had not sent his Son to redeem them.[39]

Most varieties of theism, particularly 'expanded' forms of theism that are part of a rich, historical religious tradition, make various predictions about what the world is like, and believers and non-believers can therefore 'check to see' whether those predictions turn out to be correct.

In the following section, we will look at Phillips's view that religious statements, such as 'God loves us' and 'God created the heavens and the earth', are not factual statements; that is to say, such statements do not purport to express facts in the same way as statements like 'It is raining today' and 'She won the lottery' purport to state facts. But before examining this view, we pause to consider what exactly motivates Phillips to take such an approach to religious language. The answer may lie in Wittgenstein's criticisms of Frazer's *Golden Bough*. Wittgenstein, it will be recalled, objected that Frazer was treating the beliefs of magic and religion as though they were intended to be scientific truths that rested on empirical evidence. But, Wittgenstein argued, to treat magic and religion in this way is to make these forms of life look *stupid*. For if magical and religious beliefs are evaluated by the same standards by which we assess scientific hypotheses – e.g., explanatory adequacy, predictive power, simplicity, fit with background knowledge – then the beliefs of magic and religion will inevitably turn out to be false:

> Frazer's account of the magical and religious views of mankind is unsatisfactory: it makes these views look like *errors*.
> Was Augustine in error, then, when he called upon God on every page of the *Confessions*?
> The very idea of wanting to explain a practice – for example, the killing of the priest-king – seems wrong to me. All that Frazer does is to make them plausible to people who think as he does. It is very remarkable that in the final analysis all these practices are presented as, so to speak, pieces of stupidity.
> But it will never be plausible to say that mankind does all that out of sheer stupidity.[40]

Unable to believe that the bulk of humanity could hold patently false or absurd views, Wittgenstein is led to conclude that people who are engaged in magic and religion are not offering a scientific view of the world based on evidence and conjecture, but are doing something quite different – and Wittgenstein saw it as his task to indicate just what those who participate in magic and religion are really up to.

---

39 C. Brown, *Philosophy and the Christian Faith* (Downers Grove, IL: InterVarsity Press, 1968), p. 178. Cf. William Wainwright, 'The Presence of Evil and the Falsification of Theistic Assertions', *Religious Studies* 4 (1969): 215.

40 Wittgenstein, 'Remarks on Frazer's *Golden Bough*', in Wittgenstein, *Philosophical Occasions: 1912–1951*, edited by James C. Klagge and Alfred Nordmann (Indianapolis: Hackett Publishing Company, 1993), p. 119, emphasis in the original (see also p. 125).

Phillips's thinking, we suspect, follows a similar trajectory. In particular, Phillips's philosophy of religious language seems to be motivated by the following line of reasoning: If theistic beliefs presuppose a conception of God as a metaphysically real subject – or a pure consciousness – then such beliefs would be nonsense or unintelligible; but belief in God is clearly not nonsense or unintelligible; hence theistic beliefs do not rest on a conception of God as a metaphysically real subject – or a pure consciousness. We have argued that Phillips's case in support of the main premise of this argument is fairly weak. But putting that aside, we can see why Phillips develops the kind of non-realist account of religious language that will be outlined in the ensuing section. For if theists – that is, theists not blinded by philosophical prejudices – do not think of God as a metaphysically real subject, then they must be thinking of God in some non-realist fashion. Although possible, it seems unlikely that Phillips would have taken up the non-realist cause if he had no logical qualms with the metaphysically real God – just as Wittgenstein would not have taken up his critique of the *Golden Bough* had he thought that religious beliefs are not obviously false when viewed as empirical or fact-stating statements.

In closing this section, it is probably worth noting that there is a curious discrepancy between the Wittgensteinian account of 'the magical and religious views of mankind' and the views Phillips holds about those who believe in a 'metaphysically real' God. When we turn our *anthropological* or *sociological* eye on, say, contemporary fundamentalist Christians in the United States, it seems that we are driven to the conclusion that there are millions upon millions of believers in a 'metaphysically real' God. There are, after all, thousands upon thousands of websites and printed works in which belief in a 'metaphysically real' God is expressed (and, though this is not relevant to our present point, examined and defended). On their own account – and as the vast weight of evidence attests – a huge number of these people *really do* believe that God brought the universe into existence a few thousand years ago, that God can be persuaded to intervene in human affairs by petitionary prayer, that God will take all of the deserving faithful to Heaven in the very near future while leaving the undeserving to continue to wander this Earth, and so forth. Moreover, these beliefs just *are* the core religious beliefs of these people: they pray *because* they believe that petitionary prayer is effective, etc. An anthropologist who fails to attribute 'metaphysical weight' to their religious beliefs just gets them wrong, even if – as Phillips supposes – the beliefs as thus interpreted are illusory, or confused, or downright 'unintelligible'. About these people, it seems that, on account of what is said elsewhere, Phillips and the other Wittgensteinians are committed to saying *both* that there is no intelligible content that can be given to the claims that these people make – their believing is 'sheer stupidity' – *and* that it could never be plausible to claim that these people hold all of these beliefs 'out of sheer stupidity'. At first sight – and, we think, not only at first sight – such a position is simply inconsistent: if belief in a 'metaphysically real' God is 'sheer stupidity', then it is at best an empirical question whether the bulk of humanity is the victim of 'sheer stupidity'.[41]

---

41 Of course, there is quite a bit of empirical research which suggests that, across a range of cases, the bulk of humanity is the victim of 'sheer stupidity'. Consider, for example, the research that shows how bad people typically are at statistical inference: they ignore base

Phillips might here reply that there is a crucial distinction to be made between engaging in a form of life and providing a philosophical account of that form of life. Surely religious people can fail to give a proper philosophical account of their religious beliefs and practices – whence, we cannot suppose that a 'Gallup poll' is a reliable guide to the content of those beliefs and the nature of those practices. But *this* response, even if applicable in some cases, seems entirely irrelevant to our present point. The claims that Phillips finds 'unintelligible' – e.g., that the world is just 6000 years old, that there is an intelligent being that responds to petitionary prayer, and so forth – are manifestly not the elements of a philosophical account of the religious beliefs in question; rather, these claims just *are* the first-order religious beliefs in question.[42] An anthropologist studying these people who arrives at the view that they do not believe in the literal efficacy of petitionary prayer – because to attribute that belief to them would be to burden them with 'sheer stupidity' – is just not doing his job properly. And, the desperate pronouncements of some of the Wittgensteinian philosophers of religion notwithstanding, there is no reason why this point could not carry over to the vast majority – or even entirety – of the religious and magical beliefs and practices of human societies.

There is perhaps an alternative line of reply that Phillips might try. Consider, to begin with, Alan Keightley's remarks on the Wittgensteinian idea of 'genuine' or 'true' religion:

> The Wittgensteinian conception of what genuine religion amounts to means that they do not claim to give an account of the entire range of belief and commitment we find that believers actually have. However, as the Wittgensteinians would probably say themselves, the language of the kind of religion they admire is in decline.[43]

In line with this view, Phillips might say that it is perfectly in order to hold that the vast bulk of humankind is engaged in religious and magical practices out of 'sheer stupidity', but that it is not in order to suppose that those who are engaged in 'genuine' – 'properly ordered' – religious and magical practices do so out of 'sheer stupidity'. But, of course, this immediately prompts a range of questions about the identification of 'genuine' religious and magical practices. Phillips might be inclined to claim that 'genuine' religious and magical practices have some affinity with *mysticism* and *negative theology*: we proceed aright so long as we insist that there is no way of saying what is the literal content of religious and magical beliefs. However, if that is the sole remaining 'out', then we're inclined to say that what is left is just another form of 'sheer stupidity': it is remarkable how much drivel is produced by mystics and negative theologians who simultaneously claim that there really is nothing that can be said about what it literally is that they believe. As Tom Lehrer (more or less)

---

rates, they embrace the gambler's fallacy, and so on. So long as we are prepared to allow that these failures of reason typically do no very serious harm – because, say, those who embrace the gambler's fallacy typically do not risk more than they can afford to lose – there is no evident barrier to the supposition that this evidence simply demonstrates that people very often are victims of 'sheer stupidity'.

42 Anyone who says otherwise is obviously in the grip of a philosophical theory.

43 Keightley, *Wittgenstein, Grammar and God*, p. 160.

has it, the very least that those who think they are unable to communicate what it is that they believe can do is to shut up. If you think that you *cannot* give literal expression to what it is that you believe, then whistling in the dark is not going to help; on all sides, it will be far better if you simply pass by in silence.[44]

Is Religious Language Fact-Stating?

Phillips, following the later Wittgenstein, often describes religious beliefs as forming distinctive 'language games'. Occasionally, however, Phillips expresses some misgivings about this characterization.[45] For one thing, a 'game' suggests something frivolous or hobby-like, whereas religious beliefs have momentous significance and value, at least for those who accept such beliefs. More importantly, treating religious belief as a distinct language game has often raised the suspicion that any given religious tradition would then become a self-contained esoteric game having its own criteria of truth, rationality, and intelligibility, thus rendering it immune from criticism 'from without'. Religious belief, on this view, becomes a form of fideism – 'Wittgensteinian fideism', to use Kai Nielsen's phrase.[46] In attempting to meet this criticism, Phillips points out that religious language games should not be thought of as being entirely cut off from non-religious language games and other aspects of human life. There are important connections between religious and non-religious forms of life, and these must be recognized if religious belief is not to degenerate into superstition. If, for example, a religious believer talks of death as if it were a sleep of long duration, one may accuse her of not taking death seriously, and this criticism is drawn from what we already know and believe about these matters.[47] But despite these connections between the religious and non-religious domains, Phillips emphasizes that the distinctiveness

---

44   A less tendentious way of making our point here is to say that there is a very strong case for saying that, *contra* the claims of the Wittgensteinians, it is the language of mysticism and negative theology that is 'language in decline'.

45   See, for example, Phillips, 'Religious Beliefs and Language-Games', in his *Faith and Philosophical Enquiry* (London: Routledge & Kegan Paul, 1970), ch. 5.

46   Kai Nielsen, 'Wittgensteinian Fideism', *Philosophy* 42 (1967): 191–209.

47   Phillips offers this and other examples in 'Religious Beliefs and Language-Games', p. 98 (the distinction between religion and superstition is elaborated further on pp. 101–9). See also Phillips, *Belief, Change and Forms of Life*, ch. 1, and *Religion and the Hermeneutics of Contemplation* (Cambridge: Cambridge University Press, 2001), pp. 25–30, where he argues vigorously against the equation of his views with Wittgensteinian fideism.

That Phillips does not think of religious language games as entirely divorced from, or incommensurate with respect to, other language games is often missed by his critics – see, for example, Joseph Runzo, 'Realism, Non-Realism and Atheism: Why Believe in an Objectively Real God?' in Runzo (ed.), *Is God Real?* pp. 159–60. A critic who has not overlooked this aspect of Phillips's thought is Lance Ashdown, who argues nevertheless that Phillips's position that religious language games are not completely autonomous does not cohere well with his repeated insistence that philosophers ought to stop judging religious beliefs on the basis of criteria borrowed from non-religious forms of discourse (see Ashdown, 'D. Z. Phillips and his Audiences', *Sophia* 32 (1993): 1–31). See, however, Phillips, *Religion and Friendly Fire*, pp. 8–11, where Phillips attempts to meet a similar criticism made by Stephen Mulhall.

of religious belief must not be overlooked. In particular, the language of religious believers must not be assimilated to the kind of fact-stating, physical-object discourse that characterizes the empirical sciences.

Phillips's account of religious language may be elucidated by looking at the kind of view it stands in opposition to. The opposing view – accepted, incidentally, by the majority of contemporary analytical philosophers of religion – holds that theistic beliefs purport to express 'facts' that are objective in some important sense. More precisely, theistic beliefs are thought to be true or false, and their truth-value is taken to be completely independent of what any human being thinks or believes. This, indeed, is just what realism with respect to religious belief amounts to. As Hick explains,

> Religious realism is the view that the existence or non-existence of God is a fact independent of whether you or I or anyone else believes that God exists. If God exists, God is not simply an idea or ideal in our minds, but an ontological reality, the ultimate creative power of the universe.[48]

But if theistic beliefs express facts, then their truth or falsity can be discovered by us, and many philosophers of religion believe that the projects of natural theology and natural atheology play an important role in this respect. Richard Swinburne and Michael Martin, for example, have devoted lengthy studies to the question of the existence of God, and the approach of each philosopher has involved the accumulation and evaluation of various pieces of evidence both for and against theistic belief.[49]

Phillips is adamant that this way of proceeding is entirely mistaken. In one of his early papers, for example, he writes:

> Because the question of divine reality can be construed as 'Is God real or not?' it has often been assumed that the dispute between the believer and the unbeliever is over *a matter of fact*. The philosophical investigation of the reality of God then becomes the philosophical investigation appropriate to an assertion of a matter of fact. That this is a misrepresentation of the religious concept is made obvious by a brief comparison of talk about facts with talk about God.[50]

Fact-stating language, Phillips goes on to note, has the following characteristics.

1. When claiming something to be a 'fact', we typically presuppose that we are not entirely sure or certain that what we are stating is indeed the case:

> When do we say, 'It is a fact that…' or ask, 'Is it a fact that…?' Often, we do so where there is some uncertainty. For example, if the police hear that a wanted criminal has died in some remote part of the world, their reaction might be, 'Check the facts'.[51]

---

48 Hick, 'Believing – And Having True Beliefs', in Runzo (ed.), *Is God Real?* p. 115. Cf. Stephen T. Davis's first two definitions of religious realism in *God, Reason and Theistic Proofs* (Edinburgh: Edinburgh University Press, 1997), pp. 47–8.

49 See Richard Swinburne, *The Existence of God*, rev. ed. (Oxford: Clarendon Press, 1991), and Michael Martin, *Atheism: A Philosophical Justification* (Philadelphia, PA: Temple University Press, 1990).

50 Phillips, 'Philosophy, Theology and the Reality of God', in *Faith and Philosophical Enquiry*, p. 1, emphasis in the original.

51 Ibid.

2. Fact-stating discourse, furthermore, has a contingent character, for it expresses truths that might have turned out to be false: 'A fact might not have been: it is conceivable that the wanted criminal had not died.'[52]

3. Given the contingent nature of facts, the language of facts is only appropriate when the subject-matter concerns contingent reality, such as physical properties or objects that come into being and pass away.

4. Finally, we have procedures in place for resolving disputes regarding matters of fact, and these procedures usually involve looking to the truth or falsity of other matters of fact. In all these respects, according to Phillips, the language of facts diverges from the language of religion.

Re (1): Phillips says that believers are not tentative in, or uncertain of, their (religious) beliefs. They would not, for example, think of the reality of God as a conjecture or hypothesis that stands in need of proof or evidence. Phillips is therefore scathing towards those, like Swinburne and Mackie, who like to apply the probability calculus to the question of the existence of God. He characterizes such philosophers as 'the friends of Cleanthes', referring of course to Hume's character, Cleanthes, who also enquired into God's existence by asking whether God can be probabilistically inferred from the nature or existence of the world. Phillips counsels his readers to 'give up bad philosophical friends, among them the friends of Cleanthes,' for they distort the nature or underlying 'grammar' of religious belief:

> If religious beliefs are matters of probability, should we not reformulate religious beliefs so that the natural expressions of them becomes less misleading? Should we not say from now on, 'I believe that it is highly probable that there is an almighty God, maker of heaven and earth?'; 'I believe that it is highly probable that my Redeemer liveth'; 'I believe that it is highly probable that God forgives sins'? Do these reformulations do justice to the nature of religious beliefs? Hardly.[53]

The reality of God, rather, functions as a 'bedrock' belief in the religious language game, a belief which informs an entire way of life without itself being subject to confirmation, disconfirmation or doubt. Unlike matters of fact, where we do not regard it wrong or bad to raise doubts, doubt regarding God's existence is not merely out of place, but *sinful* (analogously, faith is called a virtue).[54] Holding religious beliefs, then, 'has little in common with any kind of conjecture. It has to do with

---

52   Ibid., pp. 1–2.

53   Phillips, 'The Friends of Cleanthes: A Case of Conceptual Poverty', in Phillips, *Recovering Religious Concepts: Closing Epistemic Divides* (Basingstoke: Macmillan, 2000), p. 64. See also Phillips, 'In All Probability', *Times Literary Supplement*, 28 May 1982, p. 588, where he reviews Swinburne's *Faith and Reason* and takes him to task for holding that belief in God is belief in what is merely probable.

54   See Phillips, *Religion Without Explanation* (Oxford: Basil Blackwell, 1976), pp. 174–5, where he draws upon some remarks by Rhees and Wittgenstein.

living by them, drawing sustenance from them, judging oneself in terms of them, being afraid of them, etc.'[55]

Re (2): Phillips says that, unlike facts, religious beliefs do not express contingent truths. We might be prepared to say that it might not rain tomorrow, but 'the religious believer is not prepared to say that God might not exist'.[56]

Re (3): Phillips says that, if God is not something that might or might not exist, then God cannot be thought of as an object, a thing, or a being existing amongst other beings. Indeed, the life-transforming impact that the reality of God is often said to have indicates that God cannot properly be described as an object:

> Coming to see that there is a God is not like coming to see that an additional being exists. If it were, there would be an extension of one's knowledge of facts, but no extension of one's understanding. Coming to see that there is a God involves seeing a new meaning in one's life, and being given a new understanding. The Hebrew-Christian conception of God is not a conception of a being among beings.[57]

---

55 Phillips, *Death and Immortality*, p. 68. A similar point is made in a discussion Phillips had with J. R. Jones on BBC radio (which was first published in 1970):

JRJ: What is it that shows that, to take Wittgenstein's example, belief in the Last Judgment has obviously nothing in common with a hypothesis?

DZP: I think that if we do look at the role this belief plays in at least many believers' lives, we find that it is not a hypothesis, a conjecture, that some dreadful event is going to happen so many thousands years hence. We see this by recognizing that a certain range of reactions is ruled out for the believer. What I mean is this: if it were a conjecture about a future event, he might say, 'I believe it is going to happen' or 'Possibly it might happen' or 'I'm not sure; it may happen', and so on. But that range of reactions plays no part in the believer's belief in the Last Judgment. ('Belief and Loss of Belief', in Phillips, *Faith and Philosophical Enquiry*, pp. 112–13.)

On the 'bedrock' nature of religious belief, see also Phillips, *Religion Without Explanation*, ch. 10, where Phillips notes that the proposition 'God exists' 'does not get its unshakeable character from its inherent nature, or from the kind of abstraction which philosophy tries to make of it so often, but from its surroundings, from all the activities that hold it fast. Above all, those activities involving the language of praise and worship' (p. 172).

We should also point out that, on Phillips's view, the firmness of a religious belief does not mean that it cannot be renounced. For Phillips, however, what erodes religious faith is not evidential considerations (such as evidential arguments from evil), but factors such as the appeal of a rival secular outlook or more pervasive cultural changes. See Phillips, 'Belief and Loss of Belief', p. 116, *Death and Immortality*, pp. 73–6, and *Belief, Change and Forms of Life*, pp. 86–93.

56 Phillips, 'Philosophy, Theology and the Reality of God', p. 2.

57 Phillips, 'Faith, Scepticism, and Religious Understanding', in Phillips, *Faith and Philosophical Enquiry*, pp. 17–18. Phillips makes a similar point in response to Hick's procedure of pointing to religious believers who say that the existence of God is a matter of fact: 'I have no doubt, however, that *the same* believers who say that the existence of God is a fact would, if pressed, admit that the discovery of God is not like the discovery of a matter of fact' ('Religious Belief and Philosophical Enquiry', in Phillips, *Faith and Philosophical Enquiry*, p. 71, emphasis in the original).

Discovering the existence of an object (say, a further planet in our solar system) would result in an extension to our current body of knowledge, but such a discovery – unlike a conversion to religious belief – would not radically alter the character of one's personal life. Accepting God is quite unlike accepting the existence of some physical object. Talk of God, then, cannot to be modelled on talk about physical objects.[58] Phillips's point, as Scott and Moore explain, is that 'one cannot, by qualifying, explaining or extending the forms of expression one uses with regard to physical objects, reach an appropriate form of expression for talking about God'.[59] It is misleading, however, not only to speak of God as an 'object', but to even speak of him as an 'existent', for our notion of existence carries with it an implication of contingency: ordinarily, one cannot say that something exists unless it makes sense to suppose that it might not have existed. Phillips therefore prefers to say, along with Kierkegaard, that 'God does not exist, He is eternal'.[60] Since God does not belong to the order of contingent reality, our language about God should not be assimilated to our way of speaking about common (or contingent) objects, beings, or existents. The word 'God', Phillips states, 'is not the name of an individual; it does not refer to anything'.[61]

Re (4): Finally, Phillips says that disagreements between believers and unbelievers cannot be settled in the way in which we resolve factual disputes. Disagreements over facts usually take place against a background of shared beliefs, so that there is little or no disagreement as to (e.g.) what counts as a fact and what kind of evidence or investigation is relevant to settling a particular dispute over a matter of fact. If, for example, someone claims that there is a certain species of bacteria on the table when in fact there are none there, we can at least agree as to what kind of evidence

---

58   See Phillips, *The Concept of Prayer* (London: Routledge & Kegan Paul, 1965), pp. 21–3.

59   Michael Scott and Andrew Moore, 'Can Theological Realism Be Refuted?' *Religious Studies* 33 (1997), p. 414. As Scott and Moore note (in their fn. 18, p. 414), Phillips assumes that the religious realist suffers from the 'philosophical prejudice' that non-physical reality can be understood on analogy with physical reality. Phillips, to be sure, has further criticisms of this prejudice than those indicated in the main text. He argues, for example, that our criteria of individuation for (empirical) objects are not the same as those we have for God, and that accurate depictions of objects can be constructed, but no such images of God are available. For criticisms of these arguments, see Scott and Moore, *op. cit.*, pp. 414–18.

60   The quote is taken from Kierkegaard's *Concluding Unscientific Postscript*, trans. David F. Swenson (Princeton, NJ: Princeton University Press, 1941), p. 296. Phillips often approvingly quotes this remark – see, for example, 'Faith, Scepticism, and Religious Understanding', p. 18; *Faith After Foundationalism* (London: Routledge, 1988), p. 229; and 'Philosophers' Clothes' in Charles M. Lewis (ed.), *Relativism and Religion* (New York: St. Martin's Press, 1995), p. 138.

61   Phillips, *Religion Without Explanation*, p. 148. Cf. Phillips, 'Religious Beliefs and Language-Games', p. 85. Phillips would not want to deny, however, that 'God' is in some sense a referring expression, but he would add that the sense in which 'God' is taken as a referring expression needs to be made clear (see Phillips, 'Philosophers' Clothes', p. 138). As Rhees puts it, 'I might say that the language about God certainly does refer to something. But then I should want to say something about what it is to 'talk about God', and how different this is from talking about the moon or talking about our new house or talking about the Queen. How different the 'talking about' is, I mean. That is a difference in grammar' (*Without Answers*, London: Routledge & Kegan Paul, 1969, p. 132).

or investigation would settle the issue. Disputes amongst believers and unbelievers, however, lack any such background of shared beliefs. As a result, there is no commonly accepted decision procedure for adjudicating cases where, for example, one claims to be perceive (or experience) God and another claims that the perception is illusory. As Phillips states,

> When the positivist claims that there is no God because God cannot be located, the believer does not object on the grounds that the investigation has not been thorough enough, but on the grounds that the investigation fails to understand the grammar of what is being investigated – namely, the reality of God.[62]

Putting together the above four points of divergence between factual discourse and religious discourse, Phillips concludes that religious beliefs are not statements of fact, but confessions of faith.[63]

How plausible is Phillips's view of religious language as non-fact-stating? We believe that Phillips's position falls far short of a philosophically satisfying account of the nature of religious belief. In particular, we think that Phillips's account relies on a superficial view of the different claims that are made by religious believers. At least in part, our reasons for saying this can be exhibited in a reconsideration of the four purported disanalogies between fact-stating language and religious language that are identified by Phillips.

Consider, *firstly*, Phillips's claim that religious beliefs, unlike factual statements, are not tentative or conjectural in nature and do not require confirmation by way of proof or evidence. It is difficult to determine whether Phillips is here advancing a descriptive claim – this is just how religious beliefs are normally held – or a normative claim – this is how religious beliefs should be held – or both.[64] But, however his claim is best interpreted, it is mistaken. Descriptively construed, Phillips's claim stands refuted, or is at least challenged, by the fact that there has always been a significant group of believers who have sought to construct a rational case in support of their religious beliefs. One can find, for example, a reasoned defence of the fundamental tenets of the Christian faith in many of the 'apologists' of the early Christian centuries (including Aristides, Justin Martyr, and Athenagoras of Athens), numerous patristic

---

62 Phillips, 'Philosophy, Theology and the Reality of God', p. 2.

63 One may, of course, speak of 'religious facts', but in that case, Phillips notes, 'all the grammatical work has still to be done. We have to show how talk of facts in this context differs from talk of facts in other contexts. We would need to be clear about what finding out the facts, discovering the facts, or being mistaken about the facts, would amount to where religious matters are concerned. There would be similarities enough with other contexts, but there would be huge differences. I suspect what is important would lie in these differences' (*Faith After Foundationalism*, p. 230). As pointed out in fn. 61 above, Phillips makes a similar point in regards to calling God an object or 'God' a referring expression.

64 Given that Phillips often extols Wittgenstein's principle of 'leaving everything as it is' as an ideal to which philosophers of religion should aspire (see, e.g., Phillips's paper, 'Religion in Wittgenstein's Mirror', in *Wittgenstein and Religion*, Basingstoke: Macmillan, 1993, pp. 237–55), it would seem that Phillips is advancing a descriptive rather than a normative claim. Such an approach may be contrasted with the explicitly revisionary non-realism advocated by Don Cupitt in *Taking Leave of God* (London: SCM Press, 1980).

writers (such as Gregory of Nyssa and John of Damascus), scores of theologians in both east and west during the Middle Ages (Thomas Aquinas being the prime example), and many contemporary philosophers and theologians (Richard Swinburne and William Lane Craig, for example). To be sure, these thinkers do not claim that the only or the best way to arrive at religious belief is through philosophical argumentation. Still, they do regard natural theology or 'positive apologetics' (the project of offering arguments in support of religious belief without recourse to divinely revealed truths) and 'negative apologetics' (the project of rebutting objections to religious belief) as crucially relevant to the life and practice of the church. There is, therefore, an important strand within Christianity – and the other major theistic traditions – that treats religious belief as something that is subject to confirmation and disconfirmation. This is not to ignore the fact that within Christianity one will also find opposing streams of thought which are more sympathetic to Phillips's account of religious belief – the apophatic and mystical traditions are cases in point. But what this indicates is that Christianity, like any of the major world religions, is not a homogeneous entity, but displays an enormous variety of views about the nature and meaning of religious language. Any simple descriptive claim, such as 'religious believers do not base their beliefs on evidence', will therefore be misleading at best and patently false at worst.[65]

Phillips is no doubt aware of the diversity that exists within the theistic tradition,[66] but it is difficult to see how he could plausibly respond. He might reply, for example, that the 'proofs' of theologians such as Anselm and Aquinas are not aimed at substantiating the belief that God exists, but are rather exercises in 'faith seeking understanding', this being the attempt to understand what is *already* believed, as opposed to understanding *in order to* believe.[67] But this seems a dubious interpretation of what natural theologians, both past and present, are doing when constructing theistic arguments. For if their aim is merely to understand, and not to substantiate or persuade, then a carefully structured argument containing various premises and concluding with 'God exists' would be a most peculiar way to achieve such an aim.

Alternatively, Phillips might reply that natural theologians are an aberrant group of philosophers who attempt to import into religious practice an alien form of thinking, typically one informed by metaphysical speculation or scientific reasoning. But now Phillips would be resorting to a normative judgement – regarding the proper way religious beliefs are to be held – and here he is on weaker ground still. There might

---

65   However, as Richard Messer points out, the various conceptions of God and the competing views on the nature of religious belief that exist within historical Christianity 'overcome the simple charge that Phillips is a revisionist; for there is no single dominant conception of God, even within Christianity, to be revised' (*Does God's Existence Need Proof?* p. 55).

66   For example, in response to John Hick's fact-stating account of religious belief, Phillips writes: 'One has a vast and various range of persons, all claiming to be religious believers. I do not deny, then, that there are people whose conception of God is similar to that outlined by Hick' ('Religion and Epistemology: Some Contemporary Confusions', in *Faith and Philosophical Enquiry*, p. 127). And later on, he writes: 'I do not wish to defend those people whose religious beliefs can be described adequately in Hick's terms. I only wish to stress that there is another kind of belief in God' (p. 129).

67   See Phillips, 'Sublime Existence' in *Wittgenstein and Religion*, p. 10, and 'Return of the Monstrous Illusion' in *Recovering Religious Concepts*, p. 19.

be some reason to think that natural theology was not necessary or vitally important during the Middle Ages, given that the existence of God was rarely in dispute amongst intellectual circles and in the wider community. But today, as in the early Christian centuries, the situation is quite different. Belief in God is under attack from various quarters: scientists and scientifically-minded philosophers often claim that all natural phenomena can be adequately explained without invoking the 'God hypothesis'; in line with this view, a number of naturalistic accounts of the genesis and spread of religious belief have been offered, with belief in God portrayed as the product of ignorance and fear in the face of the hostile forces of nature (Hume), or an inequitable social order (Marx and Engels), or an immature or infantile psychology (Freud); the historical reliability of the scriptures that theists claim to be divinely inspired has been placed in question; and we are now more aware of the diversity of religious belief across the world's races and nations. Arguably, in times like these, theists who are apprised of the contemporary challenges faced by religious belief *ought not* accept the existence of God without at least attempting to meet some of the objections levelled against theism, and perhaps also attempting to find some evidence in support of theism.[68] Concomitantly, it can be argued that the only type of religious faith that is appropriate for today's well-informed theists is one that is modest and tentative, not dogmatic and self-assured.

Robert McKim, a contemporary theist, has forcefully argued in support of this conception of religious faith.[69] McKim states that theists must acknowledge both the hiddenness of God (i.e., the fact that the reality of God is not obvious to many people) and the widespread diversity in religious belief amongst people of seemingly equal integrity and competence. In the face of these phenomena, argues McKim, the only appropriate response is the adoption of a 'Critical Stance'. To adopt this stance towards one's beliefs is to critically examine one's beliefs in the light of objections and conflicting evidence, and to hold one's beliefs in a tentative manner, always open to the prospect that one is mistaken.[70] As McKim puts it,

> Religion in accordance with the Critical Stance is religion that is conducted more in the mode of longing and aspiration than in the mode of confident declaration. It has progressed from 'knowing' that it is right to acknowledging how limited is our ability to know about religious matters, and to recognizing both the ambiguity of our circumstances and the variety of responsible responses to those circumstances.[71]

---

68 A position of this sort has been defended by David Basinger, 'Plantinga, Pluralism and Justified Religious Belief', *Faith and Philosophy* 8 (1991), pp. 67–80, and Philip L. Quinn, 'The Foundations of Theism Again: A Rejoinder to Plantinga', in Linda Zagzebski (ed.), *Rational Faith: Catholic Responses to Reformed Epistemology* (Notre Dame, IN: University of Notre Dame Press, 1993), pp. 35–45.

69 See Robert McKim, *Religious Ambiguity and Religious Diversity* (Oxford: Oxford University Press, 2001), esp. chs 7–9.

70 For McKim, however, tentativeness includes more than the mere recognition of one's fallibility: 'tentative belief that p is belief that p is true that involves an awareness that p may need revision, and may even be false, and that there may be viable alternatives to p. It involves openness to inquiry and openness to change, and it may involve ongoing inquiry and experimentation' (*Religious Ambiguity and Religious Diversity*, p. 158).

71 McKim, *Religious Ambiguity and Religious Diversity*, p. 142.

Despite the fears of some religious believers, re-envisioning religious faith in the way suggested by McKim may well be a move in the right direction, an advance of some sorts, for the practice of religion. For we all know what happens to religious (and non-religious) people who do not seek to provide reasons in support of their fundamental commitments and refuse to subject their beliefs to critical scrutiny: they become intolerant, self-righteous 'fundamentalists'.[72]

Phillips's *second* purported disanalogy between fact-stating discourse and religious language is that, whereas facts express contingent truths, the truths upheld by religious believers are not of the kind that could turn out to be false. But this view is mistaken on two counts. Firstly, it is not clear why facts cannot express necessary truths. We might, for example, speak of 'mathematical facts', or we might think – along with Kripke and others – that it is a fact that water is H_2O even though it is necessarily true that water is H_2O. And secondly, even if all facts are contingently true, many theists are quite prepared to hold that the existence of God is a contingent truth. Indeed, it would be rare to find a theist who views theism as necessarily true – for one would require something to the effect of a sound ontological argument to support such a view. But theists are often prepared to accept that there are possible worlds in which God does not exist, or that there is some conceivable evidence that would falsify their belief in God. Such theists, however, need not think that God is dependent in any way for his existence on something outside himself, or that God might exist at one time but cease existing at some future time. In other words, one may hold that 'God exists' expresses a contingent truth, while at the same time holding that God is ontologically independent (or has the property of aseity) and is eternal or everlasting.[73]

Phillips's *third* disanalogy is that, whereas factual discourse is intended to refer to objects in the world, discourse about God is not intended to refer to any object or thing at all. Admittedly, there are contexts in which it is improper to describe God as an 'object'; namely, those contexts in which 'objects' are taken to *contrast with* 'subjects', or 'centres of consciousness', or 'persons', or the like. But there are many contexts in which it is perfectly legitimate to call minded beings, such as human persons or gods, 'objects'. As Swinburne states,

---

72   This, however, gives rise to a problem which, we suspect, motivates much of what Phillips has to say on the non-conjectural nature of religious belief: How can religious belief be held tentatively on the basis of (somewhat flimsy) evidence while at the same time providing the basis for an unconditional and passionate commitment (to God)? For some proposals as to how tentative religious belief can be reconciled with, and even inform and heighten, religious commitment, see McKim, *Religious Ambiguity and Religious Diversity*, pp. 166–70, and C. Stephen Evans, *Philosophy of Religion: Thinking About Faith* (Downers Grove, IL: InterVarsity Press, 1982), pp. 171–6.

73   The above discussion is premised on the assumption that the kind of necessity in question is logical. As Richard Swinburne points out, this sense of necessity – i.e., logical necessity – is not always the kind of necessity that is attributed to God. Rather, God's existence is often thought to be 'necessary' only in the sense that God does not depend for his existence on himself or on anything else. See Swinburne, *The Coherence of Theism*, pp. 263–8.

If you mean [by saying of God that he is an object] God is something of which properties are true, which causally interacts with other recognisable observable objects, which can be distinguished from others as the subject of certain predicates which he has and they don't: well, that is the case with God, and therefore on any natural understanding of 'object', God is an object.[74]

Phillips maintains, however, that the reality of God is not logically akin to the reality of an object. As mentioned earlier, Phillips attempts to support this view by arguing that, if God could be thought of as an object, then 'discovering God' – as happens in religious conversions – would have the same effect as discovering some fact or the existence of some physical object; that is to say, there would merely be an extension to one's body of knowledge without any corresponding change in one's outlook on the world or one's way of life. But the discovery of a fact or an object can, and often does, radically alter one's worldview or way of life. Consider, for example, how any of the following could lead one to see life in an entirely different light: discovering a million dollars in your garden, discovering that your partner has died in a car crash, discovering that your partner has cheated on you, discovering that you have only ten years to live, discovering that you have been adopted, and so on. There is no reason why the discovery of a fact cannot be an extension to one's knowledge *and* a life-changing experience.

However, Phillips also holds that objects are unlike God in that objects can be said to exist, whereas the sentence 'God exists' is somewhat peculiar and inappropriate as a vehicle for the expression of religious belief. For, in Phillips's view, to say that God exists is to imply that God exists contingently.[75] But, according to Phillips, God's reality is of a different order altogether: it makes no sense to say that God might not have existed or to ask such questions as: 'How long has God existed? Will he still exist next week? He was in existence yesterday, but how about today?'[76] The underlying assumption that Phillips makes here may be put as follows: If something x exists, then (a) it is possible for x to not exist, and (b) it is possible for x to come into existence and cease existing. But what reason is there to accept this? There does not appear to be any conceptual impossibility in the idea of something which cannot fail to exist and cannot come into being and pass away. For one thing, a host of abstract objects – e.g., numbers, sets, properties – have been accorded this distinction.

---

74   Quoted in Messer, *Does God's Existence Need Proof?* p. 21.

75   This view is egregious, though Phillips is not the only philosopher to have endorsed it. It is an uncontroversial modal claim that whatever is necessarily so is so. Whence it follows that, if God necessarily exists, then God exists. But, give Phillips his claim that 'God exists' entails 'It is contingently true that God exists', and we get out the absurd view that 'It is necessarily true that God exists' entails 'It is contingently true that God exists'. This is one point where Grice can help. Clearly, if you hold that it is necessary that God exists, then there will be many contexts in which you ought not to assert merely that God exists – for, if you say only that God exists, there is a clear conversational implication that you do not suppose that God necessarily exists (given that the Gricean conversational maxims are in place).

76   Cf. Norman Malcolm, 'Anselm's Ontological Arguments', *Philosophical Review* 69 (1960): 49.

And there does not seem to be any conceptual barrier in saying the same thing of a concrete object, such as a divine being.[77]

Phillips's *fourth* disanalogy is that we have commonly accepted methods for resolving disputes over matters of fact, but there are no such methods for settling disputes between believers and non-believers. Unfortunately, there is much truth in this, for in disputes over the existence of God – and philosophical matters generally – arguments that convince, or at least ought to convince, both parties to the dispute are difficult to come by, and when they are found their compelling character is not easily recognized. This, no doubt, is partly because the disputing parties often have widely divergent background beliefs with respect to, e.g., the proper methodology to be employed, what the criteria of success should be, the admissibility of certain items of evidence, and various conceptual and factual matters.[78] Hence the persistence of disagreement amongst believers and non-believers. We may lament this state of affairs, but it is no cause for supposing that there is no fact of the matter as to whether there is a God. Otherwise, we would be led to the unpalatable view that where there is widespread disagreement or dissent over the truth of *A* and the proper way to determine the truth of *A*, there is no objective, non-relative truth regarding *A* to be had. Surely, the mere contingent fact of disagreement should have no such far-ranging metaphysical implications.

Apart from these particular points, there are some more general considerations to which attention ought to be paid. Phillips places great weight on the idea that believers will not accept that it *might* be the case that God does not exist. But, we think, here – as elsewhere – Phillips is content with a quite *superficial* view of what it is that believers will and won't accept. It is well-known that the common modal terms can be used to express a great range of different modalities, and that contextual features play a very important role in determining which of the range of modalities is expressed by a given use of a modal term. So, in the case at hand, we can – and should – ask: in what sense, exactly, do Phillips's believers deny that it *might* be that God does not exist? Are they saying that it is logically – metaphysically, alethically – necessary that God exists? Are they saying that God's existence is entailed by what everybody knows? Are they saying that there is no sense to be made of the worldviews

---

77   For a similar criticism of Phillips, see Stephen Davis, *God, Reason and Theistic Proofs*, p. 53. In his paper 'Sublime Existence' (collected in his *Wittgenstein and Religion*), Phillips mentions Kierkegaard's remark that 'God does not exist, he is eternal', and then goes on to describe some similar views upheld by Simone Weil, John Wisdom, and Norman Malcolm – however, Phillips then proceeds to *criticize* such views on the grounds that they 'sublime the logic of 'existence', assuming that we can only ascribe 'existence' to things which come to be and pass away' (p. 14). But isn't Phillips himself guilty of the same charge? We don't think so. Phillips explains that to sublime the logic of our language (a phrase borrowed from Wittgenstein) is to take language out of its contexts of application (p. 12). Perhaps, then, Phillips's point is merely that, within religious contexts, God can be said to exist, though he cannot be said to exist contingently. Phillips would no doubt add, however, that if God were thought to be an object, then God would be reduced to a contingent being, and it is this we wish to dispute.

78   Cf. J. J. C. Smart, 'Why Philosophers Disagree', *Canadian Journal of Philosophy* suppl. vol. 19 (1993): 67–82.

of those who do not accept the claim that God exists? Are they saying that it is irrational to adopt a worldview that makes no room for the claim that God exists? Are they saying that it is absolutely certain that God exists? Are they saying that they possess evidence which is such that the truth of that evidence entails that God exists? Or what? Without some further specification, there is no serious theoretical work that can be done by the observation that Phillips's believers deny that it might be that God does not exist.

Another general point that deserves further attention is that the data to which Phillips appeals in order to motivate his claims about the non-factual nature of religious assertion can all be accommodated – and, in our view, much better accommodated – by the Gricean theory of conversation. Following Phillips – more or less – we can agree that, in many contexts, the point of making a claim of the form 'It is a fact that p' is to seek or to express agreement that the claim that p is not open to serious dispute given the current conversational context. If that's right, then – on the Gricean theory – we would expect that one would typically make a claim of the form 'It is a fact that p' in circumstances in which there is some genuine reason to be uncertain whether it *is* a shared belief that the claim that p is not open to serious dispute given the current conversational context. But, of course, if this is right, then – *contra* Phillips – there is no reason at all to suppose that typical claims of the form 'It is a fact that p' take as their subject-matter only that which is logically – metaphysically, alethically – contingent. It is not hard to imagine a context in which it would be perfectly appropriate – and, indeed, correct – to say that it is a fact that arithmetic is not recursively axiomatizable (even though, of course, it is *not* merely a contingent truth that arithmetic is not recursively axiomatizable). Moreover, while it is clear that, on the Gricean account, there will be many contexts in which it would be inappropriate for religious believers to say that it is a fact that God exists – since there are many conversational contexts in which all of the participants take it to be common knowledge that God exists and there are also many conversational contexts in which it is recognized by all concerned that there is deep-rooted disagreement about whether God exists – it is also clear that, as the Gricean theory predicts, there are many conversational contexts in which it is perfectly appropriate for religious believers to assert that it is a fact that God exists, e.g., contexts in which it is simply uncertain whether all of the parties to the conversation accept the claim that God exists. And, of course, there are similar points to be made about assertions that God exists: there are conversational contexts in which such assertions are appropriate, and there are conversational contexts in which such assertions are inappropriate, given the conversational purposes at hand.

While there is more to be said about the details of Phillips's view and about the general considerations that bear on that view, we think that it is quite clear that there is no good reason to accept Phillips's view that religious language is not fact-stating. While we can happily acknowledge that there are many different things that are done by way of the making of religious utterances, we reject the suggestion that no religious utterances have, in part, the function of making assertions, or stating (purported) facts. Moreover, we think that it is equally clear that a very large amount of religious utterance, religious assertion, and religious belief does involve commitment to a 'metaphysically real' God – the vast majority of religious believers do, in fact, suppose that their religious beliefs answer to an independent and transcendent reality. If there is no God, then, indeed, Augustine was in error when he called upon God on every page of the *Confessions*.[79]

---

79   We would like to thank Stephen T. Davis for providing helpful comments on an earlier draft of this paper.

Chapter 8

Theological Anti-Realism

Merold Westphal

All praise we would render – O help us to see
'Tis only the splendor of light hideth Thee!

Holy, holy, holy! Though the darkness hide thee,
Though the eye made blind by sin thy glory may not see.[1]

The term 'anti-realism' is ugly enough to scare away the faint hearted; but it is at least as well established as any of the suggested alternatives: irrealism, internalism (which has another very different meaning), perspectivism, conceptual relativism, and so forth. It is widely agreed that Kant is the paradigmatic anti-realist.[2] Always lurking in the background of current debates is his Copernican revolution according to which instead of assuming 'that all our knowledge must conform to objects' we should suppose 'that objects must conform to our knowledge'.[3] In other words, how we take what is given to us determines what gets through to us. Think, for example, of the colour-blind perceiver, or the racist.

So it leads to confusion to present as realism, or perhaps 'metaphysical realism', a view that Kant would have no trouble affirming, such as the view that the world or God exists independently of our thinking or talking about them. Kant holds that view. That is what the thing in itself is all about. Nor will it do to define metaphysical realism as the view that

> the world consists of some fixed totality of mind-independent objects. There is exactly one true and complete description of 'the way the world is'. Truth involves some sort of correspondence relation between words or thought-signs and external things and sets of things. I shall call this perspective the *externalist* perspective, because its favorite point of view is a God's Eye point of view.[4]

---

1   From the hymns, respectively, 'Immortal, Invisible' by Walter Chalmers Smith and 'Holy, Holy, Holy' by Reginald Heber, *alt.*

2   See Nelson Goodman, *Ways of Worldmaking* (Indianapolis: Hackett, 1978), p. x; Hilary Putnam, *Meaning and the Moral Sciences* (London: Routledge & Kegan Paul, 1978), p. 138; Alvin Plantinga, 'How to Be an Anti-realist', *Proceedings and Addresses of the American Philosophical Association*, Vol. 56, No. 1, (1982–83), pp. 47–9; and C. Stephen Evans, 'Realism and antirealism in Kierkegaard's *Concluding Unscientific Postscript*', in Alastair Hannay and Gordon D Marino (eds), *The Cambridge Companion to Kierkegaard* (Cambridge: Cambridge University Press, 1998), p. 161.

3   *Critique of Pure Reason*, B xvi.

4   Hilary Putnam, *Reason, Truth and History* (Cambridge: Cambridge University Press, 1981), p. 49.

Once again, Kant holds that view. That's what the thing in itself is all about. It is widely overlooked but crucial to understanding Kant's text that the noumenal world or the thing in itself is precisely the real as seen from the God's Eye point of view.[5] It is God's knowledge which Kant, as a theist, takes to be qualitatively different from our own, that does not distort the real in any way and thus, whether actual or merely possible, is the knowledge that defines the real as it truly is, that corresponds to its object, that passes the adequation test in terms of which truth has traditionally been defined.

What makes Kant an anti-realist is the further claim that we human knowers do not and cannot occupy the God's Eye point of view and thus cannot know things as they really are. He has, we might say, an Ideal Observer theory of the true and the real with God as the only possible Ideal Observer. So the distinction between the phenomenal and the noumenal, along with the equivalent distinction between appearances and things in themselves is for Kant the distinction between the perfect way God knows anything and the imperfect way we humans know that same reality. It is not an accident that the first two words of the *Critique of Pure Reason* are 'human reason'. The crucial issue in the realism/anti-realism debate is epistemic, not metaphysical. To define a realism that is incompatible with Kantian anti-realism we will require a double thesis, first metaphysical and then epistemic. Realism is the view (a) that the real is and is what it is independently of what, if anything, we may think or say about it, *and* (b) that we human knowers are capable of knowing it as it is in that independence, mirroring it without distortion.[6] Theological realism, our present concern, would be the special case of this double thesis applied to God.

Even when the need for this double thesis is sensed, it is all too easy to assume that the heart of the matter is the metaphysical thesis. Thus, for example, C. Stephen Evans, after speaking of realism in terms of 'a mind-independent reality, a reality that exists independently of human judgments and by virtue of which those judgments are true or false'[7] writes, 'What the antirealist denies is that human language can refer to [think about, talk about] the world as it is *in itself* …'.[8] But he then defines the antirealist as 'someone who denies there is any mind-independent reality'. Then, turning to the theological aspect of the question, he asks, 'Is God a metaphysical reality who exists independently of human consciousness? If so some kind of realism

---

5   For the detailed textual support of this claim, see my 'In Defense of the Thing in Itself', *Kant-Studien* 59/1 (1968), pp. 118–41.

6   I shall argue that the metaphysical thesis is secondary, that when anti-realists deny it, as they sometimes (but not always) at least seem to do, this is only as a corollary to their particular denial of the epistemic thesis. I use 'Kantian' to signify views that have a recognizable Kantian character, including, of course, Kant's own.

7   Kant holds this view. His theory of the thing in itself says, in effect, that all phenomenal knowledge, strictly speaking, is false, since it does not correspond to the way things really are, though it can have an objectivity that gives it a kind of minor league truth, truth with a lower case t. In the language of empirical realism, Newtonian physics is true, *the way the real ought to appear to a human observer*; it is *Erscheinung* and not *Schein*, appearance not illusion, fact, not fiction (or Fact). But in the language of transcendental idealism, it is False in terms of the classical definition of Truth as *adaequatio rei et intellectus*. Human understanding, even at its very best, is not the site of this *adaequatio*.

8   'Realism and antirealism', p. 155.

would seem to be presupposed'.[9] Some kind, no doubt, but not the kind that differs from Kantian anti-realism, for (forgive me if this is getting tiresome) Kant has no quarrel with such a view of God.[10] With reference to God, freedom, and immortality he writes, 'I have found it necessary to deny *knowledge*, in order to make room for *faith*'.[11] His rational faith is an antirealist faith not because it denies the independent existence of God but because it denies the possibility of our knowing God, or even thinking about God, as God truly is.

Of course, when one denies the independent reality of this or that (type of) entity, say universals, or the theoretical entities of sub-atomic physics, or God, one has denied the first thesis of realism as defined above with reference to that (type of) entity. But it is better to call such a person an existential anti-realist or, in the case of God, simply an atheist, than a Kantian anti-realist;[12] for the distinctive genius of Kantian anti-realism is the combination of metaphysical realism (the first thesis) with epistemic anti-realism (the second thesis).

Alvin Plantinga, recognizing a certain counterintuitive character to any Kantian style anti-realism, poses the question, 'What leads its protagonists to adopt it?'[13] As a protagonist of a version of Kantian theological anti-realism, I wish to respond to this question.[14] But first I want to distinguish the theory I'm trying to propound and defend from two other views presented by Plantinga, one sympathetically and one unsympathetically.

After critiquing the anti-realisms of Putnam and Rorty, Plantinga insists 'that anti-realism is not at all a mere confusion; there is strong intuitive support for it or something like it'. This intuition or impulse has the form of the question, 'How could there be truths totally independent of minds or persons?'[15] He attributes the view that there are such independent truths to Plato and calls it 'realism run amok; and it is this that the impulse towards anti-realism is an impulse *against*'. Plantinga then suggests that the theistic tradition is the proper satisfaction of this impulse, citing a passage from Aquinas. 'Even if there were no human intellects, there could be truths because of their relation to the divine intellect. But if, *per impossible*, there were no intellects at all, but things continued to exist, then there would be no such reality as truth.' Thus, Plantinga comments, 'truth is independent of our intellectual activity but not of God's' because, on the view in question, 'truth and *being believed by God* are distinct but necessarily coextensive properties ...'.[16] On this view, propositions necessarily have the property of '*being true if and only if believed*

9   'Realism and antirealism', p. 156.

10   Nor need those who follow in his footsteps, though, of course, some Kantians do have such a quarrel.

11   *Critique of Pure Reason*, B xxx.

12   Alvin Plantinga makes this helpful distinction in 'How to Be', p. 48.

13   'How to Be', p. 54.

14   For an earlier discussion of these issues, see my 'Christian Philosophers and the Copernican Revolution' in *Overcoming Onto-theology* (New York: Fordham University Press, 2001), pp. 89–105.

15   'How to Be', p. 67.

16   It looks as if Aquinas was a Kantian before Kant was, as I have argued in *Transcendence and Self-transcendence: On God and the Soul* (Bloomington: Indiana University Press, 2004), ch. 5.

by God. Plantinga concludes, 'So how can we sensibly be anti-realists? Easily enough: by being theists'.[17]

This *theistic anti-realism*, as we might call it, is an integral part of Kant's anti-realism both because he is, at least as I read him, a quite classical theist[18] and because this claim, which makes God the measure of the true and the real, is essential to his crucial contrast between divine and human knowledge. But by itself, precisely because it does not draw that contrast, this *theistic anti-realism* is not the *Kantian anti-realism* here under consideration and *a fortiori* not the *theological anti-realism* I defend as a special case thereof. It leaves open the possibility that our knowledge, if not essentially at least occasionally, is a perfect duplicate of God's, in which case we know things as they are in themselves.[19] Kantian anti-realism, while it may presuppose some version of this theistic anti-realism, is most distinctively a claim not about divine knowledge but about human knowledge.[20] In Kant's case and my own, it *explicitly* draws a sharp, essential contrast between the real as seen by God and the real as seen by us, even in our most excellent epistemic exploits. So, while affirming theistic anti-realism, Plantinga is free to abominate Kantian anti-realism and all its works, including theological anti-realism.

There is a second view I wish to contrast with Kantian anti-realism as I understand it, and that is Kantian anti-realism as Plantinga understands it or 'creative anti-realism' as he calls it. Distinguishing the existential anti-realist from the Kantian anti-realist, he writes, 'Kant didn't deny, of course, that there are such things as horses, houses, planets and stars; not did he deny that these things are material objects. Instead his characteristic claim is that their existence and fundamental structure have been conferred on them by the conceptual activity of [human] persons ... Such structures as those of space and time, object and property, truth and falsehood – these are not to be found in the world as such, but are constituted by our own noetic activity'. Turning to the theological dimension, Plantinga calls creative anti-realism 'the view that there is such a person as God, all right, but he owes his existence to our noetic activity' and he calls this view 'at best a bit strained' and 'at best a piece of laughable bravado'.[21]

---

17 'How to Be', pp. 68–70, citing Aquinas from *De Veritate* Q. 1, A. 6 Respondeo.

18 Let us remember that one can be a theist without accepting the theistic proofs and, as I shall argue, while being a theological anti-realist (in a Kantian sense of that term).

19 In this case Kantian anti-realism can be replaced by a robust (or is it arrogant?) realism as defined by the two-pronged definition given above. It is my impression that this fallibilist, anti-Kantian realism is shared by Descartes (at least in relation to the world) and Plantinga. Such a view quite naturally presupposes a Platonic view of propositions that is anything but self-evident. See my 'Taking Plantinga Seriously: Advice to Christian Philosophers', *Faith and Philosophy*, 16/2 (April 1999), pp. 173–81.

20 Which is why the Kantian tradition can include both theists and atheists.

21 'How to Be', pp. 48–9, 54. Plantinga's hostility to 'creative anti-realism' is expressed in his Stob Lectures in the claim that the two primary opponents of Christian theism are perennial naturalism going back to Epicurus, Democritus, and Lucretius, and creative anti-realism going back to Protagoras. *The Twin Pillars of Christian Scholarship* (published as a pamphlet by Calvin College and Seminary, Grand Rapids MI, 1990), pp. 14–15. See also Part I of *Warranted Christian Belief* (New York: Oxford University Press, 2000).

Given this account, it is not surprising that Plantinga is unsympathetic to this anti-realism, both in its general and in its specifically theological form. But unless properly qualified it is neither Kant's view nor the Kantian anti-realism I wish to defend. Plantinga qualifies his claim that the existence of the world and of God owe their existence to our noetic activity with a 'perhaps' and an 'if they couldn't exist without displaying that structure', namely the structure they do in our experience and thought.[22] But that insufficiently illuminates the ambiguity of the claim that they owe their existence and structure to our noetic activity. In one sense that is trivially true, but in another sense it is simply false.

A homely illustration will help us make the necessary distinctions. Suppose I turn on the TV to watch a football game.[23] The brightly coloured uniforms will appear to be various shades of grey, because I am watching on a black and white set. What we have here is a pretty good model of the Kantian view of things, for he views the human mind as a kind of receiving and processing apparatus not unlike the black and white TV set. It gives us access to the real, but not direct and undistorted access. The three-dimensional world with brightly coloured uniforms is the noumenal world, the world of things in themselves, the *world as it appears to those who are there*. The two-dimensional, shades-of-grey world is the phenomenal world, the world of appearances, the *world as it does and should appear to anyone watching on the black and white set, assuming it is properly functioning*. We can make the following, Kantian observations about the situation:

1. There is only one game and I am watching it. I am in touch with the real.
2. This game is real independently of my watching or even thinking about it.
3. I do not see this game as it is in itself, in all its glorious colour, because I am not in a position to do so. I am observing it indirectly through a receiving and processing apparatus that (a) presents it to me but (b) systematically distorts it in the process.
4. Although there is only one game going on, I could speak of two games or two sets of uniforms if I wanted to make an epistemic point. In other words, I could distinguish the game *as it appears to any perceiver who has direct, undistorted access to it* from the game *as it appears to any perceiver who has only indirect, distorted access to it*.
5. It is trivially true that the latter game owes its existence to the activity of TV sets. If there were no such sets there would be no shades-of-grey uniforms nor true and false judgements about them,[24] though there would still be true and false judgements about the real, bright uniforms of which the grey ones are (mis)representations.
6. While it would be 'a bit strained' or 'laughable bravado' to say that the game itself owed its existence to the black and white TV sets, it would also be plainly false and a deep misunderstanding of the situation. The brightly coloured game could and would go on quite nicely in the absence of any

---

22 'How to Be', pp. 48 and 50.
23 Take your pick, American football or 'soccer'.
24 Excepting counterfactuals.

observers watching it on black and white sets. The only game that owes its existence to the TV sets is the game *as seen by means of those sets*, which is not the game itself.

7. Insofar as the term 'creative' anti-realism connotes or even entails this misunderstanding, it is thoroughly misleading. To be sure, the TV sets might be said to 'create' the world that would disappear with their disappearance. But this language would be misleading unless accompanied by the constant reminder that it is not the game (or the world or God) who disappears, but only a certain (type of) thought or perception of them. A less misleading phrase would be distortive anti-realism, though of course it is not anti-realism as a theory that creates or distorts but the TV set or the human mind for which it stands.

One further clarification is needed. The version of Kantian, theological anti-realism I wish to defend holds (a) that both the world and God are and are what they are independently of what, if anything, we may think or say about them (no quarrel with the realist here – remember the thing in itself), and (b) that we human knowers are not capable of knowing them as they are in that independence, mirroring without distortion the way they are known to God.[25] But there are Kantian anti-realists whose position differs significantly and for whom, accordingly, the language of misperception and distortion are not fitting and for whom the independence of the world is considerably mitigated. I shall call them Rortian by analogy with 'Kantian', to signify both Richard Rorty's position, as I understand it, and a number of related positions that bear a strong family resemblance thereto.[26]

Rortian anti-realism begins with two significant departures from Kant. First, it is atheistic; theologically speaking it is an existential anti-realism.[27] But since it is not an existential anti-realism in relation to the world, it has a significant family resemblance to Kant's theory and belongs to the Kantian family. Second, in place of a single, universal receiving and representing apparatus, it interprets human understanding in terms of a plurality of paradigms, horizons, systems of construal, conceptual schemes, pre-understandings, language games, epistemes, call them what you will. While Kant would not welcome this pluralism of the *a priori* (unless he were alive today), Rortians are nevertheless a species of Kantians because they hold that human understanding is not a direct, intuitive mirroring of the real but an act of construal that reflects the (historically contingent and particular) nature of the subject and not just that of the object. The Copernican revolution is alive and well here.

---

25 'Distortion' and 'misperception' do not signify a failure of our cognitive apparatus to be properly functioning but only its 'failure' to occupy the God's Eye point of view, to see God and the world through divine eyes.

26 At the very least it does not appeal to God as an actual knower, so perhaps Kaufman and Hick, as critiqued by Plantinga in *Warranted Christian Belief,* belong to this particular species of Kantian anti-realism.

27 As presented in *Philosophy and the Mirror of Nature* (Princeton: Princeton University Press, 1979) and *Contingency, irony, and solidarity* (Cambridge: Cambridge University Press, 1989).

The third element in Rortian anti-realism is the quite Kantian denial that any version of human understanding can occupy the God's Eye view of the world and give us the world in itself. But neither can God, who does not exist, and so the thing in itself disappears. There is no Ideal Observer, only a diverse plurality of human, all too human observers.[28] Sharing with Plantinga the anti-realist intuition that truth cannot be entirely independent of minds, Rortians find the notion of THE world or THE truth no longer meaningful since there is no mind whose construals are THE measure of the real. In the absence of any mind, human or divine, whose beliefs would stand in an if and only if relation to the true and thus to the real, Rorty himself prefers to talk about tools and coping rather than about truth as correspondence or mirroring.

We should notice several things about our friends the Rortians.

1. They are but one species of Kantian anti-realism, and objections to their views are not necessarily objections to Kantianism as such and its Copernican Revolution.[29]
2. They deny, or at least seem to deny, that the world is and is what it is independently of what, if anything, we may think or say about it. So they provide whatever excuse there may be for talking as if the issue were about 'metaphysical realism', a quarrel between realists who affirm this independence and Kantians who deny it.
3. But, so far from being the essence of Kantianism, this denial is not even the essence of Rortianism. This metaphysical claim about the world, if that is what it is, is rather a corollary of the epistemic claim about the relativity of human understanding to a variety of perspectives combined with an atheism that forbids making God the Ideal Observer that we can never be.
4. Finally, the Rortian abandonment of the in itself is more nuanced than is sometimes noticed. While it would be misleading to use the language of distortion or misperception here, it would be equally misleading to speak of 'creative' anti-realism, for the world as we perceive it is, in good Kantian fashion, the product of our perspectives AND a world not of our making. Rorty insists on 'a distinction between the claim that the world is out there and the claim that truth is out there. To say that the world is out there, that it is not our creation, is to say, with common sense, that most things in space and time are the effects of causes which do not include human mental states'. To say that the truth is not out there is to say that there are no descriptions, vocabularies,

---

28 The Nietzschean reference is not accidental. Rortian pragmatism and Nietzschean perspectivism, if not identical twins, at least bear a strong family resemblance to one another.

29 In addition to Kant's version and the Rortian, there is also the Peircean version. Without appealing to God as the actual Ideal Observer, Peirce's pragmatism, unlike Rorty's, retains the notions of Truth and The Real by making the Ideal Observer a regulative ideal of human understanding. He writes, 'The opinion which is fated to be ultimately agreed to by all who investigate, is what we mean by the truth, and the object represented in this opinion is the real'. Charles Hartshorne and Paul Weiss (eds), *Collected Papers of Charles Sanders Peirce* (Cambridge: Harvard University Press, 1931–35), 5:407. I believe Habermas and Sellars are Peircean Kantians, and I find it helpful to think the same about Gadamer, Kuhn, and Quine, though that is perhaps not as clear.

or language games out there, that these are both necessary conditions for truth and human creations. 'The world does not speak. Only we do. The world can, once we have programmed ourselves with a language, cause us to hold beliefs. But it cannot propose a language for us to speak. Only other human beings can do that.'[30] The world's constraints on our belief are filtered through our language games but they are not created by our language games. In both respects Rortians belong to the Kantian family.

*

I turn now to the long postponed question Plantinga asks about Kantian anti-realists, 'What leads its protagonists to adopt it?' I shall offer reasons for being a theological anti-realist, though some of the reasons will offer support for a broader anti-realism. The view in question holds (a) that God is and is what God is independently of what, if anything, we may think or say about God, *and* (b) that we human knowers are not capable of knowing God as God truly is, mirroring without distortion the divine self-knowledge which stands in an if and only if relation to God's being. As an overtly theistic theory, this one sides with Kant and against the Rortians and the Peirceans.[31] Its Copernican Revolution draws an emphatic distinction between divine and human knowing.[32] But it sides with the Rortians and at least many of the Peirceans in holding to an historically pluralized understanding of the of the human mind as a receiving and representing apparatus. I speak of THE world and THE divine mind, but not of THE *a priori* conditions of possible experience. I think the question, Whose Reason? Which Rationality? is always appropriate.[33] So then, why hold to this fourth species of Kantian anti-realism? I offer three types of reason, some of which, but not all, might well be found compelling by theistic and non-theistic thinkers alike.

The Metaphysics of Finitude

The basic intuition here is quite simple: *finitum non est capax infiniti*. The human mind is finite and suited to grasp finite realities. But God is infinite and will always exceed our grasp. Our images and our concepts will never be able to pass the adequation test when applied to God (though they may well be adequate to lead us to saving faith and holy living).

Pseudo-Dionysius sums up this line of thought by saying that God is only known by God. He writes

> For, if we may trust the superlative wisdom and truth of scripture, the things of God are revealed to each mind in proportion to its capacities; and the divine goodness is such that, out of concern for our salvation, it deals out the immeasurable and infinite in limited measures. Just as the senses can neither grasp nor perceive the things of the mind . . . by the same standard of truth beings are surpassed by the infinity beyond being, intelligences

---

30 *Contingency*, pp. 4–6.
31 See note 29 above.
32 Of God and everything else, for that matter.
33 With apologies to Alasdair MacIntyre.

by that oneness which is beyond intelligence. Indeed the inscrutable One is out of the reach of every rational process. Nor can any words come up to the inexpressible Good, this One, this Source of all unity, this supra-existent Being. Mind beyond mind, word beyond speech, it is gathered up by no discourse, by no intuition, by no name. It is and it is as no other being is. Cause of all existence, and therefore itself transcending existence, *it alone could give an authoritative account of what it really is.*[34]

It is worth noting that this comes, not in *The Mystical Theology*, which tells us how not to speak of God, but in *The Divine Name*, which tells us precisely how to speak of God. Mystical silence, yes; but human discourse as well, though we are only to use the names given to us in scripture, where we find that 'authoritative account'. But lest we think that by means of divine revelation we are raised above all the 'negative theology' of the passage just cited, Dionysius continues

In the scriptures the Deity has benevolently taught us that understanding and direct contemplation of itself is inaccessible to beings, since it actually surpasses being. Many scripture writers will tell you that the divinity is not only invisible and incomprehensible, but also 'unsearchable and inscrutable', since there is not a trace for anyone who would reach through into the hidden depths of *this infinity*. And yet, on the other hand, the Good is *not absolutely incommunicable* to everything. By itself it generously reveals a firm, transcendent beam, granting *enlightenments proportionate to each being*, and thereby draws sacred minds upward to its permitted contemplation, to *participation* and to the state of *becoming like it.*[35]

It is also worth noting that Pseudo-Dionysius is not starting something new but rather expressing a broad consensus in the church. In his response to Jacques Derrida on 'negative theology', Jean-Luc Marion lists the following as having a strong apophatic dimension to their theologies: Justin Martyr, Athenagoras, Clement of Alexandria, Origen, Athanasius, Basil, Gregory of Nyssa, John Chrysostom, and John of Damascus from the eastern church, along with Augustine from the western church.[36]

Augustine is not shy about describing God; but at the same time he recognizes the inadequacy of human thought and language to mirror the divine. He writes:

You, my God, are supreme, utmost in goodness, mightiest and all-powerful, most merciful and most just. You are the most hidden from us and yet the most present amongst us, the most beautiful and yet the most strong, ever enduring and yet we cannot comprehend you ... Can any man say enough when he speaks of you? Yet woe betide those who are silent about you! For even those who are most gifted with speech cannot find words to describe you.[37]

---

34 *The Divine Names*, in Colm Luibheid (trans.), *Pseudo-Dionysius: The Complete Works* (New York: Paulist Press, 1987), pp. 49–50, emphasis added.

35 *The Divine Names*, p. 50, emphasis added. The editor takes the quoted words to be a reference to Romans 11:33.

36 'In the Name: How to Avoid Speaking of "Negative Theology"', in John D. Caputo and Michael J. Scanlon (eds), *God, the Gift, and Postmodernism* (Bloomington: Indiana University Press, 1999), pp. 34–35.

37 *Confessions*, I, 4. For a fuller treatment on Augustine on this point, see ch. 4 of *Transcendence and Self-Transcendence*.

Nor is Augustine unique in the west on this point. The apophatic affirmation of the incomprehensibility of God is crucial for John Scotus Eriugena, Hugh and Richard of St. Victor, Gilbert of Poitiers, Robert Grosseteste, Albert the Great, Thomas Aquinas, and Bonaventure.[38] *The Cloud of Unknowing* might be said to summarize the mystical side of these traditions:

> And then I think that soon after you will have a true knowledge and experience of God as he is: *not as he is in himself, for no one can experience that except God himself,* nor as you shall experience him in blessedness, both body and soul together, but in as much as this is possible, and as it is his good pleasure to be known and experienced by a humble soul living in this mortal body.[39]

For the more strictly metaphysical side of these traditions, Aquinas is both eloquent and unambiguous. Like many of those already named, he has strong neo-Platonic elements in his thought and speaks the language of participation which signifies an ontological ground for the epistemic dialectic embodied in the citations from Augustine and Pseudo-Dionysius. Only God knows God as God truly is, but when, either by nature or by grace we participate in that self-knowledge, there is a dialectic of affirmation and negation. We know and yet don't know. It is as if the ancient and medieval Christian traditions have been reading Heidegger when he insists that unconcealment and concealment are inseparable.[40]

But Aquinas also speaks Aristotelian with its emphasis on the ineluctable dependence of human knowledge on the senses. Knowledge occurs when the intellect grasps the essence of its object. When the form in the intellect is (non-numerically) identical with the form in the object, truth occurs as the *adaequatio rei et intellectus*. This is the language of mathematical equations, where one side is exactly equal to the other. But all our concepts are derived by abstraction from sensible reality. 'In the state of the present life, in which the soul is united to a corruptible body, it is impossible for our intellect to understand anything actually, except by turning to phantasms.'[41] By virtue of this *nisi convertendo se ad phantasmata*, Aquinas regularly insists that in this life we are not able to see the essence of God.[42] The doctrine of analogical predication is a reminder that none of our judgements about God can pass the adequation test, whether they are derived from reason or revelation. *Strictly speaking* they are all False, for Aquinas is among the foremost in defining truth in terms of adequation. This does not mean, as any reader can easily see, that

---

38   The list is drawn from Jean Leclercq, 'Influence and Noninfluence of Dionysius in the Western Middle Ages', in *Pseudo-Dionysius: The Complete Works*, pp. 26–9 and could easily be extended.

39   James Walsh, S.J. (ed.), *The Cloud of Unknowing* (New York: Paulist Press, 1981), ch. XIV, emphasis added.

40   See, for example, *Identity and Difference*, trans. Joan Stambaugh (New York: Harper & Row, 1969), pp. 64–7.

41   *S.T.*, I, Q. 84, A. 7. See Karl Rahner's sustained commentary in *Spirit in the World*, trans. William Dych, S.J. (New York: Continuum, 1994).

42   For a detailed textual study see John F. Wippel, 'Quidditative Knowledge of God', in his *Metaphysical Themes in Thomas Aquinas* (Washington, D.C.: Catholic University of America Press, 1984).

Aquinas does not affirm some ways of speaking about God as appropriate to our finite capacity and thus true (but not True), while others are inappropriate and thus false, or that he denies that the truth available to us by revelation is adequate for our salvation and moral guidance.[43]

Aquinas is no mere fallibilist here, asserting that sometimes we get it Wrong but sometimes we get it Right. With many voices of Christian tradition he makes the finitude of our knowledge of God qualitative and not merely quantitative. Our inability to think or talk about God as God truly is systemic.

Then, as if to rub salt into the wound, he insists that we will have to remain Kantians in heaven. In the life to come we will be able by divine grace to see the divine essence, but God will still exceed our grasp essentially and not only occasionally. No longer dependent on the senses, the intellect remains finite.

> Now no created intellect can know God infinitely. For a created intellect knows the divine essence more or less perfectly in proportion as it receives a greater or lesser light of glory. Since therefore the created light of glory received into any created intellect cannot be infinite, it is clearly impossible for any created intellect to know God in an infinite degree. Hence it is impossible that it should comprehend God.[44]

Or again, commenting on 'We shall see Him as He is' (I John 3. 2), he writes, 'But what is supremely knowable in itself may not be knowable to a particular intellect, because of the excess of the intelligible object above the intellect . . . Hence it does not follow that [God] cannot be known at all, but that He transcends all knowledge: which means that He is not comprehended.'[45] Aquinas is a Kantian anti-realist with reference to God because he is a theist who distinguishes Creator from creature.

Although Reformation traditions are not especially friendly to neo-Platonism, Aristotle, or Pseudo-Dionysius, they are Augustinian, and were it not for limitations of space and fear of overkill, these motifs could be traced in Luther and Calvin. Instead I shall let Karl Barth speak for these traditions when he warns against thinking of the revelation in Christ 'as though it were a visible thing in the midst of other visible things, and not, on the contrary, visible only in its invisibility'.[46] Actually, with such talk he sums up a far wider and more ecumenical swath of Christian tradition than that of the Reformation, as indeed he does when he later writes,

> God is known only by God. We do not know Him, then, in virtue of the intuitions and concepts with which in faith we attempt to respond to His revelation. But we also do not know Him without making use of His permission and obeying His command to undertake this attempt. The success of this undertaking, and therefore the veracity of our human

43 I'm quite sure my teacher, Kenneth Kantzer, was thinking about Calvin, but he might have been thinking of Augustine, Pseudo-Dionysius, or Aquinas, when he spoke of the Bible as the divinely revealed misinformation about God. Here one hears neither simple affirmation nor simple negation.

44 *S.T.*, I, Q. 12, A. 7. Like Kant's anti-realism, Aquinas' rests on the distinction between Creator and creature.

45 *S.T.* I, Q. 12, A. 2.

46 *The Epistle to the Romans*, trans. Edwyn C. Hoskyns from the sixth edition (New York: Oxford University Press, 1968), p. 92.

knowledge of God, consists in the fact that our intuiting and conceiving is adopted and determined to participation in the truth of God by God Himself in grace.[47]

Except in the case of Barth, it may seem a bit anachronistic to call all these voices from Christian tradition Kantian. But I think it is clear that they affirm the two theses that define Kantian, theological anti-realism: (a) God's reality is independent of human thought, and (b) human thought and discourse never grasp God as God truly is. At times implicitly and at times explicitly, the second thesis is made in terms of the distinction between the way God knows God and the way we know God, the very heart of Kant's own anti-realism.

No doubt a search of these sources would find a rich variety of appeals to scriptural texts that are seen to suggest the radical finitude of human understanding found in the Platonic discourse of participation and the Aristotelian discourse of analogy. For example,

> For my thoughts are not your thoughts,
>   nor are your ways my ways, says the LORD
> For as the heavens are higher than the earth,
>   So are my ways higher than your ways
>   Any my thoughts than your thoughts. (Isa. 55:8–9 NRSV)

Or again,

> For now we see in a mirror, dimly, [in a riddle, ἐν αἰνίγματι]
> but then we will see face to face.
> Now I know only in part; then I will know fully,
> even as I have been fully known (1 Cor. 13:12 NRSV).

The Hermeneutics of Finitude

In Kant's own distinction between divine and human knowing the contrast between time and eternity is at least as basic as that between finite and infinite. The reason why such categories such as unity, causality, or existence cannot be applied to things in themselves is because as we employ them they are all schematized as modes of temporality, whereas God, and only God, sees all things, including God, *sub specie aeternitatis*. In other words, the problem in the case of God is not that God is not one, is not cause, or does not exist, but that we cannot employ these categories univocally to God. Just as for Aquinas our concepts are infected with the finitude of the senses, so for Kant our categories are infected with time as the form of both inner and outer sense.

---

47   G. W. Bromiley and T. F. Torrance (eds), *Church Dogmatics*, II/1, *The Doctrine of the Word of God* (Edinburgh: T & T Clark, 1957), p. 179. I have changed the translation of *Anschaungen* and *anschauen* to 'intuitions' and 'intuiting' to highlight the Kantian character of Barth's vocabulary, unfortunately obscured by rendering them 'views' and 'viewing'. Note well the language of participation. Nor should his insistence that the analogy of being be replaced by the analogy of faith lead us to overlook his dependence on the language of analogy. See ch. 6 of *Transcendence and Self-Transcendence*.

If Aquinas is a Kantian, Kant is no less a Thomist with an implicit doctrine of analogy. My teacher, Wilfrid Sellars, understood this when he used to say that things in themselves were in 'sprace' and 'trime'.

Even theists who want to say that God is somehow in time, everlasting rather than eternal,[48] could, and I would think should, draw a qualitative distinction between God's temporality and human temporality as it 'infects' knowledge, thus distinguishing between knowledge of things in themselves and knowledge of things as they appear to human knowers.

One can think of Kant's distinction between time and eternity as just another metaphysical way of distinguishing finite from Infinite, creature from Creator. But already in Kant's century, with thinkers such as Montesquieu and Herder, and then with a host of thinkers in the following two centuries, led by Hegel and Nietzsche, human knowledge came to be seen as infected not merely with time as a mode of sensation but even more profoundly with time in the mode of history. Reason was seen to be finite by virtue of its embeddedness, not merely in the body (which can be thought of as a universal condition of human understanding, at least as long as gender is ignored), but also in the contingencies and particularities of language and culture. Embedded reason is a matter of paradigms, presuppositions, pre-understandings, or perspectives; in other words, reason is not one but many. Whose reason? Which rationality? 'Human reason' cannot occupy the God's Eye point of view, given the contingent and conditioned character of each conceptual scheme; accordingly only arrogance could claim for any one of the Baskin Robbins 31 flavours of reason that it is both superior to all other extant versions and unsurpassable by any possible successor. In the language of philosophy of science, what paradigm would claim be the ultimate paradigm, precluding all possible future revolutions?

This pluralistic understanding of the *a priori* can be called the hermeneutics of finitude. It is a hermeneutical understanding of the finitude of human understanding (a) because it takes all understanding (and not just the reading of texts) to be interpretation, construal, seeing-as that is underdetermined by its object, and (b) because it understands interpretation to take place within the hermeneutical circle, which means, of course, within a variety of such circles. Understanding is guided and governed by pre-understanding, judgement by pre-judgement (pre-judice),[49] normal science by a paradigm. Instead of the linear relation between the *a priori* and the experience (= judgement, as Kant has it) whose condition it is, the relation is circular because each *a priori* or governing perspective, being the product of contingent historical processes, is at both revisable and replaceable.[50] To speak of historical (cultural, linguistic) processes is to remind ourselves that we are speaking

---

48 For example, Nicholas Wolterstorff. See 'God Everlasting', in Stephen M. Cahn and David Shatz (eds), *Contemporary Philosophy of Religion* (New York: Oxford University Press, 1982), pp. 77–98.

49 See Hans-Georg Gadamer, *Truth and Method*, 2nd ed. rev., trans. Joel Weinsheimer and Donald G. Marshall (New York: Crossroad, 1991), pp. 265–307 on the rehabilitation of pre-judice. For my interpretation of the hermeneutical turn, see chs. 3 and 6–8 of *Overcoming Onto-theology*.

50 See Gadamer, *Truth and Method*, p. 267.

of language games, socially shared forms of life, interwoven complexes of belief and practice, which become the perspectives to which various interpretations of this or that are internal.

Although Kant's ahistorical understanding of human finitude has been replaced here by an historical interpretation of understanding as interpretation, the hermeneutical turn retains a clearly Kantian character. The 'object' of our experience and judgement is neither mere fact nor mere fiction but the product of the real and the receiving apparatus through which it is filtered in becoming present to us. As Gadamer reminds us, because understanding is interpretation, it is 'not merely a reproductive but always a productive activity as well'.[51] That was true of our black and white TV above, but given the historicized, pluralized account of the *a priori* now before us, another model might be helpful. Consider racists. They know *a priori* that individuals from certain groups are morally and intellectual inferior to them because the receiving and representing apparatus (racist language game) only permits such individuals to appear to them under those conditions. What people in another language game might consider evidence to the contrary will be ignored or explained away, if necessary. Most of the time it will not be necessary, because our racists will 'just see' the victims of their racism to be inferior, even subhuman. This model fits the hermeneutics of finitude because this pre-judice is both particular (not everyone is a racist) and contingent (the conditions of its existence might disappear, taking it with them).

The Hermeneutics of Suspicion

Our racism example points us in a third direction, namely that our thinking and talking about God do not correspond to God's reality because they are distorted by our fallenness. Elsewhere I have described the hermeneutics of suspicion, which is a radicalization or deepening of the hermeneutical turn, as '*the deliberate attempt to expose the self-deceptions involved in hiding our actual operative motives from ourselves, individually or collectively, in order not to notice how and how much our behavior and our beliefs are shaped by values we profess to disown*'.[52] Paul Ricoeur calls Marx, Nietzsche, and Freud the 'masters' of the 'school of suspicion',[53] but I call them the great, secular theologians of original sin. Not only do they expose the self-deceptions by which personal and corporate sin hides itself from itself; they also show how shameful desire distorts not only our practices but also our beliefs. Thus do we edit God to our convenience.

There is a theological tradition that stretches from Augustine through Luther and Calvin to Kierkegaard and Barth that places great emphasis on the noetic effects of sin. The biblical source is most especially Paul, who announces the wrath of God 'against all ungodliness and wickedness of those who by their wickedness suppress

---

51 *Truth and Method*, p. 296.

52 *Suspicion and Faith: The Religious Uses of Modern Atheism* (New York: Fordham University Press, 1998), p. 13.

53 *Freud and Philosophy*, trans. Denis Savage (New Haven: Yale University Press, 1970), p. 32.

the truth', so that 'they became futile in their thinking, and their senseless minds were darkened. Claiming to be wise, they became fools', with idolatry as the result (Rom. 1:18–23).

Discussing the hermeneutics of suspicion with students at a Christian college, I once said that I suspected I had never prayed to a God who wasn't an idol. They were horrified, but they began to see my point when I explained (1) that I believed the God who heard my prayers was no idol, but the living God, and (2) that God as I intended, represented, conceived of God was always an imperfect, distorted approximation, not only in relation to God's inherent reality but even in relation to God as we humans ought to think of God. Not only the finitude of our createdness but also the fallenness of our current condition keeps our God-talk from being the mirror of the divine nature.

The two crucial premises at work here are (1) that sin darkens the intellect just as it degrades the will, and (2) that believers are not immune to the noetic effects of sin. It seems to me that there is abundant support, both theological and philosophical, for these claims. With regard to the second point, saving faith is not total sanctification, and believers who acknowledge that residual sin distorts their love of God and neighbour (and themselves, for that matter) should also acknowledge that it damages their knowledge.

For these three (types of) reasons, I say to philosophers and theologians alike, so how can we sensibly be theists? Easily enough: by being anti-realists.

Chapter 9

God's Aseity

John Webster

Philosophers of religion and dogmatic theologians often eye one another over the ramparts. Like most disputes, theirs has a history (perhaps several), simplified and distorted versions of which are rehearsed by their respective adherents, which satisfy their narrators yet fail to enlighten them. Tensions may be eased, however, and friendly relations fostered, by careful, courteous and self-critical self-explanation. What follows tries to do this from the side of Christian dogmatics by some doctrinal and historical remarks on a concept in which both philosophers of religion and theologians have had considerable, if somewhat differently distributed, investment: the aseity of God. The concept is a keenly sensitive register of the divergences between some kinds of philosophical and theological inquiry, over such matters as the sources of teaching about God, the relation of non-biblical concepts to Scripture, the ways in which classical Christian texts are most fittingly read, and the ends of an intellectual conception of God. It also illustrates the way in which – particularly over the last three hundred years or so – the fault lines do not simply run between philosophy and theology but often across them.

I

What Christian doctrine has to say about the attributes of God is shaped by the church's confession of the Holy Trinity. When it inquires into divine aseity, therefore, theology is not asking 'What must be true of a god?', but a rather more unwieldy question: 'Who is the God, the enactment of whose utter sufficiency as Father, Son and Holy Spirit includes his creative, reconciling and perfecting works towards his creatures?' A Christian theology of the divine attributes is a conceptual schema for indicating the identity of the God of the Christian confession. God's identity is, further, to be considered both with respect to its unfathomable depth in itself and with respect to his enactment of a wholly gracious turn to creatures. That is, a theology of God's attributes attempts to describe his immanent and his relative perfection. Within such an account, the concept of aseity indicates the glory and plenitude of the life of the Holy Trinity in its self-existent and self-moving originality, its underived fullness. In every respect, God is of himself God. God's originality and fullness, moreover, form the ground of his self-communication. He is one who, out of nothing other than his own self-sufficiency, brings creatures into being, sustains and reconciles them, and brings them to perfection in fellowship with himself. A theology of God's aseity is an indication of the one who is and acts *thus*, who is the object of the church's knowledge, love and fear, and whose praise is the church's chief employment.

The concept of aseity tries to indicate God's identity; it seeks not so much to offer a comprehensive definition of God as to point towards God's objective and self-expressive form. The task of the concept is not to establish conditions for conceivability but rather to have rational dealings with the God who is, and is self-communicative, anterior to rational work on our part. God is objective and expressive form, enacting a particular identity, presenting himself to us as a specific gestalt, and so making himself perceptible, intelligible and nameable (this is part of the meaning of 'revelation'). Consequently, in theology aseity is a positive or material concept, determined by the particular form of God's self-expressive perfection. Its content is governed by those acts in which God enacts his being before us and so gives himself to be known. Because of this, theology will not over-invest in whatever generic sense may be attached to the concept of aseity (or of any of the other divine attributes). This, not because of intellectual sectarianism, a desire to segregate the *usus theologicus* in an absolute way from all other speech about deity – after all, aseity, like nearly all Christian theological concepts, is a borrowed term with a wider currency. Rather, theology is simply concerned to ensure that its talk of aseity concentrates on that which is proper to *this one*, on what Kaufman calls 'the particular concreteness of the self-existent one'.[1]

All this is simply an application of the rule which is basic to the Christian doctrine of the Trinity: *deus non est in genere*. Concepts developed in articulating the Christian doctrine of God, including the concept of aseity, are fitting insofar as they correspond to the particular being of the triune God in his self-moved self-presentation. A further extension of this rule is that in theological usage aseity is not primarily a comparative or contrastive concept. That is, the content of the term cannot be determined simply by analysis of the difference between God and contingent creatures. Although the contrast between divine self-existence and creaturely contingency is a corollary of the concept of God's aseity, disorder threatens when that contrast is allowed to expand and fill the concept completely. The point is worth pausing over, especially because the modern career of notions of aseity and self-existence has been quite deeply marked by comparative interpretations, particularly by theologians and philosophers with heavy investments in natural religion and its theological derivatives.

That there can be a relatively uncontroversial appeal to the contrastive aspects of divine aseity, and that such appeal has a long history in Christian theology, is beyond dispute. This way of filling out the content of aseity is used to best effect when deployed in an informal, non-fundamental way, simply for the purposes of

---

1   G. D. Kaufman, *Systematic Theology: An Historicist Perspective* (New York: Scribner's, 1968), p. 152, n. 8. Barth, similarly, proposes that 'a doctrine of the divine attributes is strictly to be understood and expounded as that which alone it can be – a repetition and development of the being of God': K. Barth, *Church Dogmatics* II/1 (Edinburgh: T&T Clark, 1957), p. 340. See further the impressive essay by J. Ringleben, 'Gottes Sein, Handeln und Werden. Ein Beitrag zum Gespräch mit Wolfhart Pannenberg', in *Arbeit am Gottesbegriff. Bd 1: Reformatorische Grundlegung, Gotteslehre, Eschatologie* (Tübingen: MohrSiebeck, 2004), pp. 203–34: 'Nur wenn Gott das *esse a se* nicht nur faktisch zukommt, sondern er auch *a se* und *per se* das *esse a se* und *ex seipso* hat, ist Aseität ganz aus sich, d.h. *ihm*, selbst gedacht' (p. 227).

explication and elucidation, and not as a guide to the entire scope of the concept. Consider two passages from Augustine:

> See, heaven and earth exist, they cry aloud that they are made, for they suffer change and variation. But in anything which is not made and yet is, there is nothing which previously was not present. To be what was once not the case is to be subject to change and variation. They also cry aloud that they have not made themselves: 'The manner of our existence shows that we are made. For before we came to be, we did not exist to be able to make ourselves.' And the voice with which they speak is self-evidence. You, Lord, who are beautiful, made them for they are beautiful. You are good, for they are good. You are, for they are. Yet they are not beautiful or good or possessed of being in the sense that you their Maker are. In comparison with you they are deficient in beauty and goodness and being.[2]

> God exists in the supreme sense, and the original sense, of the word. He is altogether unchangeable, and it is he who could say with full authority 'I am who I am'.[3]

The changeless dignity and beauty of God's uncreated being, because it 'exists in the supreme sense', are ultimately beyond comparison. They can also be glimpsed by contrast with what is 'made': 'You are, for they are'. Yet there is no sense that God's supreme, self-existent being somehow requires this contrast with the creaturely, as a kind of background without which its splendour could not be seen. God simply *is*, originally, authoritatively and incomparably, and no creature can say, as does God, 'I am who I am'.

Something of the same pattern of thought can be found in Anselm (towards whom 'perfect being theology' often expresses much devotion):

> You alone then, Lord, are what you are and you are who you are ... And what began [to exist] from non-existence, and can be thought not to exist, and returns to non-existence unless it subsists through some other; and what has had a past existence but does not now exist, and a future existence but does not yet exist – such a thing does not exist in a strict and absolute sense. But you are what you are, for whatever you are at any time or in any way this you are wholly and forever.[4]

> He alone has of himself all that he has, while other things have nothing of themselves. And other things, having nothing of themselves, have their only reality from him.[5]

Once again, the contrast of divine self-existence and creaturely contingency is informal, simply a corollary of the fundamental affirmation about the being of God: 'You alone ... Lord, are what you are and you are who you are' (the echo of Ex. 3:14 is not to be missed). God's aseity is not a mirror image of contingency; rather, in both Augustine and Anselm it is an aspect of the divine *solus*, the irreducible uniqueness and incommensurability of God.

---

2 *Confessions* (Oxford: Oxford University Press, 1991), XI.iv (p. 224).

3 *On Christian Teaching* (Oxford: Oxford University Press, 1997), I.xxxii (p. 24).

4 *Proslogion* XXII, in B. Davies and G. R. Evans (eds), *Anselm of Canterbury. The Major Works* (Oxford: Oxford University Press, 1998), pp. 99f.

5 *On the Fall of the Devil* I, in *Anselm of Canterbury. The Major Works*, p. 194.

A compromise of this proper attention to the divine identity occurs whenever an abstract contrast between self-existent and created being is allowed too large a role in determining the notion of aseity. When this takes place, aseity transmutes into a reverse concept to contingency. This is in large part because the derivation of the concept of aseity shifts. No longer arising in the context of explicating the enacted, self-expressive being of God, it emerges instead out of a consideration of the nature of contingent reality. Moreover, the content of the notion of aseity begins to be altered accordingly. It is no longer a (doxological) affirmation of God's matchless and utterly replete being in and from himself, but simply that which must be said of *deitas* if contingent reality is to be secured by a ground of existence beyond itself. This takes place as the concept of aseity migrates away from the doctrine of the immanent Trinity and of the triune God's economy of grace, and instead finds its place in a metaphysics of created being. With this migration, aseity becomes a 'paired' concept, inseparably attached to and expounded in terms of the contingency of the world. In a curious irony, divine self-existence becomes a derivative concept.

Tracing the history of this deformation is an important and instructive task, not the least because lack of historical perspective has meant that more modern philosophical and theological construals of aseity have often been read back into patristic and mediaeval texts. There is no substantial recent history of the concept.[6] Even a brief account is well beyond the scope of a constructive essay;[7] but attention might be drawn to one or two examples.

A deformed notion of aseity is already firmly in place very early in the eighteenth century in Samuel Clarke's *Demonstration of the Being and Attributes of God* (1704). Clarke's account of aseity is especially interesting because within it one can still find preserved the residue of an older, non-comparative and non-derivative conception (such as we saw in Augustine and Anselm) which fits with severe difficulty into the modern frame of his argument. '*There has existed from*

---

6   There is a good deal of material in J. Ringleben, 'Gottes Sein, Handeln und Werden', however, which may be consulted along with the brief treatments in *Die Religion in Geschichte und Gegenwart*, 4th edition, vol. 1, cols. 808f. or *Handwörterbuch der Philosophie*, vol. 1, cols. 537f.

7   One of the most important recent treatments of aspects of the history, though one which focuses on the parallel concept of God as *ens necessarium* rather than on *aseitas*, is that by Eberhard Jüngel, in *God as the Mystery of the World: On the Foundation of the Theology of the Crucified One in the Dispute between Theism and Atheism* (Edinburgh: T&T Clark, 1983), pp. 14–35. Here Jüngel argues the inadequacy of the concept of divine necessity (central, in his view, to much modern metaphysics) for a Christian construal of God. In part this is because the implied notion of omnipotence is uncorrected by Christological considerations, and in part because 'necessity' is an inadequate rendering of divine freedom: 'God is interesting for his own sake', whereas 'the necessary is always thematic or interesting for the sake of something else' (p. 34). Jüngel's account suffers from the schematism which is often the fate of histories of ideas strongly influenced by Heidegger's genealogy of Western philosophy; and he fails to allow a sense in which divine necessity is not an essential correlate of contingency but a way of speaking of the absoluteness of God (Jüngel is rightly criticized along these lines by W. Pannenberg, *Systematic Theology*, vol. 1 [Grand Rapids: Eerdmans, 1991], p. 83, n. 55). Nevertheless, Jüngel has surely identified a crucial aspect of the history which ought not to be overlooked.

eternity some one unchangeable and independent Being', Clarke proposes.[8] This – notably abstract and anonymous – being is required ('something must needs have been from eternity') otherwise we face the absurdity of 'an infinite succession of changeable and dependent beings'.[9] Consequently, aseity is attributed to this being, not, as it were, doxologically, from a stance in the presence of the divine self-naming as 'I am', but functionally, as a property required of this being if contingent reality is adequately to be explained. 'That unchangeable and independent being which has existed from eternity, without any external cause of its existence, must be self-existent, that is, necessarily existing.'[10] Further, the qualities of this being, because they are determined by its function, are largely non-agential and non-personal. The self-existent being is 'a most simple being, absolutely eternal and infinite, original and independent'.[11] God is simple cause, not (say) luminous and self-presenting personal goodness and beauty; still less is God the bearer of the triune name. Yet in one crucial respect Clarke retains the older conception: the self-existent being is *in se*, and not merely an element in a process of explaining the world's origin. 'To be self-existent is not to be produced by itself, for that is an express contradiction, but it is (which is the only idea we can frame of self-existence, and without which the word seems to have no signification at all) – it is, I say, to exist by an absolute necessity originally in the nature of the thing itself.'[12] This necessity, he continues, is

> antecedent in the natural order of our ideas to our supposition of its being. That is, this necessity must not be barely consequent upon our supposition of the existence of such a being (for then it would not be a necessity absolutely in itself, nor be the ground or foundation of the existence of anything, being on the contrary only a consequent of it) but it must antecedently force itself upon us whether we will or no.[13]

Yet this conception does not break free from the use which Clarke has assigned to it: the apologetic aim traps Clarke into a comparative approach. And because his account lacks any operative sense of the immanent divine life, concentrating instead upon the cosmological functions of the concept of God, it remains a-personal and functional.

Clarke's argument found, and continues to find, theological echoes. Schleiermacher did not consider aseity 'a special attribute',[14] on the grounds that nothing more is said in it than has already been said in the notions of omnipotence and eternity. Aseity is, in fact, 'a speculative formula which, in the dogmatic sphere, we can only convert into the rule that there is nothing in God for which a determining cause is to be posited outside God'.[15] Thus far, of course, Schleiermacher simply repeats

---

8   S. Clarke, *A Demonstration of the Being and Attributes of God*, ed. E. Vailati (Cambridge: Cambridge University Press, 1998), p. 10.

9   S. Clarke, *Demonstration*, p. 10.

10 S. Clarke, *Demonstration*, p. 12.

11 S. Clarke, *Demonstration*, p. 14.

12 S. Clarke, *Demonstration*, p. 12.

13 S. Clarke, *Demonstration*, p. 13.

14 F. D. E. Schleiermacher, *The Christian Faith* (Edinburgh: T&T Clark, 1928), p. 218.

15 F. D. E. Schleiermacher, *The Christian Faith*, p. 219.

a traditional formulation; what is distinctive about his account is his reference to the earlier discussion in *The Christian Faith* §4.4, according to which 'the *Whence* of our receptive and active existence … is to be designated by the word "God"'.[16] This for Schleiermacher is 'the really original signification of that word'.[17] As with Clarke, the content of aseity and its function tug in different directions. Even in his lack of external determination, God has become inseparable from 'our receptive and active existence'. And so 'in the first instance God signifies for us simply that which is the co-determinant in this feeling [of absolute dependence] and to which we trace our being in such a state; and any further content of the idea must be evolved out of this fundamental import assigned to it'.[18]

A similar derivation of aseity can be found much more recently in Tillich. Here the language of causality is particularly strong. 'The question of the cause of a thing or event presupposes that it does not possess its own power of coming into being. Things and events have no aseity.'[19] In effect, Tillich offers an anthropological reworking of what Clarke had expressed in cosmological terms. 'Causality expresses by implication the inability of anything to rest on itself. Everything is driven beyond itself to its cause, and so on indefinitely. Causality powerfully expresses the abyss of nonbeing in everything.'[20] Causality thus generates the anxiety of 'not being in, of, and by oneself, of not having the "aseity" which theology traditionally attributes to God'.[21] To speak of divine aseity is therefore to indicate that God 'is the power of being',[22] beyond the bifurcation of essential and existential being which characterizes the finite.

In their various ways, Clarke, Schleiermacher and Tillich exemplify a basic disorder introduced into the concept of aseity when expounded in close relation to cosmology or anthropology: as the function of the concept shifts, its content is adapted accordingly. Aseity becomes less an affirmation of the underived beauty and goodness of God, and more a property which must be ascribed to *deitas* if it is properly to fulfil its function of supporting the contingent. The sheer originality of God's aseity, the perfection and completeness of his existence in and from himself, is in some measure eclipsed, overtaken by a kind of 'finite' transcendence or aseity, comparatively rather than absolutely different. In the course of his extraordinarily perceptive treatment of the doctrine of God in his *System of Christian Doctrine*, Dorner remarks that '[t]here belongs to the divine idea something determinate, which raises Deity above comparison or mere quantitative difference. The same is true of his absolute essence, his aseity'.[23] When this is lost in a theological account of the matter, the Christian character of the relation of God and creatures is jeopardized, as it turns into the reciprocal presence of two realities, each of which is in some measure necessary for the other, so that God *a se* and the world *ab alio* together form a whole. Aseity becomes detached from the

16   F. D. E. Schleiermacher, *The Christian Faith*, p. 16.
17   F. D. E. Schleiermacher, *The Christian Faith*, p. 16.
18   F. D. E. Schleiermacher, *The Christian Faith*, p. 17.
19   P. Tillich, *Systematic Theology*, vol. 1 (Chicago: University of Chicago Press, 1951), p. 196.
20   P. Tillich, *Systematic Theology*, vol. 1, p. 196.
21   P. Tillich, *Systematic Theology*, vol. 1, p. 196.
22   P. Tillich, *Systematic Theology*, vol. 1, p. 236.
23   I. Dorner, *A System of Christian Doctrine*, vol. 1 (Edinburgh: T&T Clark, 1880), p. 203.

theological metaphysics of God's immanent and economic love, and is reduced to bare self-positing cause of created reality.

Such is the pathology; the corrective is Trinitarian. To this we now turn.

II

If theology is to move beyond a stripped-down conception of aseity, it must do so by following the instruction offered in the actual exercise of God's self-existence; that is, it must take its lead from what is given to creatures to know of God's self-willed and determinate form as *autotheos*. 'We have to be taught first, by the decision made in his actual existence, that God is free in himself. This statement has to come first as the content of a knowledge whose object cannot be an idea, but only God himself in his self-evidencing free existence.'[24] Aseity as a synthetic concept, correlative to and so in some way a function of creaturely contingency, can only be supplanted by something materially rich – by a notion of aseity beyond that of a merely comparative absolute, speculatively derived. In Christian dogmatics, such a materially rich notion of aseity cannot be articulated apart from the doctrine of the Trinity, for it is that piece of teaching which offers a conceptual paraphrase of the life of God, both in his inner depth and in his gracious turn to that which is not God. It is as Father, Son and Spirit that God is of himself, utterly free and full, in the self-originate and perfect movement of his life; grounded in himself, he gives himself, the self-existent Lord of grace. God *a se* is the perfection of *paternitas*, *filiatio*, and *spiratio* in which he is indissolubly from, for and in himself, and out of which he bestows himself as the Lord, saviour and partner of his creature. This triune character is the distinguishing feature of the Christian confession of God's aseity. As Calvin puts it: 'God ... designates himself by another special mark to distinguish himself more precisely from idols. For he so proclaims himself the sole God as to offer himself to be contemplated clearly in three persons. Unless we grasp these, only the bare and empty name of God flits about in our brains, to the exclusion of the true God.'[25]

How might Trinitarian teaching fill out the notion of aseity? First, in speaking of God's aseity we have in mind both the 'immanent' and the 'economic' dimensions of the divine life. *God is from himself, and from himself God gives himself.* There is a certain priority to the first statement ('God is from himself'): the immanent dimension of God's self-existence stands at the head of everything else that must be said. This is because only in this way can the concept of aseity be kept free of the degrading synthetic or comparative elements. First and foremost, aseity is a statement of the divine 'I am'; only by derivation is it a statement that God is the groundless ground of contingency. Nevertheless, the priority of the immanent would be badly misperceived if it were not related to the necessary further statement: 'from himself God gives himself'. Without this second statement, the first would risk abstraction from the actual exercise or form of God's life. The perfection of

---

24   K. Barth, *Church Dogmatics* II/1, p. 308.
25   J. Calvin, *Institutes of the Christian Religion* (London: SCM, 1960), I.13.ii (p. 122).

God's life as *autotheos* includes his works as Father, Son and Spirit in creation, reconciliation and redemption.

With this in mind, how might God's immanent aseity be further described? God's aseity is to be understood, not formally, but materially. Aseity is not to be defined merely in negative terms, as the mere absence of origination or dependence upon an external cause. If this is allowed to happen, then a subordinate characteristic of aseity (God's 'not being from another') comes to eclipse its primary meaning (God's 'being in and from himself'). 'It was,' Barth notes, ' a retrogression when the idea of God's *aseitas* was interpreted, or rather supplanted, by that of *independentia* or *infinitas*, and later by that of the unconditioned or absolute.'[26] It is much more fruitful to understand aseity in terms of fullness of personal relations. Aseity is *life*: God's life *from* and therefore *in* himself. This life is the relations of Father, Son and Spirit. Crucially, therefore, aseity is not a property to be affirmed *de deo uno* anterior to God's triune life, but indicates the wholly original character of the relations which are God's life (failure to see the constitutive role of this in the conception of aseity is at the root of its modern disarray). The self-existence of the triune God is his existence in the *opera Dei personalia ad intra*, the personal, internal activities of God. These activities are personal relations, that is, modes of subsistence in which each particular person of the Trinity is identified in terms of relations to the other two persons. To spell this out fully would require an account of (for example) the act of the Father in begetting the Son, and the acts of the Father and the Son in spirating the Spirit. Expressed as relations, God's life *a se* includes the Son's relation to the Father as the one whom the Father begets (passive generation), and the relation of the Spirit to the Father and the Son (passive spiration). By these activities and relations, each of the persons of the Trinity is identified, that is, picked out as having a distinct, incommunicable personal property (*character hypostaticus sive personalis*): paternity, filiation, spiration. Together, these acts and relations *are* God's self-existence. Aseity is not merely the quality of being (in contrast to contingent reality) underived; it is the eternal lively plenitude of the Father who begets, the Son who is begotten, and the Spirit who proceeds from both. To speak of God's aseity is thus to speak of the spontaneous, eternal and unmoved movement of his being-in-relation as Father, Son and Spirit. This movement, without cause of condition, and depending on nothing other than itself, is God's being from himself. In this perfect circle of paternity, filiation and spiration, God is who he is.

The aseity of the triune God thus means a good deal more than absence of derivation. Indeed, if that privative construal of aseity is accented too forcefully, it can suppress the elements of generation and spiration which are basic to the proper Christian theological sense of the term, on the grounds that begetting and proceeding seem to introduce precisely the troublesome notion of derivation which aseity is intended to exclude from the conception of the divine. Classical Trinitarian theology takes a different tack to exclude an inappropriate notion of derivation, and attendant ideas such as composition. It develops a distinction between the aseity common to all three persons by virtue of their sharing in the divine essence, and the aseity which is the personal property of the Father alone: although all the persons of the Trinity

---

26   K. Barth, *Church Dogmatics* II/1, p. 303.

are *a se* according to essence, the Father alone is *a se* according to person. Phrased in rather more technical language: all three persons are ἀγένητος (uncreated) by virtue of their common divine essence; but only the Father is ἀγέννητος (unbegotten) because he alone is the *principium* of the Son and the Spirit. The consensus on the point is neatly encapsulated by John of Damascus: 'The Father alone is ingenerate, no other substance having given him being. And the Son alone is generate, for he was begotten of the Father's essence, without beginning and without time. And only the Holy Spirit proceeds from the Father's essence, not having been generated but simply proceeding.'[27] The Father accordingly, is *a se*, not only according to essence (as God) but also as a property of his own person; but neither to the Son nor to the Spirit, who are begotten and proceed from the Father respectively, can aseity be attributed as a personal property.

At first glance, this set of distinctions appears to undermine a construal of divine aseity in terms of the personal relations which make up the triune life, precisely because it distinguishes between a 'common' aseity and an aseity proper to the Father. This might be judged to focus too much on the relations of origin within the Trinity, with the result that the reciprocally-constituting character of the immanent relations of the godhead is threatened, resulting in some kind of subordinationism. If the Father's 'unbegottenness' becomes definitive of the divine essence, then the personal properties *ad intra* of the Son and the Spirit (that is, filiation and spiration) may easily seem secondary, derivative from and not equiprimordial with paternity. And when that happens, aseity once again is associated with a common divine essence 'behind' the relations of the divine life.

This retreat into a monistic concept of aseity is not necessary, however, and can readily be corrected by appeal to the reciprocally determinative character of the divine persons. The Son, for example, is eternally begotten of the Father. As such, he is not, as Son, *a se*, since he does not share the Father's property of being ἀναρχον. But this does not entail that the Son is in some manner subsequent to or inferior to the Father. The Son's generation is eternal: not a 'coming-to-be' as the Father's creature, but a relation which is constitutive of the divine essence and of the identity of the Father as well as of the Son. John of Damascus again (here stating a commonplace of the tradition in interpreting John 14.28): 'If we say that the Father is the origin of the Son and greater than the Son, we do not suggest any precedence in time or superiority in nature of the Father over the Son (for through his agency he made the ages), or superiority in any other respect save causation'.[28] Causation and filiation, because both are eternal, do not relate as fullness of being and absence of being. Filiation is not a lack but a mode of God's eternal perfection, intrinsic to the wholly realized self-movement of God. Begetting – and likewise spiration – are the *form* of God's aseity, not its result or term, still less its contradiction.

To make affirmations along these lines requires, of course, that we do not draw too sharp a distinction between the unity of the divine essence and its triunity: the aseity of the Son and the Spirit which they possess as sharers in the one divine essence is not wholly separate from their distinctive personal properties as the one

---

27 John of Damascus, *Exposition of the Orthodox Faith* (Oxford: Parker, 1899), I.8 (p. 8).

28 John of Damascus, *Exposition of the Orthodox Faith*, I.8 (pp. 8f.).

who is eternally begotten and the one who eternally proceeds. Further, it requires that we allow that the relations of the godhead are not secondary, and that they are mutually constitutive and conditioning. The Father is, according to his person, *a se* only as he stands in relation to the Son; his aseity is not anterior to the act and relation of begetting. This does not mean that the relation of Father and Son is reversible (the Son does not beget the Father); but the relation is reciprocal, because both 'Father' and 'Son' are relative terms.[29] Above all, we need to grasp that God's aseity is his self-existence *in* these relations. God is from himself as he enacts his life in the reciprocity of paternity, filiation and spiration.

> God as originated and as originator stands in the relation of reciprocal action. The Deity as originated is eternally one with the Deity originating, in this way, that the former is referred again to the cause, and is related in a causal and conditioning manner to that cause, just as the effect was immanent in the cause from the beginning. And thus God is not simply to be defined as absolute Causality, but there is to be predicated of him, so to speak, a double-sided causality (as absolutely reciprocal action), as a circular motion of originating that is at the same time originated, of being originated that is at the same time activity, to be expressed in the proposition that *God is absolute Life*. For God is absolute Life in himself, not by his being realized once for all, but by eternal Self-realization; thus the absolute Potentiality or Possibility of himself is not lost in action, but is securely preserved therein.[30]

There is, perhaps, some lack of caution in what Dorner has to say, possibly some loss of the conception of God's perfection (in a footnote, he has to distance himself from Hegel); but his appeal to the concept of 'life' to explicate aseity is very sure-footed. Moreover, Dorner grasps that only a theology of the immanent triune life could adequately protect theology from resting content with a notion of aseity which reduces God to mere causative force or absolute substrate of the contingent.

We may close this account of aseity as a characteristic of God's inner-trinitarian life with some comments on two closely associated concepts which have been used to state God's self-existence, namely God as *causa sui*, and God as *ens necessarium*. Both illustrate the need to ensure that concepts used in the course of explicating the Christian confession should be kept in the closest possible proximity to substantive theological doctrine, and not simply introduced already full of content derived from their deployment elsewhere.

The concept of God as *causa sui* has a long history in patristic and mediaeval usage; the locus classicus is a comment of Jerome's on Eph. 3.15:

> Other things receive their substance by the mediation of God, but God – who always is and does not have his beginning from another source but is himself the origin of himself and the cause of his own substance – cannot be understood to have something which has existence from another source. Warmth, indeed, is something which belongs to fire, but something which has been warmed is something else. Fire cannot be understood without heat; other things which become warm from fire borrow its heat and, if the fire should withdraw, the heat gradually decreases and they return to their own nature and are by no means referred to as warm.[31]

29   Further on this, see W. Pannenberg, *Systematic Theology*, vol. 1, p. 312.
30   I. Dorner, *A System of Christian Doctrine*, vol. 1, pp. 257f.
31   R.E. Heine (ed.), *The Commentaries of Origen and Jerome on St Paul's Epistle to the Ephesians* (Oxford: Oxford University Press, 2002), p. 158.

Towards the end of the nineteenth century, the concept was revisited by the Roman Catholic dogmatician Herman Schell, who appealed to the language of God as *causa sui* to achieve much the same as Dorner sought to achieve by speaking of God's 'life', namely to overcome what he judged to be a static conception of God as *ipsum esse subsistens*, and so to draw attention to God's eternal self-activation.[32]

When pressed, the concept soon shows itself incoherent and dogmatically precarious. At a purely formal level, it seems to suggest that God in some way precedes himself as his own cause, and 'it is absurd to suppose that something is *explanatorily prior* to *itself*'.[33] The dogmatic difficulties are equally serious. Talk of God as his own cause cannot easily cohere with teaching about divine eternity or immutability, since it appears to introduce an actualist concept of God's 'coming-to-be' as the result of some causal process. Further, it imperils divine simplicity, introducing distinctions between *causa* and *causatum*, or *potentia* and *actus* which, by attributing potentiality to God, undermine the all-important identity of essence and existence in God (reasons such as these led to Schell's work being placed on the *Index* in 1898). By suggesting that God produces himself, it seems to require the possibility of God's non-existence as a kind of background to his being. In effect, a God who is his own cause lacks an integral element of perfection. If the concept of *causa sui* is to be used, therefore, the notion of 'cause' must first be stripped of any associations with 'becoming' or 'coming-into-existence' – of anything that might corrode the eternal fullness of God's being. Further, it must be used, not to conceive God on the basis of a general metaphysics of causality, but to indicate what Ringleben calls 'the divine livingness' and 'the uniqueness and incomparability of the divine being itself'.[34] In the end, however, causal concepts are less than adequate to the task; what is needed is the language of person and action.

Similar difficulties attend the idea of God as necessary being. We have already noted that this way of speaking of aseity is commonly dominated by the idea of 'necessity for…'.[35] Necessity thereby becomes a determination of God, reduced to a merely functional relation to the creatures of whom he is the necessary ground. These problems can, certainly, be eased by deploying a more complex modality of necessity, according to which necessity is not simply 'necessity for another'. The necessity predicated of God when he is spoken of as *ens necessarium* is *necessitas absoluta*. It is equivalent to absolute existence, existence without ground or determination, and so different from functional or contingent existence. Consequently, the necessity of God for the world is properly to be understood as *necessitas consequentiae*, that which simply follows from God's will or self-determination, and has no further reference to realities beyond that will. Strictly speaking, divine necessity is not a

---

32 See H. Schell, *Katholische Dogmatik*, vol. 1 (Paderborn: Schöningh, 1889), pp. 238–41.

33 J. Hoffman and G. S. Rosenkrantz, *The Divine Attributes* (Oxford: Blackwell, 2002), p. 91; cf. R. Swinburne, *The Coherence of Theism* (Oxford: Clarendon Press, 1977), p. 262: 'Certainly given that at some time God is, his subsequent existence will indeed be due to his actions. But what has no cause, and so is inexplicable, is the non-existence of a time before which God was not.'

34 J. Ringleben, 'Gottes Sein, Handeln und Werden', pp. 229f.

35 See *supra*, n. 7.

matter of *necessitas coactionis*, according to which God and the world would be mutually constitutive, thus reducing God to finitude. Yet even if *ens necessarium* can be construed in this way, as equivalent to pure self-original existence, it remains a rather blank, empty concept. Like the parallel notion of 'the absolute', it invites filling out from elsewhere. Accordingly, as with the notion of God as *causa sui*, it has to be judged materially inadequate as an account of God's life.

III

God is *a se* in the eternal fullness of the loving relations of Father, Son and Spirit. From himself he has life in himself. But God is not only from himself in his inner life, in the *opera immanentia per se*, but also in the external works which correspond to his inner life, in the *opera Dei exeuntia*. With this, we can complete the material description of God's aseity by expanding the second statement that 'from himself God gives himself'.

A theology of aseity finds itself under a very specific constraint at this point: if it is diligently to follow the logic of the triune self-movement, then it cannot remain content with a definition of divine self-existence which refers exclusively to the being of God *in se* apart from his relation to creatures. If theology were to try to do this, it would in fact fail to grasp the real content of God's aseity, even in its 'internal' dimension. The movement of God's triune life has its perfection in and of itself, and is utterly sufficient to itself; but this perfect movement is not self-enclosed or self-revolving. In its perfection, it is also a movement of self-gift in which the complete love of Father, Son and Spirit communicates itself *ad extra*, creating and sustaining a further object of love. Of himself, God is *gracious*. 'Since, then, God, who is good and more than good, did not find satisfaction in self-contemplation, but in his exceeding goodness wished certain things to come into existence which would enjoy his benefits and share in his goodness, he brought all things out of nothing into being and created them.'[36]

God is from himself not simply in absolute independence but in his 'exceeding goodness'. The inclusion of the *opera exeuntia* in the description of aseity is, however, not common in the Christian doctrinal tradition, especially when the doctrine of God is expounded in terms of the metaphysics of self-existent substance, or if the theology of the divine processions is isolated from that of the divine missions. But some precedents may be found in the exegetical tradition, notably in the interpretation of John 5:26: '[A]s the Father has life in himself, so he has granted the Son also to have life in himself.' Two examples are particularly instructive in holding immanent and economic aspects of aseity.

In his treatment of the Johannine text in the twenty-second Tractate on the Gospel of John, Augustine suggests an understanding of God's 'life in himself' (that is, of what will later be signified by the term 'aseity') in both its intra-trinitaran and its soteriological dimensions. His reflections stem from a vivid sense of the present fulfilment of the Son's promise of life, recorded in the previous verse: 'the hour

---

36   John of Damascus, *Exposition of the Orthodox Faith*, II.2 (p. 18).

is coming, and is now here, when the dead will hear the voice of the Son of God, and those who hear will live' (John 5:25). 'This hour is now occurring, and this is assuredly occurring and is not at all ceasing,' Augustine tells his congregation: 'Men who were dead are rising, they are passing to life, they live at the voice of the Son of God, from him persevering in his faith.'[37] Immediately, however, Augustine traces this saving reality of new life in Christ back to its foundation in the Son's eternal relation to the Father. If there is indeed a present reality of resurrection life for believers, it can only be because 'the Son has life; he has that by which the believers may live'.[38] This, in turn, prompts the question which guides the rest of what Augustine has to say: 'How does he have it?'.[39] That is: How does the Son have life, by virtue of which he can bestow life on believers? The answer runs: the Son has life '[a]s the Father has it', that is, 'in himself'.[40] *Et quomodo habet? Sicut habet Pater ... in semetipso.*[41] 'For the Father has life in himself, the Son also has life in himself':[42] Why is this point so significant for Augustine? Because the Son's having life *in semetipso*, as a mode of divine aseity, at one and the same time distinguishes the Son absolutely from creatures and grounds the believers' partaking of life.

Accordingly, Augustine explicates God's life *in semetipso* and so *a se* in terms of the eternal relations of Father and Son. The Father, he says, '"has given to the Son also to have life in himself." As he has, so he has given to have. Where does he have it? "In himself". Where has he given to have it? "In himself"'.[43] Here Augustine seeks to articulate an understanding of paternity and filiation in which the Father's giving does not in any way entail the Son's inferiority: what the Father gives the Son is what he, the Father, has – life in himself; and the mode of life which is the Son's by the gift of the Father is characterized, not by its being 'in another', but, again, by its being in himself. '[T]he Son of God was not as if at first without life and [then] he received life. For, if he so received it, he would not have it in himself. For what does "in himself" mean? That he himself is life itself'.[44] This is why the relation of Father and Son is wholly unique, consisting as it does of a giving and receiving which is devoid of any subordination, so that of the Son to whom the Father gives life it can be said: *ipsa vita ipse esset*, he himself is life itself.[45] '"As the Father has life in himself, so he has given the Son also to have life in himself", so that he [sc. the Son] does not live by participation, but lives without change and in every respect he, himself, is life.'[46] Thus the logic of 'life-giving' is strictly parallel to that of 'begetting': 'what is said, "He has given to the Son" is such as if it were said, "He begot a Son"; for he gave only by begetting. As [the Father] gave that he

37 Augustine, *Tractates on the Gospel of John 11–27* (Washington: Catholic University of America Press, 1988), 22.8.2 (pp. 204f.).
38 Augustine, *Tractates on the Gospel of John 11–27*, 22.8.2 (p. 205).
39 Augustine, *Tractates on the Gospel of John 11–27*, 22.9.1 (p. 205).
40 Augustine, *Tractates on the Gospel of John 11–27*, 22.9.1 (p. 205).
41 Augustine, *In Iohannem Evangelium Tractatus CXXIV* (Turnhout: Brepols, 1954), p. 228.
42 Augustine, *Tractates on the Gospel of John 11–27*, 22.9.2 (p. 205).
43 Augustine, *Tractates on the Gospel of John 11–27*, 22.9.2 (p. 205).
44 Augustine, *Tractates on the Gospel of John 11–27*, 22.9.3 (p. 206).
45 Augustine, *In Iohannem Evangelium Tractatus CXXIV*, p. 228.
46 Augustine, *Tractates on the Gospel of John 11–27*, 22.10.3 (p. 207).

might be, so he gave that he might be life, and so he gave that he might be life in himself'.[47]

This is rather distant from later notions of aseity as independence; it is aseity as the eternal and lively perfection of Father and Son. Yet to this immanent reality there corresponds the Son's mission; the life which the Son receives and has in himself is that which he in turn bestows upon creatures. Augustine is, of course, sharply aware of the gulf between God and creatures. The apostle or the believer only has life in Christ, not in himself: life *in semetipso* is entirely incommunicable, and so the identity of 'Son' and 'life' cannot in any way be replicated in the creaturely realm. But if aseity differentiates the divine Son from creatures, it is also at the same time the ground of his saving gift. The Son has, and is, life; and 'as he has, so he has given'.[48] Indeed, the full scope of the Son's being life in himself must be understood both immanently and economically. As the one who has life *in semetipso*, the Son 'would not need life from another source, but would be fullness of life by which others, believing, might live the life they live'.[49]

Augustine's exegesis, then, directs us to two primary aspects of a theological conception of aseity: (1) that aseity is materially to be understood out of the eternal relations which constitute God's inner triune life; (2) that this aseity is as it were the eternal impetus of the Son's life-giving mission of salvation. Something of the same can be found in Calvin's rather more terse remarks on the same verse in his 1553 commentary on John's Gospel:

> [Christ] shows the source of the efficacy of his voice – that he is the fountain of life and by his voice pours it forth on men. For life would not flow to us from his mouth unless its cause and source were in himself. For God is said to have life in himself, not only because he alone lives by his own inherent power, but because he contains the fullness of life in himself and quickens all things. And this is peculiar to God; as it is said, 'With thee is the fountain of life' (Ps. 36:9). But because God's majesty, which is far removed from us, would be like a secret and hidden spring, he has revealed himself in Christ. And so we have an open fountain at hand to draw from. The words mean that God did not want to have life hidden and as it were buried within himself, and therefore he transfused it into his Son that it might flow to us.[50]

If Augustine is concerned to emphasize how the immanent Trinitarian dimensions of the Son's life in himself form the deep ground of his saving gift of life, Calvin appears to be concerned primarily with Christ who is of himself saviour and life-giver. The immanent dimension is certainly rather more muted in what Calvin has to say, and he concentrates on Christ's *efficacia*, Christ as *fons vitae*. Yet Calvin

47   Augustine, *Tractates on the Gospel of John 11–27*, 22.10.4 (p. 207). With this emphasis on 'begetting', Augustine safeguards the distinction between the aseity which is the personal property of the Father alone and the common divine aseity in which both Father and Son participate: the Son's aseity is not identical with that of the personal aseity of the Father who begets him.

48   Augustine, *Tractates on the Gospel of John 11–27*, 22.10.3 (p. 207).

49   Augustine, *Tractates on the Gospel of John 11–27*, 22.10.4 (p. 207).

50   J. Calvin, *The Gospel According to St John 1–10* (Edinburgh: St Andrew Press, 1959), p. 131.

does root what he says on this matter in the immanent reality of Christ's deity; only as one who *is* life can he give life. '[L]ife would not flow to us from his mouth unless its cause and source were in himself.' Having life *in se* is 'peculiar to God', the one who is alone 'the fountain of life'; for Calvin, therefore, the deity of the Son, his co-equality with the Father who 'contains the fullness of life in himself', is the presupposition of the Son's saving acts. Without this immanent aseity, the Son's work would be entirely lacking in the power to vivify. But Calvin is equally firm that the Son's life *in se* is superabundant, overflowing. His imagery – *fons*, *causa*, *origo* – is telling, indicating what he clearly considers to be the chief practical aspect of aseity, namely that 'God is said to have life in himself, not only because he alone lives by his own inherent power, but because he contains the fullness of life in himself and quickens all things'. The sole perfection of God *a se* is unquestioned, for God is the one who *propria virtute et intrinsica solus vivat*. But the life with which God alone lives of himself is the fullness of life which *quickens*. The form of this life-giving overflow of God's life is the Son. '[B]ecause God's majesty, which is far removed from us, would be like a secret and hidden spring, he has revealed himself in Christ', in whom 'we have an open fountain at hand to draw from'. The divine will is not simply to possess life as something 'hidden and as it were buried within himself', but rather to transfuse that life 'into his Son that it might flow to us'. Calvin is characteristically reticent about the Trinitarian dimensions; he is less concerned than is Augustine to clarify that filiation ('transfusing' life into the Son) does not entail subordination. What Calvin offers is an account of the aseity of God from the economic perspective.

Taken together, Augustine and Calvin suggest a number of characteristics for an adequate theology of divine aseity. Aseity is not only the absence of external causation, but the eternal life which God in and of himself *is*. It is, therefore (following the Gospel's usage) *in*seity as much as *a*seity. That life cannot be conceived apart from the mutual relations of Father and Son; its perfection includes the perfect mutuality of the Father's giving of life to the Son who in his turn has life in himself. Nor can it be conceived apart from its overflowing plenitude in giving itself to creatures. God's aseity, although it marks God's utter difference from creatures, does not entail his isolation, for what God is and has of himself is life, and that life includes a self-willed movement of love.

IV

Both the pathology and the material exposition sketched here suggest that an account of aseity goes wrong when it is alienated from its proper Trinitarian setting and deployed to perform different functions. When this alienation takes place, its content is reworked into something more basic (less positive); the biblical and theological texts in which its primary Christian sense is encapsulated are either pushed to the margins or reinterpreted in line with what is taken to be a more basic sense; above all, the location of the concept drifts from Trinitarian to cosmological teaching. These are, it should be emphasized, not simply the errors of philosophers, for it is at least arguable that the development of a bare, non-Trinitarian concept of aseity owes as much to abstract theological notions of God's *independentia* as it does to philosophical apologetics for natural religion. In this matter, and others, theology has not always successfully resisted the forces which lead to the alienation of inquiry from Christian confession and praise.[51]

Little is to be gained, therefore, by a theological repudiation of philosophy. Theology is not a pure science, and can never extract itself wholly from the wider domain of intellectual inquiry. A gesture of withdrawal on theology's part may be at times a necessary protest against neglect of the integrity of the object of theology, which is the Christian gospel. But such defiance can only be occasional and fairly short-lived; when it becomes a matter of unyielding principle, it usually succumbs to the kind of supernaturalism which generates excessive claims about the perfectibility of theology (and theologians). More than any other science, theology ought to be alert to the idolatries of comprehension.

What matters more than any contingent conflict of the faculties – a conflict which is largely a modern invention, even if it does echo some older debates – is that both theological and philosophical inquiry into the Christian faith be led by the material content of the church's confession. In terms of the concept of aseity, we have seen that this involves making sure that its Trinitarian and soteriological dimensions are allowed to determine its sense from the beginning, and not simply restricted to mere adjunct status. But the point has wide application. Both philosophers and divines are responsible to the enactment of God's identity set out in the gospel. That *positum*, and not some generalization such as 'deity', is the matter to which and by which philosophical and theological reason are directed, and in the service of which both may be engaged.

---

51 A compelling analysis of these forces can be found in G. Schner, *Essays Catholic and Critical* (Aldershot: Ashgate, 2003).

Name Index